"Once again Floy Turner and Sherrie Clark's latest book, Behind Her Special Agent Badge, was a great read. Once I started reading it, I dropped everything until I finished it. It really shows the complexity of a law enforcement job, the stress it entails, and the range of emotions the job brings. As a retired federal agent from South Florida, the book brought back memories of cases that we worked together. I am ready for their next book!"

VICKI MELLON
Special Agent, Retired,
Federal Bureau of Investigation

"Turner and Clark are masterful storytellers, and you'll be hooked from the get-go. The only time I wasn't glued to a page was when I was turning it, and I did that as quick as possible so I could read what happened next."

SUSAN AMBROSINO
Police Officer,
NYPD
District 32

"I enjoyed reading the first book and couldn't wait for the second book. Floy is the perfect example of compassion, passion, and professionalism during her years as a law enforcement officer. I am so honored to know Floy and truly recommend everyone to read her memoirs. Thank you, Floy, for your years of commitment and dedication to serve the residents of Florida."

ANNA RODRIGUEZ
Author, Founder & Executive Director,
Florida Coalition Against Human Trafficking

"As a retired Police Sergeant who spent 10 years in Homicide, this is such a timely book. Everyone should read it, especially during this time when cops are getting a lot of negative publicity. Through Turner's transparency, she shows us that there are good cops; in fact, most cops are good. Her honest perspective can't help but encourage readers to look at law enforcement through a fresh and fair set of eyes."

DONNA BROWN
Homicide Detective Sergeant, (Retired),
Tallahassee Police Department

"This is quite simply a must-read book. It is characteristically brutal, tragic, humorous, and riveting. I recall many of the cases described by Floy as I was a Special Agent with the Florida Department of Law Enforcement from 1997 through 2010 and had the honor and privilege to work with Floy.

"Floy has given the reader an inside peek into the craft of criminal investigations which is ever evolving. Her story reveals how the police actually work their craft under extreme pressure dealing with statistics, politics, the media, and what they must confront at crime scenes.

"Additionally, the reader learns how police work has been hardwired into Floy to such an extent that it infects how she experiences the everyday world to include work and home-life bleeding into each other and how police struggle to reconcile what they've seen in their day jobs when they close their eyes at night."

ROBERT BIONDOLILLO, (Retired)
Sunrise Police Department Chief of Detectives,
FDLE Special Agent,
Deputy Chief of Police Coconut Creek Police Department

"What an exciting book! Turner and Clark had me hooked from the first sentence. With each adventure, I felt as if I was walking through Turner's career with her, and I couldn't wait to read what happened to us next."

JANE DOUGHERTY-MCGOWAN
Police Officer, (Retired),
NYPD

"Special Agent Turner is a repeat offender – but in a great way! Her second book gives us another peek behind the badge, and you will not be able to turn the pages fast enough."

GARY MARTIN HAYS
Attorney, Best-Selling Author,
TV and Radio Show Host,
Board Member, Elizabeth Smart Foundation

"Behind Her Special Agent Badge is a must-read book! Floy Turner has an authentic, real voice that demands respect, that demands to be listened to, while at the same time a soft and often funny touch when recalling some of her more awkward experiences in a male-dominated profession. I cheered for her the whole way through!"

JILLIANE HOFFMAN
Best-Selling Author

Behind Her Special Agent Badge

MURDER, MAYHEM, AND LIFE IN THE
FLORIDA DEPARTMENT OF LAW
ENFORCEMENT

Floy Turner
and
Sherrie Clark

Storehouse Publishing, LLC
St. Augustine, FL

Storehouse Publishing, LLC
Saint Augustine, Florida 32092
www.StorehousePublishers.com
Author@StorehousePublishers.com

Ordering Information:
Quantity sales. Special discounts are available with the Publisher at the email address above and type in subject line "Special Sales Department."

The views expressed in this work are solely those of the author(s) and do not necessarily reflect the views of the publisher, and the publisher hereby disclaims any responsibility for them.

Behind Her Special Agent Badge / Floy Turner and Sherrie Clark—1st ed.

ISBN-13: 978-1-943106-10-3 (sc)
ISBN-13: 978-1-943106-11-0 (ebk)

Library of Congress Control Number: 2016961471

Printed in the United States of America

Dedication

I want to dedicate this book to my husband Gary Carmichael, my love and my best friend, and to our family Kally, Reg and Mary Ellen, Chris and Kellie, and Scott. Life has blessed us with a loving family and friends who have supported my endeavors.
   FLOY TURNER

I want to dedicate this book to my five children Devlin, Tristan, Liam, Micah, and Janna, the loves of my life.
   SHERRIE CLARK

We would both like to dedicate this book in memory of our fallen brothers and sisters in the thin blue line all over the country. God bless you for your service and for making the ultimate sacrifice.
   FLOY TURNER AND SHERRIE CLARK

Epigraph

The wicked flee when no man pursueth:
but the righteous are as bold as a lion.
–Proverbs 28:1–

Disclaimer

The purpose of this book is to entertain while enlightening readers to what happened in South Florida during the 1990s and into the new millennium from the perspective of state law enforcement officer Floy Turner. It's based on actual events that occurred during the first half of her tenure as a Special Agent with the Florida Department of Law Enforcement. Turner has made every effort to recreate events, places, and conversations as accurately as possible from her memories of them as well as through research.

Turner's immediate family gave her permission to use their real names. Also, the actual names of those who have been written about in the news have been used. To protect the privacy and anonymity of everyone else involved in this book, she has changed their names, the names of places, and any identifying characteristics and details, and she has modified some of the circumstances. Any similarities to anyone you think you may know are coincidental.

This book does include a few words that some may find offensive. They are written as they had been spoken so that the stories retain their authenticity.

The authors and publisher shall have neither liability nor responsibility to any person or entity with respect to any loss or damage caused, or alleged to have been caused, directly or indirectly, or disruptions caused by errors or omissions, whether such errors or omissions result from negligence, accident, or any other cause, by the information contained in this book.

Contents

Preface

Co-Author Floy Turner

During my career in law enforcement, my girlfriends questioned me about my cases. When I told a verbal story of my experiences, they responded by telling me that I should write a book.

As an avid reader, I came to admire four specific authors who wrote about investigations, solving crimes, and police work:

- I was fortunate to work with best-selling author Jillian Hoffman when she was a regional legal advisor for the Florida Department of Law Enforcement in the Miami Regional Office Center (MROC). I had been a consultant for her book *Pretty Little Things*.
- Best-selling author Jon Jefferson had been referred to me by Art Bohannan to assist as a subject matter expert in *The Bone Yard*, a *Body Farm* novel.
- The other two authors who I have never had the privilege of knowing are Sue Grafton and Janet Evanovich. Grafton caught my attention with her female character Kinsey Millhone. Evanovich grabbed me with her funky humor that had me laughing out loud as I read.

When Sherrie Clark approached me about this endeavor, I was excited and thrilled to jump into the process of sharing my life and adventures with other women. What I did not expect was how many of my fans would turn out to be men.

Sherrie and I shared that cop connection, and we make a good team.

Co-Author Sherrie Clark

After the release of our first book BEHIND HER MIAMI BADGE, readers wanted to understand who Floy Turner and Sherrie Clark were as a team, how we came about writing this series, and what we did to make it happen. We began to realize that our story as a team was a crucial part of this series, and I truly believe that the success of our relationship contributed to the success of our first book together.

The Journey

Several years ago while hosting the online radio show GOD, WHERE WERE YOU WHEN? I wanted to do a show on human trafficking. Of course, Floy Turner came to mind immediately as an expert in that field. She sent me her bio for the show. Simply stated, I was blown away by her experience and credentials! As an author, book editor, and author coach, I saw the same potential in her story that she did, so we decided to write a book together.

As she shared her experiences with me, I developed a passion to make them as significant to you, the reader, as she had made them to me. So what started out to be an exciting project evolved into a mission of bringing her story to life.

This Book

BEHIND HER SPECIAL AGENT BADGE (BHSAB) is different from the first and more humorous book BEHIND HER MIAMI BADGE. Although BHSAB has gone in a more serious direction due to the types of crimes written about on its pages, we managed to conserve that "Floy humor" that we've all come to know and love.

Working with Floy Turner has been an honor and a pleasure. Throughout the writing process, I came to know and appreciate her compassion and her wit.

As you read the pages that follow, I am confident that you will also see that Floy Turner is a professional in her field, and she's a real human being behind the badge.

Acknowledgements

Thank you to everyone who joined us in our journey of writing this book. Each of you played a significant part and is appreciated more than you can know.

Although we both have different groups of people we want to thank, our appreciation crosses over to each other's supporters. We recognize that what you gave was for the benefit of the whole book.

We want to thank everyone who supported us for the last book BEHIND HER MIAMI BADGE. We are convinced your efforts contributed to its success. Thank you to Jane Dougherty-McGowan, Annarita Elliff, Linda Evans, Janet Howard, Allyson Machate, Malaki, and the many other readers who spread the word about our first book, recommending it to others without hesitation. Your affirmation of and confidence in both the book and us are priceless.

We want to give a special thanks to Sandy Sledge and Vicki Mellon for proofreading our manuscript. You both did a fantastic job.

Also, thank you to Devlin Kidney for creating our book trailers. You've captured the essence of the stories wonderfully.

Thank you to Lee Ann Howlett for being our voice and narrating BEHIND HER MIAMI BADGE'S audiobook. You did a wonderful job. We especially appreciate how your family served and protected with the Florida Highway Patrol and the legacy they left behind through you.

Thank you, Chandronette Mobley, for patiently working with us on the social media and for giving your professional advice as to its direction, always with our books in mind.

Floy:

I want to thank my husband Gary Carmichael, who helped me lay out my story and for his technical input on different elements. Gary, I love you.

I also want to thank my family Kally Turner (Kally O'Mally), Reg and Mary Ellen Haid, Chris and Kellie Thomas, and Scott Carmichael for your love and support with this endeavor.

I want to thank the PLOCK Book club: Freda Blackmar, Janey Fox, Shannon Harbour, Susann Hayes, Beth Jansen, Judy Lind, Karen MacClaren, Mary Morgan, Laura Rhodes, Cherie Wilson, and Nancy Klopfenstein for your feedback and encouragement through the writing of this book.

To my friends at the Barco Newton YMCA in Fleming Island, Florida, I want to give thanks. Thank you to my workout buddies, the staff, and trainers for all of your support through this journey, especially the veterans, current military and their spouses who have sacrificed so much for our country.

A thank you to my church family at the First Presbyterian Church Green Cove Springs for your continual encouragement in moving forward in the writing of this book.

Thank you to my co-author Sherrie Clark for all of your friendship and hard work and for helping me bring my story to life.

Sherrie:

My deepest thanks and appreciation go to my husband Darryl Clark and all five of my children: Devlin Kidney, Tristan Kidney, Liam Kidney, Micah Clark, and Janna Clark. Your continual support, encouragement, and never-ending patience with me during the writing of this book mean more to me than you know.

A big thank you too my wonderful friend and business partner Malaki. You listened, you encouraged, and you gave me your honest feedback, telling me what I needed to hear, not necessarily what I wanted to hear. I believe this book (and me) are better as a result of your friendship and professional advice.

Another big thank you to my son Devlin. You did a fantastic job helping me smooth out some of those rough areas. I couldn't have done it without you. Those sections, and thus this book, are richer as a result of your golden touch.

Marsha Geoghagan, thank you for being real and for readily sharing your much sought-after wisdom on so many levels. I truly enjoy talking with you about writing and running things by you. Your honest input has been very much appreciated.

I would be remiss if I didn't thank my long-time, wonderful friends Rhonda Biondi, Debbie Dykes, Fran Futril, Janet Howard, Audrey Kendrick, and Rosilyn Spencer for your continual, genuine interest and excitement in my endeavors. I can always count on your cheerleader-like support. It keeps me encouraged during those times when I really need it.

Last but definitely not least, I want to thank my co-author Floy Turner. I am truly enjoying our journey together of writing your story. You are more than my co-author; I'm proud to call you my good friend.

CHAPTER 1

A Dream Come True

had finally arrived. I was now Special Agent Floy Turner, and my childhood heroine Nancy Drew had nothing on me!

After all, Florida's top law enforcement agency—the Florida Department of Law Enforcement (FDLE)—had asked me to join them, and I had eagerly accepted the invitation. I was now a member of this elite group whose agents were considered the cream of the crop in law enforcement.

Attaining my dream career as special agent didn't come easy, though. I had no fairy godmother who waved her magic wand. Instead, I had worked hard to qualify for this coveted position ever since I had attended the Florida Highway Patrol Academy eleven years earlier.

Although I loved my job as a trooper, I knew I was ready to make the change to special agent when given the chance. I knew the contents of my resume piqued the FDLE's interest when it came to hiring agents. I knew my experience of working in the most violent neighborhoods in Miami, engaging in dangerous drug investigations that resulted in the confiscation of over twelve million dollars of illegal narcotics, and participating in numerous undercover-operative opportunities had served me well.

That chance to fulfill my dream came in the summer of 1993, after learning that the FDLE had special agent openings. I applied, throwing my name in the hat with all of the other law enforcement officers, detectives, and agents who had shared my same dream, and I proceeded to jump through all of the necessary hoops.

Then one morning in September 1993, I got that life-changing phone call before going to work as a trooper. I'll never forget the caller's words telling me that the FDLE wanted to hire me as a special agent. *Me!*

Yes, the time had finally come for me to reap the rewards of my hard work. I was given three weeks to prepare physically, mentally, and emotionally. Who would have thought that the most difficult of the three would have been the latter?

Still, I made peace with leaving the familiar behind, and I embraced the unknown. I exchanged my Stetson hat for a business suit. I exchanged the highways and byways for the opportunities to investigate complex, statewide cases that involved high-profile homicides, public corruption, narcotics cases, and counterterrorism. I closed the old doors, and I walked through the new ones.

I looked forward to life, and from where I stood, it couldn't get more exciting. The only thing left for me to do was to embrace the ride ahead of me and enjoy it.

Meet South Florida's New Agents

Mine wasn't the only dream fulfilled in the fall of 1993. The FDLE hired around thirty more agents throughout the state, and I was one of four hired in the South Florida area.

I already knew two of the new agents in South Florida— Vaughn Wolf and Jerry Smith. If anyone had asked me if I approved of the selections of who would move forward in the hiring process with me, I would have given my thumbs up. But no one did, and that was okay.

When I learned the identity of the fourth newbie, Eric Pollen, I couldn't recall ever meeting him. I was satisfied with starting my new adventure with knowing two out of three, though. I would get to know Eric in due time.

The four of us made an interesting team. Vaughn Wolf had been a trooper with the Florida Highway Patrol (FHP), and Jerry Smith had worked as an undercover narcotics detective with the Miami-Dade Police Department. Eric had been a retired homicide detective for the Hollywood Police Department.

Vaughn had left the FHP to work for the DEA, and they assigned him to Manhattan. Evidently, he didn't like the DEA, Manhattan, or both, so he decided he'd rather return to Miami and work for the state of Florida, which led him to apply to the FDLE.

He was single and took great advantage of his good looks by accepting the role of a ladies' man. Vaughn stood over six feet tall. His light green eyes sparkled when he flashed that beautiful smile, and his light blond hair complimented his perpetually tanned skin. Cops who knew him from when he worked in Miami said he modeled men's underwear while living in New York. I didn't doubt it, although I tried not to envision him in men's underwear. Business was business, and I always tried not to veer away from those tenets.

Jerry had been one of the most likable guys I knew, so I was happy to learn that he was part of our group. He and I had worked together on a narcotics case, so I had come to respect him and trusted his instincts as a cop.

Eric looked more like an Ivy Leaguer than a cop because of his meticulous attire consisting of starched shirts and pressed pants. His clothes seemed tailored-made because they always fit his slim build and average height perfectly.

Our shared mutual interests in law enforcement, and in particular the FDLE, caused the four of us to quickly become a cohesive group. Although the FDLE had hired us, our employment was contingent upon passing the drug-screening pee test, which we all did, and the psychological, which consisted of a multiple-choice test and an interview with a state shrink. Since we were hired at the same time, our tests and one-on-one meets with the psychologist were scheduled at the same time. We drove together to Tampa to complete this last component of our hiring process.

Afterward on our way back to Miami, we laughed about the question on our written psychological exam that asked about our reading preference: *Alice in Wonderland* or *Popular Mechanics*.

Jerry and Eric both stated they chose *Popular Mechanics*, and I chose *Alice in Wonderland*. When Vaughn said he checked *Alice in Wonderland*, the rest of us laughed and teased him. Regardless of our choices, our group collectively determined that we were all more normal than the doctor evaluating us.

As it turned out, the four of us passed the psychological, but we weren't surprised. Still, I think we were all silently relieved that the final step in the hiring process was over, and we could move on with our new career.

To make it all official, the FDLE gave each of us our new special agent badge and identification card. When I received mine, I stared at both for the longest time with a mixture of pride and surreality.

Breathing a sigh of relief was still not an option, though. I had one more obstacle to overcome.

Miami had three openings, and the Key West field office had one. Since I lived in Homestead, I really, *really* preferred to work in Miami. I didn't want to face a move of a hundred-twenty-five miles away that required me to travel on a road containing lots of stopping and going, but I would have accepted the assignment anyway.

Therefore, I devised a plan so that I could make the Key West assignment work. I would move my travel trailer to the Keys and live in it and then travel home on the weekends when I wasn't on call. I knew firsthand that my trailer was habitable since I had lived in it for about eight months while my house was being reconstructed after Hurricane Andrew had demolished it. Although the rebuilding of my home had since been completed, I had kept the travel trailer on my property. Now it may come in handy once again because no way was I going to let a measly one hundred twenty-five miles come between me and my dream career.

When we were handed our assignments, I couldn't hold back my smile. Jerry, Eric, and I were assigned to Miami, and Vaughn got assigned to the Key West Field Office. I guess the command staff figured he was a natural for the Keys with his good looks and tan.

To make life a little sweeter, the FDLE assigned all of its agents an unmarked car. Admittedly, I was a bit disappointed that mine happened to be a six-year-old Chevy with faded bronze paint and faded blue-velour interior. In fact, it looked so bad that I felt the need to apologize to my neighbors for parking such a rundown car in my driveway.

My keen police mind told me that this car must have been used for one too many surveillances. The driver's seat sunk as I sat in it. It was a good thing I was tall; otherwise, I would be looking through the steering wheel. It also contained an assortment of crumpled fast-food wrappers and chicken bones under the front seat.

Professionally, I was concerned that that it looked nothing like a police car. Before, I had always used a marked patrol car, which deterred a lot of crime. In this car, I knew that in certain neighborhoods, or "hoods" as they were affectionately called, I could be mistaken for a lost tourist or citizen. Thugs didn't just happen upon these vulnerable drivers; they sought them out and took advantage of them, turning them into victims.

Although my new "wheels" may not have been the envy of the neighborhood, its beat-up appearance made it perfect for undercover surveillance.

Next on the special agent checklist was attending the ten-week FDLE Academy in Tallahassee. I had been required to go to our state's capitol for training in the past. My first time was as a cadet with the FHP and then several subsequent times to acquire additional training for different task forces to which I had been assigned during my career with them.

Back then, I had struggled with my emotions every time I had left Homestead to attend training in Tallahassee. I knew I would miss my family. But back then, my daughters were young and needed their mother, so leaving them behind created a tremendous amount of guilt.

This time around, though, things were different. My daughters had grown up. In fact, my youngest daughter lived in Tallahassee and was a student at Florida State University. Both of us attending different schools in the same city at the same time would just be one of those delightful coincidences.

Now I looked forward to going to Tallahassee to spend time with part of my family.

Welcome to the FDLE Academy

The time had finally arrived for me to leave for the FDLE Academy. So on a Sunday morning in the fall of 1993, I drove to a rest area off the Florida Turnpike to meet Jerry, Vaughn, and Eric. We loaded both my and Vaughn's FDLE cars with Jerry's and Eric's suitcases and duffle bags.

Jerry rode with me, and Vaughn and I followed each other as we all drove to Tallahassee to begin our new adventure. Our excitement trumped any exhaustion we felt. During the drive, Jerry and I shared the anecdotes we both had heard from other agents and made assumptions of what attending the academy would be like.

When we stopped at a rest area on I-10 in the northern part of the state, we realized (and appreciated) how the weather had changed from the hot humidity of South Florida to a nice, dry, cool day with a breeze.

As we entered Tallahassee, I could feel the excitement building inside me. I followed Vaughn's car to the Cabot Lodge and pulled into its parking lot. Although I had heard stories about this place, I had never personally experienced it. Every time I had attended training in Tallahassee as a trooper, I always stayed in the FHP Academy dorm and ate in its cafeteria. I couldn't help but let out an involuntary gag as I flashbacked to our meals of "Red Death" and the fried mullet served every Friday. All of the trooper cadets just knew they reused the same grease to cook subsequent meals.

This time around, though, we were going to stay in a legend. I knew the Cabot Lodge offered a lot of amenities for state employees. First of all, it was located in a fashionable side of Tallahassee with lots of upscale eateries nearby, and its excellent location provided ease in getting on and off I-10.

Secondly, the Cabot Lodge boasted about its free happy hour with its top-shelf liquor, wine, and beer every night, not to mention the unlimited buttered popcorn. In fact, this event was so popular that I believe it may have even superseded the free breakfasts every morning, or maybe its popularity merely prevented some from taking advantage of the breakfasts due to possible hangovers.

To add to the hotel's lure, it also offered close proximity to the "Ice Palace," FDLE's state-of-the-art building that housed its administration, laboratory, local field offices, and academy. For those agents who missed the breakfasts due to fully engaging in its happy hour the previous evening, the short drive to headquarters was much appreciated.

With all of this in mind, I looked forward to experiencing this illustrious establishment and creating my own stories at the Cabot Lodge.

Upon checking into our individual rooms, we learned that Florida State University's home games would be played during four of the weekends of our ten-week stay. Therefore, we would need to pack up our belongings and move elsewhere while the hotel catered to football fans, who had usually booked their rooms a year in advance. The hotel offered to store our luggage while the FDLE flew the four of us back to Miami on those weekends. We were the only four new hires who would qualify for the flying perks since Miami was almost five hundred miles away.

Forcing myself to go to sleep that first night was difficult. As I lay in bed, I recalled how it felt trying to go to sleep when I was a little girl on Christmas Eve with visions of new toys and the adventures they offered dancing through my mind. Now I was an adult, and my visions consisted of new adventures.

The next morning when the alarm clock buzzed, I kept my eyes closed, not wanting to move. I wanted to lay there and continue enjoying the luxury of my soft bed.

Wait a minute, I thought. *My bed isn't this soft. Oh, yeah, I'm not in my own bed.*

My eyes flew open when I remembered *why* I wasn't in my own bed; I was in Tallahassee, and today was my first day of training as a special agent with the FDLE.

I jumped out of bed, my heart racing with excitement. I didn't want to feel rushed, so I had made sure to set my alarm clock early enough to give me plenty of time, and I took full advantage of it. I was eager to meet the academy staff and my fellow classmates, and I wanted to make a good first impression. So, I took great care with my hair and makeup and made sure I chose just the right attire—a conservative navy-blue suit with an off-white blouse and navy-blue flat shoes.

I met Jerry in the lobby. We decided to leave the motel an hour before our reporting time even though the drive to the Ice Palace took about fifteen minutes. We would rather get there early and wait then take the chance of getting delayed by heavy traffic, a vehicle accident, or construction, and thus arrive late.

Our drive was uneventful, so we pulled into the Ice Palace's parking lot forty-five minutes early. I took my time gathering my belongings, which basically included a notebook, a purse with my gun and mandatory credentials, and a pair of sunglasses.

Upon entering, I stepped into an atrium with shiny granite floors. A staircase sat behind it.

A young man dressed in a dark-blue suit welcomed us. "Good morning," he said with a smile.

We returned his smile and showed him our credentials. "We're here for the academy."

He pointed to the right. "Sure, Agents, it's down that hallway, last door on the right."

"Thank you," Jerry and I said in unison.

I followed the young man's directions and walked down a blue-carpeted hallway. The soft flooring continued into the training room. Its businesslike setting gave it a corporate ambiance as opposed to the military-like setting of the FHP Academy.

The room consisted of padded conference chairs and rows of clean, white modern tables. I felt as if they were rolling out the red carpet to us, recognizing our years of service in law enforcement. For sure, there would be no rookies here.

Over the course of the next ten weeks, we learned so much information. A large section of the training covered RICO, or Racketeer Influenced and Corrupt Organizations. As the name indicates, these types of investigations targeted organized criminal activity. Other sections included investigating financial crimes, such as fraud and money laundering, homicide cases, criminal profiling, narcotics, and crimes against children.

As I got to know my classmates, I understood why the FDLE chose them. Undoubtedly, all thirty of them were top-notch, very smart law enforcement officers, and just being part of this elite group confirmed what I already knew: I had achieved a magnificent turning point in my career. They brought their vast experiences garnered from many years of working with local, state, and federal agencies. Some had been part of a command staff, such as sergeants, lieutenants, and captains, and others were experts in their fields, such as narcotics and homicide investigations.

As a result, I shouldn't have been surprised at finding this new venture a bit more challenging academically than I did while attending the highway patrol academy, the DEA narcotics school, and Barry University. The academic competition here had increased substantially, and therefore my grades were smack-dab in the middle when compared to my colleagues' grades.

It turned out that my time in Tallahassee gave me some of my fondest memories both inside and outside of academy life. Foremost, I took advantage of staying in the same town as my daughter, and we met for evening runs. We used these times to talk and catch up on each other's lives as we propelled ourselves up and down the hills. We stayed fit while enjoying our time together.

Of course, I spent a lot of time with my colleagues as well. After my runs with my daughter, I sometimes joined several class members at a couple of local establishments, namely Studebakers' and the Brown Derby. State police circles considered them to be the best watering holes in Tallahassee. They provided opportunities for us to meet and greet new colleagues, old friends, and seasoned agents who were in town for business.

Regardless of our reasons for visiting these establishments, fun was to be had by all. We packed the dance floors as sixties rock-and-roll music played in the background. For those sitting it out from the dance floor, they listened as the who's who of law enforcement told and retold cop stories, also known a "war stories."

We might have let our hair down, but those of us who had seen the destruction firsthand when investigating traffic accidents knew that mixing drinking with driving was a bad combination. A few Tallahassee police officers were recruited from time to time to provide transportation, similar to the FSU students who were obliged to utilize the "drunk bus."

The Friday before Thanksgiving, I graduated from the academy and returned to Miami as a FDLE Special Agent. Although I enjoyed my time in Tallahassee, I was glad to be back home. Not only did I have a new job to plan for over the weekend, but I needed to get busy planning our Thanksgiving dinner.

Despite my excitement, the weekend came and went, and Monday morning came soon enough along with my reporting to my new field office.

My First Day on "The Job"

I tried to contain my exhilaration as I opened the small front door to the gray, two-story Miami Regional Operations Center (MROC) building that housed the FDLE Miami office. I think I succeeded in my efforts.

The large airplane that flew about two hundred feet overhead felt almost like a celebratory salute to the occasion. The shaking of the ground beneath my feet and the vibrating of the building upon my entering it didn't distract me one bit. Plus, it was all par for the course since we were located in the flight path of the Miami International Airport with only a parking lot, fence, and street separating us from the runway.

Once inside, I glided across the visitor reception area. I looked over at the two small, stained, and threadbare gray chairs that waited for visitors to plop down on them. In fact, I remember sitting in one of them not too long ago as I anxiously waited for my interview.

I smiled and took in a deep breath, reminding myself that I was no longer a visitor; I was now a bona fide special agent who belonged here.

I walked to the dispatch center's small glass window where the communications officer, an attractive woman with curly blonde hair, sat. I recognized her from my previous visits, but I wasn't sure if she recognized me.

While reaching into my jacket pocket for my new credentials, she smiled and dismissed my attempts with a wave of her hand. With a strong southern drawl, she said, "I know who you are, Agent Turner. We've been waiting for you. Come on in."

Her relaxed tone sounded like a friend inviting me into her house for a cup of coffee.

I returned her smile. "Thank you."

She buzzed me into a hallway with several doorways that led to offices. I stepped onto dirty blue industrial carpet. You'd thought that my OCD tendencies would have caused me to be repulsed at its condition, but instead my heart swelled with pride.

In fact, there wasn't anything the FDLE could have done wrong at the time.

I passed by a large whiteboard hanging on the wall near the elevators that contained a list of names and official identification numbers handwritten with a blue marker. I figured they belonged to the agents assigned to the MROC since each name was preceded with the initials "S.A." for Special Agent.

I continued to follow the communications officer to the end of the hallway. We walked through the last doorway and into a large meeting room.

"Take a seat, Agent Turner," the communications officer said. "We're expecting a few other people to join you. Ya'll be having a meet and greet first. Should be fun." Then she left.

I sat down and looked around at my surroundings. A lot of different thoughts and emotions went through my head as I waited. I read somewhere that changing jobs can be a known stressor, and I couldn't agree more. As happy as I was, I still felt apprehensive and a bit awkward because of the newness. The FHP was my comfort zone, and I had stepped out of it in a big way.

Naturally, I couldn't help but think about my colleagues at the patrol and how I already missed them. I did find some solace knowing that we'd be crossing paths again since we'd be working in the same town.

I glanced down at my new business suit to make sure it was lint-free. I grinned when I thought about how excited I first was over the requirement to wear a professional—and hallelujah—feminine wardrobe, especially after years of wearing a uniform and tactical gear. As a result, I didn't own a single business suit.

This void had armed me with an excuse to shop 'til I dropped at the Dadeland Mall, and shop I did. In fact, I didn't waste any time. Within just a few days of getting that momentous phone call informing me that I was hired, I could be found in some of my favorite stores trying on and buying clothes that not only accommodated my job but fed my femininity.

My excitement refused to be dampened by the functionality challenges that a lot of female officers faced when buying regular clothes for police work. Suit pants must have belt loops on the waistband to ensure that the belt supporting your holster stayed in place. The waist sections on jackets or blazers needed to be roomy enough to accommodate a gun, extra gun magazines, handcuffs, a pepper spray container, and a collapsible baton. Shoes must be sturdy without any heels in case you needed to run.

Purchasing a new wardrobe was not the only perk that came with this job. I felt like I had made the big time when the FDLE provided me with a Visa card and American Express card to be used for expenses incurred during investigations, like hotels, flights, and gas. The only charge card the patrol gave to troopers was a state card to purchase gas.

Before my mind wandered anymore, Jerry Smith walked into the meeting room followed by Eric Pollen. I was so glad to see their familiar faces. The bond we had developed in Tallahassee turned us into kindred spirits, so I smiled at them and gave a thumbs up.

Seeing them dressed in their business suits, watching them take a seat, and realizing why we were gathered together in that room that morning created an emotional high. At that moment, it hit me, I mean *really* hit me that I was not dreaming anymore.

Back with RID (Robbery Interdiction Detail)

After going through orientation in the FDLE's meeting room, I spent the rest of the morning getting introduced to the command staff and field agents.

In a twist of fate, I learned that my first assignment as an FDLE Special Agent was back on the Robbery Interdiction Detail (RID), a multi-jurisdictional and hazardous task force where I had worked as a felony trooper with the FHP. RID was a proactive approach to quell the violence in high-crime areas where the homicide rates were the highest. We targeted the thugs who were gaining control of their communities.

The FDLE recognized that through my training as a trooper, I was well-suited to situations where possessing a tactical edge could make the difference in survival. In other words, I knew how to handle myself on the streets of Miami. Furthermore, I was one of the few agents who already knew the police codes unique to Miami law enforcement.

Although we worked in different locations, we targeted two neighborhoods known for extreme violence and that were located in very close proximity to each other. They were referred to as the Scott Projects and "Pork and Beans." The sale of narcotics took place on every street corner with armed "dope boys" employed as lookouts and protectors.

We utilized what were known as "jump outs," which was a swift tactical movement of driving quickly into the suspected "dope hole" and then exiting our vehicles to ensure the element of surprise. This put us at the advantage in that the lookouts and dope boys might not have time to react by either drawing their guns or hiding or moving their dope or money.

These maneuvers turned out to be very successful. The task force took more guns and lots of dope and drug money off the streets. All of this went hand in hand with shootings and gang wars.

Chasing teenagers with guns was the scariest part, though. I always worried that they couldn't grasp the seriousness of the consequences from shooting a gun. These kids were merely a product of a society that glorified violence because the street culture of shootings, illegal activities, and gang warfare flourished in this area. I always felt bad for the innocent families who tried to raise their children among this lawlessness.

We also spent our time locating stolen vehicles with stolen license plates and then conducting traffic stops. We knew that these offenders used stolen cars to further their criminal and gang activities, and if the police stopped them, they could bail and try to outrun the cops. To counter these attempts as well as discourage any violence from the drivers and vehicle occupants, our car stops involved multiple task force members responding to the scene.

Unfortunately, many of these car thieves were juveniles. Consequently, we called them "shorties" since some were so young they could barely see over the steering wheels.

The car stops proved to be more productive than merely locating and recovering stolen vehicles and arresting the car thieves. While performing legal safety sweeps of the vehicle's passenger compartments, we found lots of guns hidden under the front seats or between the seats, and many of them had been stolen.

I recall one evening during the late summer of 1993. I was still a trooper and part of the RID Task Force. I had conducted a traffic stop for a minor violation, and a few of the FDLE agents came to back me up.

One of the agents was a very pleasant-looking man named Mark Harper. He was about five-foot-eleven and appeared to be in his early forties. His full, dark moustache accentuated his dark complexion and brown eyes. Mark was also a member of the FDLE SWAT team.

I had ordered the driver to exit his vehicle and sit on the curb. He complied.

I asked, "Mind if I search your car?"

"Sure," he said with a shrug of his shoulders and smirk on his face.

Out of the corner of my eye, I saw Mark standing near me. I tilted my head toward the driver and asked, "Hey, Mark. Would you mind keeping an eye on my guy while I look through his car?"

"Okay."

I donned my black leather gloves and began looking under the car seats and discovered a loaded semi-automatic gun. As I pulled it out, I grasped its grip with my thumb and pointer finger with the barrel pointed downward. I lifted up my arm in a stupid show-off moment as if to say to the FDLE agents, "Look what I found!"

My show-and-tell moment deflected Mark's attention from the suspect, who now realized he had a split second to run, but a split second was all he needed. Off he went with the FDLE agents running after him.

A perimeter was quickly established, and my then partner's K-9 Sniffer located the runner hiding in an abandoned shed. For the "runner," the worst part was meeting up with Sniffer. I'm sure that if these perps had known their fates with Sniffer on the job, surrendering would have been much easier and less bloody. Most of them ended up with torn clothes and bite marks on their legs, buttocks, arms, and/or hands. Although Sniffer was known to show no mercy to those he hunted, he didn't completely discriminate against fleeing felons; he also bit a few cops, but he never bit me.

Now less than a year after my not-so-smart showoff moment, Mark was back in my life and this time as my field training agent. I found this match comforting in that we already knew each other and our respective abilities. His role would be to provide assistance and guidance with the FDLE case-management system and report-writing style.

Of course, they didn't ask me for my preference of assignments, but if they had, I would have chosen RID anyway. I felt confident working it, especially since I knew what was expected and had the tactical advantage that some of other agents may not have had.

As a felony narcotics officer with the FHP, I had been trained exceptionally well when it came to conducting felony traffic stops. Regardless of the reason, any traffic stop has the innate possibility of becoming dangerous. Those that involved narcotics trafficking, however, had a stronger propensity of becoming extremely violent in the blink of an eye and without any warning.

This time around would be somewhat different. As a trooper, I had initiated traffic stops from violations to felonies, but as an agent, any car stop performed was for a suspected felony only.

Also, I would drive into an area in my unmarked car and conduct surveillance.

This assignment was really the best of both worlds. In fact, it was almost like a family reunion. Not only would I be working with RID as a special agent and with Mark, but I was fortunate enough to have the opportunity to work with my former FHP squad. Jacob, Sniffer, and I were together again but in a different capacity.

We were no longer "partners," and I no longer trained with the FHP K-9 unit. Although I had enjoyed both, I didn't miss the training. I always had to play the bad guy since I was the only Miami felony trooper without a K-9. As a result, the dogs chased me. Falling backwards as the dog jumped on me from a fast run and the pain from the strong jaws clamping onto my wrist, even with a protective "hidden sleeve," never got any better. As far as I was concerned, I was glad to leave that part of my career behind.

In my heart, though, I would never leave Jacob and Sniffer behind. They may not be my official "partners" anymore, but I still knew that if I ever needed them for backup, I wouldn't have to look far. I knew that wherever I was, they'd be close by watching my back.

During my absence, RID's hours hadn't changed (from six at night to two in the morning), but the robberies and murders of English, German, and American tourists had stepped up several notches, and shootings were out of control. These statistics caused our tactical and mental stress levels to step up several notches as well.

FDLE agents from all over the state were deployed to Miami for a couple of weeks at a time. They quickly learned how to traverse from Liberty City to Hialeah in the late-night hours to seek refuge in front of Café Cubano's coffee window for a caffeine jolt. The Miami-Dade Police Department (MDPD), Miami Police Department (MPD), Hialeah Police Department (HPD), and state troopers also used this late-night window's sidewalk as a meeting spot to network and exchange information during their downtime.

Some of those officers who had come from other areas of the state tended to address situations with a bit of naivety. For instance, one of the agents from North Florida witnessed a fight in the littered, dirt-filled courtyard of a large three-story apartment complex off NW 54th Street in Liberty City.

We heard him say over the radio, "I see a man armed with a bat fighting another man. I'm going in to break up the fight."

This well-intentioned agent was alone when he jumped out of his unmarked patrol car in an effort to intervene. Of course, both fighters jumped on him. Then other nearby thugs who had just been hanging around saw an opportunity for some entertainment. They joined in to fight this lone ranger too, even though he had clearly identified himself as a cop. The rest of RID had to respond to the scene and rescue him before his clock was completely cleaned.

By the time we arrived, the crowd had jumped him and had given him some blows. We saved the agent from what was only going to get worse. The rescue turned into a free-for-all fight before we could all get out of there, arresting anyone who was part of the attack.

Those of us from Miami knew that when the odds were stacked against us, responding alone placed us in too much danger. We always knew to wait for backup unless someone was in imminent danger or being killed.

After all, we knew that many of the gang members, dope boys, and career criminals didn't demonstrate any respect for police officers, and they weren't about to start now.

Have Gun, Will Travel Too

Taking on gunfire was not an anomaly while working RID. Thankfully, none of the rounds hit their intended targets—the cops.

Some shootings took place on the rooftops of buildings or from other areas of large buildings occupied by innocent people.

In those circumstances, the shooter wasn't easy to spot, so it was impossible for us to shoot back.

Then there were those close encounters when armed perpetrators accosted or shot at the officers. When these situations occurred, a crime scene needed to be established.

In fact, squad members made it a point to carry large rolls of crime scene tape in their car trunks so that they could expedite securing the scene of the shootings.

Since everyone who crossed into the crime scene area was considered a witness for court purposes, we always roped off a section for the various departments' command staff who subsequently arrived at the site. We used this tactic so that they could stay close to the scene yet off the witness list.

This was just the beginning. An investigation of that shooting then followed to ensure the shoot was justified. So when a police officer discharged his or her weapon, a crime scene investigator seized the discharged gun for an evidence examination. The investigation couldn't be completed immediately, but the officer still needed a gun for protection after leaving the crime scene.

The cop's colleagues, as well as supervisors, recognized this vulnerability. Consequently, most of us kept a spare gun in our trunks to provide that officer with a weapon. After all, we of all people knew better than to leave our partners without a gun.

From the Mouths of Babes

Early one evening while working RID, I met a young fourteen-year-old boy named Claude Baptist. He rode a bicycle and wore a big grin on his nice-looking face.

Claude wanted to talk with the task force members. I could tell he was curious about our work.

The guys ignored him, so I talked to him. As he and I chatted, he told me he wasn't allowed to be on the streets after dark and would soon need to get home.

Claude then dropped a bombshell. "I know where the bad guys stash their dope."

He really had my attention now. A flash of excitement went through my body. "You do? Can you tell me where?"

"Yes. I live in an apartment on the second floor, and I look out my window and watch people buy the drugs. I see them give money. Then I see where the people who take the money go and pull out the drugs to give it to the buyers."

I listened intently to Claude as he volunteered all of this valuable intel. I knew he was credible because I knew what he described was a tactic the sellers used for two reasons. First, if the police searched them, they wouldn't have any contraband on their person. Second, the buyers wouldn't be able to grab the dope and run before paying for it. They must wait for the drugs to be retrieved by the sellers first, and before that happens, you can bet the seller had their money in hand.

Later that evening after Claude got safely in his house, I shared this information with the rest of the task force. I drove my unmarked car and parked down the street from the location Claude had described. I placed my window shade over my dash, which is common in Miami to preserve dashboards from the intense Florida sun. I scrunched down in my seat, using the shade to hide me. I then used my binoculars to watch the dopers operate behind a chain-link fence that surrounded the front and backyards of a ground-level concrete house.

A large ficus tree stood nearby. After the buyer gave the seller money, he walked behind the tree, bent over, and reached inside a pouch to retrieve the dope. Once in a while, the money guy disappeared temporarily into the house. I figured he went to hide the money so that he wouldn't have it on his person in case someone tried to rip him off or the cops frisked him.

After verifying Claude's information along with seeing exactly where the dope was hidden, I drove back to my team and gave them my report. We decided to go ahead and apply our "jump-out" strategy.

The dopers didn't have enough time to run and/or hide the drugs. We arrested them and confiscated the dope from their hiding areas.

Thanks to Claude's excellent information, we seized four ounces of crack cocaine, seven thousand dollars, and two guns. We also acquired quite a bonus. We arrested a doper who had been previously charged in the murder of an English tourist. The doper's manslaughter charge was dismissed on a technicality, but because of Claude, this guy now had collected new charges for new court battles.

When the Christmas season arrived, I wanted to pay my little "snitch" for his great intel. I bought Claude and his two younger brothers gift certificates to McDonalds. He and his brothers could walk to the one close to his apartment and buy Happy Meals. I considered this to be a small price for his contribution to RID.

When I went to his house to give him the gift certificates, he showed me a cloth portfolio with a news network logo. He got it during one of the few school field trips outside the "hood." Claude told me that he watched the news every night and wanted to be a broadcaster.

I met Claude's mother and got to know her. She was a single parent and a lovely Haitian lady with the same beautiful smile as her son. Initially, she didn't speak English. Eventually, though, she learned the language and became a U. S. citizen. Each time I visited them in their modest home, she offered me refreshments or a meal.

I knew the Baptist family struggled financially. Over the years when other holidays rolled around, I always counted on my two girlfriends Linda and Diane from Homestead to send food, new clothes, and great gifts to this wonderful family. In addition, my FDLE colleagues sent gifts at Christmas time. Later on, the Presbyterian Church Circle in Boynton Beach pitched in with food and gifts.

This family appreciated all of these contributions so much. They had never celebrated holidays with dinners and presents until then. They had only walked to the nearby Catholic Church where they worshipped.

Claude ended up involved with the morning broadcast at his school. He also initiated a beautification project for an inner-city park.

Meeting Claude blessed me. I knew him as an exceptional teenager and watched him grow into an outstanding man. I witnessed him progress through his inherent ability to network with the people he came to know. He always picked up the phone or sent me an email just to say hello and wish me well.

Claude never lost sight of his goals. Currently, he is now with a local Miami affiliate where he contributes to the news broadcast as an editor and reporter.

I consider him an inspiration. He never dwelt on the hardships he faced; instead, he always looked for the good and never wavered in his strong faith in God.

The Pain of Letting Go

Although my job was going great, by Christmas and New Year I was experiencing a lot of stress on the home front. The underlying unhappiness of my marriage over the years had taken its toll. I felt hopeless and helpless.

So on Christmas Day, while exercising with my daily run, I cried. It wasn't just a cry, but a grieving that I knew came from the very core of my being.

In my heart, I realized my marriage was over, but understanding it and facing it seemed like two different issues. Of course, I didn't want to admit that I had failed in my marriage, and falling in love again with my husband was no longer an option. Too much had occurred over the years in some areas, and too little had occurred in others. Collectively, all of our unresolved issues had been ignored and swept under the rugs of our careers. When I stopped to pay attention to them, I felt as if I was reopening the unhealed wounds. I was no longer convinced that the overwhelming pain that accompanied my attempts was worth the effort.

I knew the job had added insult to injury. For cops, protecting and serving others could be a challenge when balancing it with our families. Not only did our loved ones have to adjust to the crazy hours, but they needed to learn to accept broken plans due to an arrest made, a court subpoena, an unexpected occurrence that mandated the parent or spouse to work past the time his or her tour ended, or an endless number of other reasons. When both parents and spouses were on the job, then the chances of the unexpected doubled. It's tough on the kids, and it's even tougher on the marriage.

Some marriages do make it, and I had hoped mine would be one of them. I had hung in there probably longer than I should have, playing the eternal optimist. But admittedly, that's all I did...just hung in there. I wasn't exactly proactive. The job and my children took all of my time, and I guess I just didn't have anything left over to give to my husband.

The tears continued to flow, and I let them. I was alone with my thoughts, not realizing I had already run well beyond my normal route. The pain fueled me, and I didn't feel tired as I pondered my circumstances and what I should do.

On one hand, I had finally achieved my passion, my dream career. Ideally, my husband would have shared in my success, and I in his, and we would have retired, grown old together, and lived happily ever after. After all, we had two daughters. For the longest time, I think they had been the glue that kept him and me together. Undoubtedly, they had been the light that kept me focused.

They were growing up, though, and I wanted to set an example for them where they saw a strong mom who excelled in the career she loved. I wanted them to feel confident that they had the capabilities to become strong and independent women and that they didn't need to compromise when it came to relationships.

Sometimes I may have fallen short of being the perfect mom, but regardless, I loved my two girls. They had always been a blessing to me. I think when all was said and done, they taught me quite a few lessons, and they gave me the strength to do what I may not have otherwise believed I was capable of doing.

I turned back to head home, my vision blurred from crying. I tried to remember the good times my husband and I had shared, but our problems besieged my thoughts. Maybe one day I would be able to complete this task, but not today.

I rounded the corner and saw my house. Seeing the concrete block structure reminded me that I shared my sanctuary with a man who felt like a stranger. I realized I had been trying to balance it all—motherhood, my career, and my marriage. The first two were stable, but the third component had been teetering for too long. The teeter had now become more of a sway, not unlike the winds we experienced a few years back with Hurricane Andrew.

I made it to my house and stopped. I took in a deep breath before continuing, and as I walked through my front door, I came to the conclusion that my marriage would not survive another holiday.

CHAPTER 2

A Christmas Eve Murder

While my marital issues caused me to endure a lousy Christmas holiday, others across town suffered through the most horrific Christmas they could have ever imagined. Ronald Brooks, a tax collector with the Florida Department of Revenue, experienced his worst and last holiday season.

Ronald's position, which earned him almost a meager twenty-two thousand dollars a year, forced him to perform some functions that weren't always acceptable to everyone. For instance, when a business defaulted on paying its state taxes, and an investigator deemed it appropriate to freeze its bank accounts, the onus to sign the notifying letters and send them to those delinquent business owners fell on Ronald.

Because Ronald was merely a paper pusher and not a decision maker, he never thought he needed to protect his personal contact information from the public. He allowed his North Miami Beach home telephone number and address to be listed in the Miami phone book.

While Ronald worked hard performing his job as a state employee, entrepreneur Pascal Romano lived the great American dream. To begin, he owned the notorious Italian restaurant Bianchi's located in Coconut Grove, otherwise known as the "Grove."

In Pascal's defense, though, realizing his dream didn't come easy. Italian-born and-raised, he literally worked his way to the United States as a waiter on a cruise ship. After the ship docked in the Port of Miami, he walked off its gangway and never returned. The boat subsequently sailed away and continued on its journey with one less waiter.

Pascal spent the next four years waiting tables in local Miami restaurants until he *allegedly* saved enough money from his tips to purchase Bianchi's Restaurant with a four-hundred-sixty-thousand-dollar cash down payment. It ended up earning a reputation as an upscale establishment.

However, food and expensive wine weren't the only items served at Bianchi's. It also served discretion to high-powered judges and mobsters as they held their private "courts" in its dining area, conducting under-the-table cash transactions and accepting bribes for favorable court rulings.

All good things must come to an end, though, and these illegal activities were no exception. Bianchi's later became known for the scandalous 1993 Operation Court Broom judicial scandal.

This investigation started when the FBI and FDLE had gotten wind of complaints and rumors that some court cases appeared to have been fixed. Some credible criminal attorneys and state prosecutors began to approach the FDLE and FBI regarding the constant decisions handed down by a few judges. As a result, informants were developed, and surveillance began at Bianchi's.

While these judges and mobsters enjoyed two-hour lunches at their reserved Bianchi's tables, FDLE and FBI agents sat across the dining area near the restrooms or kitchen, watching and documenting the illegal activities. Of course, the agents had to eat the excellent food so that they appeared to "fit in" with the other diners, making this assignment that much more appetizing. The downside was that they started having difficulties "fitting into" their clothes as their waistlines expanded from consuming Bianchi's delectable food.

This scandal became known as Operation Court Broom, the largest judicial corruption investigation in Florida's history. Five Miami judges and a half a dozen lawyers were arrested for offering and taking bribes to fix court cases.

Pascal was a minor player and was subpoenaed for his restaurant's participation. In April 1993, the state had had him in court testifying in the matter. However, serving food to officers of the court, who were on the take, wasn't really a crime.

Now, though, Operation Court Broom seemed to be in Pascal's rearview mirror. He didn't *appear* to be any worse for the wear, keeping up the semblance of living the great American dream. In addition to his popular restaurant, he had a wife and baby. They lived in a large, yellow stucco two-story home with a barrel-tiled roof in the affluent city of Coral Gables, south of the Grove.

Another component to Pascal's American dream was an attractive attorney by the name of Hilda Fletcher. Police who had Pascal under surveillance reported him to frequently be at her home late at night and alleged her to be his mistress. Coincidentally, Hilda and her five-year-old daughter lived near Pascal. Of course, her close proximity to him provided a convenience in more ways than one.

Rounding out his great American dream was his membership in the inner circle of movers and shakers supporting the University of Miami football games. He and these fans, who affectionately called themselves members of the "Mile High Club," traveled in leased airplanes to many of the away games.

Pascal's engagement in the high-society life and having these high-powered patrons dine in his restaurant was a status symbol.

In return, he served them gratis meals and wine and wrote off the costs of both. However, catering to the upper crust created a lack of cash flow at Bianchi's, which in turn limited the restaurant's finances, which in turn limited Pascal's personal finances.

His inability to pay his taxes had been ongoing before finally coming to a head on December 23, 1993, when he received the letter signed by Ronald Brooks notifying him that his bank accounts had been frozen. The pressure of needing to purchase expensive gifts for his wife, his son, and his girlfriend, of appeasing his high-society patrons, plus all of the expenses involved with running Bianchi's caused Pascal to go into a rage. He couldn't access any cash funds. He drove to the state building that housed the Department of Revenue, only to find it closed.

His fury remained. Pascal found Ronald Brooks' address in the phone book and drove to his house on Christmas Eve. While Brooks shopped for Christmas dinner preparations, Pascal smoked a cigarette on the sidewalk in front of Ronald's small and modest home, watching and waiting for Ronald to pull into his driveway. Using his nonsmoking hand, he fingered his Brazilian-made Taurus .38-caliber gun in the right pocket of his jacket.

In the meantime, Mrs. Brooks sat in her wheelchair eagerly waiting for her husband to come home. She kept her eyes fixed on the small Christmas tree that sat on top of their large boxed television, enjoying the multi-colored lights, tinsel, and decorations as she listened to Christmas carols coming from the tabletop radio next to Ronald's recliner.

She now depended on Ronald for everything since her heart, diabetic, and breathing issues had caused her to retire early from her school-teaching job. A smile spread across her face when she heard Ronald's car approaching. She then felt a tinge of excitement as she remembered that since tomorrow was

Christmas, her husband wouldn't have to work, and she could spend more time with him.

Ronald parked his small, battered, and faded gray Honda at the curb in front of his house. He reached into the passenger's side and retrieved his groceries.

Pascal took one last drag from his cigarette and dropped it on the ground. As Ronald walked from his car, he saw Pascal facing him.

Pascal pulled the gun from his jacket pocket and shot Ronald four times point blank in the chest.

Mrs. Brooks heard the shots over the Christmas carols. She wheeled herself to the front door, opened it, and saw her husband and her lifeline in a pool of blood dying in front of her home.

When the homicide unit from the North Miami Beach Police Department (NMBPD) got the report, the detectives rushed to the scene to begin the investigation of Ronald's murder. They initially determined this to be a robbery attempt gone bad.

They located a couple of witnesses in the neighborhood. Both stated they saw a small-framed man with olive skin, dark hair, and a black beard standing and smoking near Ronald's house. One witness saw a gold station wagon parked near where this man stood.

The day after Christmas, the detectives were able to start speaking with Ronald's coworkers. They discovered that restaurant owner Pascal Romano had called and spoken to a secretary at the Revenue office moments before closing. After she told him that Ronald had left for the day, he screamed at her and used profanity. She could feel his rage coming through the phone lines.

The homicide detectives made their way to Bianchi's. Pascal wasn't there, so they interviewed all of the restaurant employees. The staff stated that they hadn't seen Pascal since late on Christmas Eve when he came to the restaurant and emptied out the cash drawer. They said he seemed upset and left in a hurry. Now the employees worried about maintaining service, and thus their jobs, at Bianchi's during this busy holiday season.

The detectives began to zero in on Pascal as the shooter

Since I was a new FDLE agent, I had been assigned as the duty agent from Christmas Eve through New Year's Day. Early in the morning, two days after Christmas, I received a telephone call at my office from an FDLE supervisor. He told me to attend a meeting at the NMBPD homicide unit about a state employee who had been the victim of a homicide.

The supervisor said, "Since Eric Pollen has extensive homicide investigative experience, he'll also be at this meeting. Since you were the duty agent, you'll be the case agent, and we'll need you to open an investigation."

My heart skipped a beat or two or maybe even ten, and I felt my jaw drop. Fortunately, my supervisor couldn't see me. I was ecstatic that he assigned *me* to be the case manager. This meant that I would be responsible for the investigation, which included the investigative case file and case management records. In a high-profile case like this one, though, my supervisor and the FDLE regional legal advisor would be the final decision makers.

Admittedly, this news also made me a little nervous. My mind raced as I realized I had to be on top of my investigative skills and write meticulous reports since this case would make a large impact in Tallahassee, good or bad. More importantly, though, I had to obtain justice for this state employee, so I felt some comfort knowing Eric was with me since he was so experienced.

My supervisor then gave me the details surrounding the circumstances of the murder and the identity of the suspect. "Tallahassee's going to be briefed as well," he said, "because the victim's murder may be the result of his performing his official state duties. And oh, the governor and other state officials are going to be monitoring this case."

I thought, *No pressure here.*

He continued. "Furthermore, the NMBPD's taking the lead. You've got the state connection, so you're going to need to work together as a team. But first you'll need to report to a Lieutenant Lynn Russo. She's in charge of the NMBPD's homicide unit."

I was relieved that she would be the person I would work with on my first homicide case. Lynn and I already knew each other. Every time I thought about her, I couldn't help but see her piercing green eyes and flaming red hair sitting on top of a pretty and petite keg of dynamite. Her colorful suits always came with plunging necklines and very high-heeled shoes.

Professionally, I trusted and respected her judgment. She had also acquired a lot of respect from the Miami-Dade State Attorney. I admired her tenacity when investigating a suspect. A lot of her passion probably came as a result of the murder of her police officer husband, who had been killed in the line of duty. Maybe her own senseless loss caused her to transfer her pain and hunger for justice into each homicide case that came across her desk.

Lynn would eventually rise to become the police chief at NMBPD. She went down in history as being the first woman to serve in that position with that department.

When my supervisor finished briefing me, I drove to the NMBPD station. I pulled into its almost-full parking lot and walked toward the aesthetically pleasing two-story building framed mostly with glass.

Once inside, I approached a balding man sitting and writing something at a large desk. The three stripes on his sleeves signified that he held the rank of sergeant.

I stood in front of him and tried to sound as casual as possible. "Excuse me. I'm Special Agent Turner, and I'm here to see Lieutenant Lynn Russo."

His head lifted slowly from his paperwork. His expressionless face stared at my badge and ID and then up at my face for a moment as he quickly summed me up. In a tone that sounded almost bored, he said, "They're waiting for you in the conference room. Up the stairs and to the right. It's at the end of the hall."

He then looked back down and continued writing.

I thanked him and turned to walk up the stairs, each one taking longer than I wanted. Admittedly, I wanted to run up them and take two steps at a time to quickly reach the destination of my first homicide case as a special agent, but I suppressed my desire.

I arrived in the homicide conference room for the meeting. Lynn sat at one end of the table and looked up when I walked through the door.

"Hi, Floy. Good to see you. Have a seat." She pointed with her perfectly manicured hand to the seat across the table from her.

Also in the room was a very handsome, clean-shaven man with dark, curly hair. He carried a cup of steaming coffee as he walked from the coffee machine to the conference table. I was able to get a glimpse of his build, which turned out to be trim, and it fit nicely into his Ralph Lauren suit.

Lynn motioned to the good-looking man. "Floy, this is Detective Hal Cohen. He's one of the homicide detectives here with me."

He said, "Hi, Floy." He continued standing as he sipped his coffee.

Eric then entered the room. He walked over to Hal, and they greeted each other by smiling and shaking hands. Hal then slapped Eric on the back. Obviously, they already knew each other and were friends.

BEHIND HER SPECIAL AGENT BADGE • 33

Lynn said, "Well, okay then. Looks like everyone is present and accounted for, so let's get down to business."

Hal briefed us again on the case, most of which I had already heard. Then he said, "Have either of you got any information to add?"

"Yes," I said. "Prior to the meeting, I asked the FDLE analyst to run a public record check for Pascal. She found that he has an additional leased residence in a large apartment building located on Kendall Drive. She also discovered that he owns a 1990 gold Ford Taurus station wagon. We think he might have fled Miami in it."

The detectives and I agreed that enough probable cause existed to obtain search warrants for all of Pascal's properties— the one he shared with his wife, his restaurant, and his additional apartment on Kendall Drive. I guess he had so much going on that he needed some place where he could get away and spend some "me" time.

At that point, obtaining these warrants was the priority. By searching his properties, we hoped to secure evidence for the murder and apprehend the murderer. We also set in place surveillance units on all three properties.

Next on the agenda, we wanted to have a conference meeting with the agents who had worked the Court Broom case. We wanted to learn more about Pascal's associates.

We all left the meeting with a plan in place. Hal and Eric volunteered to write the warrants.

Hal said, "We'll keep you informed of our progress and let you know when a judge signs them."

My tasks included making preparations and recruiting FDLE supervisors and agents to make up three search teams. We needed the additional assistance in serving all three sites simultaneously.

My efforts paid off because we were able to assign six agents per team. Since all of the places to be searched were out of the NMBPD's jurisdiction, the FDLE agents would be in charge of this part of the investigation.

My gut instinct told me that Pascal kept his most confidential information in his "me" apartment. I didn't believe he wanted to risk his wife learning more about *all* of his personal information, such as his mistress and other residence.

I drove to the apartment complex office and informed the manager that I was anticipating serving a warrant at Pascal's unit. I asked him for a key and said, "I promise I won't use it until I have possession of the signed warrant in my hand."

He was cooperative and didn't seem a bit surprised. As the manager of a big apartment complex in Miami, he had probably been served with warrants before because of all of the drugs.

Not long after I left the manager's office, Eric called me. "Hey, Floy, just wanted you to know we got the warrants signed."

I said, "Great. You search the house where Pascal lives with his wife, and Hal can search the restaurant. I'll search the apartment."

I notified the rest of the teams about the signed warrants. We agreed that the three teams would meet at the two residences and the restaurant at nine o'clock that night and then search all three properties at the same time.

By the time I got back to Pascal's building a few hours later to serve the warrant, the night seemed to have gotten darker. The weather also had cooled down quite a bit, but I was so focused on the task at hand that the chill didn't bother me like it usually would.

I saw the surveillance van parked across the street. The FDLE agent and NMBPD detective that had manned it for the past four hours exited the van and walked over to us.

The FDLE agent said, "The apartment doesn't look like anyone's home. We haven't seen any lights turned on, and no one has entered or left it since we've been here."

I said, "Okay, then. Let's canvass the area to see if we can find anyone who may know something. We'll meet back here when we're done."

We all split up in search of someone who could give us more information and/or confirm what my surveillance team concluded.

I proceeded to perform my due diligence by walking around the apartment and talking with neighbors. Fortunately, the late hour didn't hinder our plans since so many Miami residents go in and out of their apartments until really late.

Two of the agents intercepted a couple leaving their apartment located below Pascal's. The woman said, "I hadn't seen the man who rented the apartment in the last few days."

The male neighbor said, "Yeah, I'd see him leave around midmorning, and I think he'd come home late at night."

When my whole search team rejoined me, we walked to Pascal's apartment. I held a copy of the search warrant in my left hand and used my right hand to unlock the door with the apartment key. When I tried to fit the key into the key hole, I realized the lock had been changed.

I looked at the two guys standing closest to me. They stepped back and then used the alternative method of entry—kicking in the door.

I stepped inside and looked around. I must say that Pascal's digs did not impress me. The drab apartment looked like a dirty, sparsely furnished flop house.

The typical white and bare walls looked like they had been painted and repainted by the apartment maintenance crew. Plastic beige blinds covered the dirty windows, and soiled beige carpet covered the floors.

I thought, *This guy has two women he's romantically involved with, and both are living well while this pig lives in a sty.*

The search team split up to search the various rooms. Two searched the living room, looking under the cushions on the small tropical-print sofa and two cheap armchairs.

A wall separated the living room from the small dark kitchen that had a checkered linoleum floor and white appliances. Two other agents searched through the white cabinets and drawers.

A fifth agent and I entered a single bedroom to search it. The first thing that caught my eye was a torn-up computer sitting on top of a small wooden desk. The hard drive was missing.

We toppled over the queen-size mattress. I emptied out all of the dresser drawers while the other agent searched the closet.

We didn't succeed in finding any paper records during our search.

"I guess that's it," I said. "Let's go."

I called Hal to ask if they had found something at the restaurant. Unfortunately, that search came up empty as well.

He said, "The employees here say they're closing the restaurant. They aren't being paid, and no one knows where Pascal is or if he's ever coming back. We're leaving now and heading back to the office."

I then called Eric to see if they had found anything at Pascal's family home.

"Sorry, Floy. It was quite the dramatic venture. His wife held their baby and cried the whole time we were there. When we asked her about her husband's apartment, she cried harder and insisted she didn't know anything about it. I believed her. I did ask if she knew Hilda Fletcher. Oh, boy, she really came unglued then. She was so hysterical, she couldn't even talk, so we just had to stop the interview."

By the time the searches were over, my adrenaline went into low gear. I felt exhausted and couldn't wait to go home. But first, we all needed to meet up at the FDLE offices and discuss our findings as a team. Thankfully, someone had offered to bring donuts, and someone had offered to make the much-needed coffee.

I finally got home around two in the morning. Lying in bed, I revisited the night's events. I didn't consider them failures. After all, we did learn a few things. First, his wife was ignorant of Pascal's criminal activities as far as we could discern. His hard drive was missing, and those things don't go missing without a reason. More importantly, Pascal was missing, and a person doesn't go missing without a reason.

Now all we needed to do was find both Pascal and the hard drive. Once we did, I was certain a lot of our questions would be answered.

Once we did, we may even solve this case.

Strategic Runs

I woke the next day with the case on my mind. It seemed to consume my every waking moment these days. If truth be known, it probably took up some of my dreamtime as well.

Its high-profile nature, as well as it being my first homicide case, motivated me to reach out to my assigned mentor and training agent Mark to guide me in those areas of his expertise. I needed to see whether or not I was on target with this investigation.

We had already scheduled a "meeting" at the Doral Golf Course to run together, and the timing couldn't have been better. Since the FDLE offices were nearby, the golf course's security chief had offered its three-mile cart path for agents to use on their early morning runs.

Mark and I figured we could get our exercise in for the day and discuss business all at the same time. Plus, the paths and time of day gave us an element of privacy.

As I got dressed in my running clothes, I made a mental list of things I wanted to discuss with Mark. I stepped outside into the cool December morning, glad that the weather was perfect for a run.

I drove to the golf course and pulled into the parking lot five minutes early. I saw Mark stretching off to the side.

This morning's run went quickly. We ran, and we talked. I laid everything out to him, including my actions and gut instincts. Mark listened attentively and periodically injected a question.

After our run and speaking with Mark, I felt confident that I hadn't ventured off track with my investigative efforts.

These morning runs soon evolved into a routine for us. About once a week, Mark and I met and ran through this beautiful quiet area before the golfers ventured out onto the courses and before we ventured off into our workday.

Is Anybody There?

That morning, Mark and I went back to the FDLE after our run where I showered and dressed for the day. I then scheduled a midmorning meeting with the Operation Court Broom agents at the FDLE offices and invited the NMBPD investigative team to join us.

We developed a list of Pascal's known associates, and I coordinated everyone's activities in locating and interviewing everyone on it. From that list, we hoped to develop additional leads that would show us where Pascal was as well as develop any information that might link him to the murder.

The associates to whom Eric and I were assigned included his girlfriend Hilda Fletcher, a young lawyer named Brent Patrick, and some owners of companies at the Port of Miami. Eric and I decided to go to Hilda's house first. I figured she probably knew the most.

We drove down Hilda's quaint tree-canopied road that provided lots of shade from the mid-afternoon sun. While looking for her house, we passed by long driveways, veranda porches, and well-maintained landscaped lawns that adorned the beautiful homes lining her street. Mercedes-Benzes, Land Rovers, and BMWs occupied the driveways.

We pulled up to Hilda's gray brick home. Expensive-looking wicker furniture sat on her veranda. A fresh Christmas wreath hung on her red door, and red shutters decorated both sides of her windows. Manicured trees were scattered throughout her impeccable yard.

I wondered if Hilda had ever visited Pascal's sleazy apartment. I thought, *Why would a successful lawyer be attracted to this guy?* I mean, he was uneducated, a waiter who had suddenly obtained money to buy his restaurant, and he drove a beat-up station wagon.

I didn't think the attraction could be about his looks, not according to the pictures I had seen of him. Plus, he was married. He hung around with criminals, albeit some of those crooks were judges and lawyers. Regardless, I just could *not* wrap my head around this romance.

I knocked on Hilda's door, but she didn't answer. We thought that she might be at work, so we decided to go to her office.

We drove about two miles just off of a once high-end shopping area known as Miracle Mile. Since the advent of the much-more fashionable malls over the last couple of decades, these shopping areas had lost most of the allure they had held back in their day. One thing the malls didn't have, though, were the pink sidewalks that this part of the Gables had.

When we pulled up to her office, we saw that it was closed. With Christmas over and New Year's Eve just around the corner, many people had taken the whole week off between the holidays.

Eric suggested we drive to the Port of Miami, also known simply as the "Port." We figured these businesses were open and wouldn't shut down for another few hours. We hoped we may be able to find some of those who we wanted to interview still at work.

The Port was accessible from downtown Miami and contained docks, cruise ship buildings, customs, and other related offices. Some of these enterprises were legal, but lots of members of the mafia could also be found around all of the ports.

We parked in front of an attractive and well-kept sand-colored building. Big letters on a sign read "Merle Containers," which was one of the businesses on our list. Its CEO was allegedly connected to Pascal through the University of Miami football fans' Mile-High Club.

We walked inside and didn't see anyone except for one man walking down the hall with his back to us.

I spoke in a loud voice. "Excuse me, sir. We're looking for Frank Brown."

The man stopped and turned. His eyes went down to the objects on my waist—my badge and my gun—which sat next to each other. Both items seemed to irritate him. He lowered his eyebrows and flared his nostrils. I got one of those cop feelings that this guy didn't like law enforcement.

He looked directly into my eyes. "Frank's not in, and you need to get outta here." He accentuated his gruff tone with a jutted chin.

I refused to let him intimidate me. I squared my shoulders and in a firm tone asked, "When is Frank expected back?"

Mr. knuckle-dragging thug's eyes narrowed more as they darted back and forth between Eric and me. He shrugged. "Don't know. Now go!" He turned as if dismissing us and walked away.

Eric and I left, knowing we weren't getting anywhere. As we left the building, I said to Eric, "Did you feel the love?"

Eric just looked at me and shook his head.

Next, we visited a shipping business. The treatment we received improved by just a notch and a small one at that.

I turned to Eric and said, "They all hate the police."

Eric said, "Well, it is the Port."

I felt that both of these businesses were connected to some sort of illegal activity. I didn't think my theory was farfetched. The Port was known for transporting stolen vehicles out in containers and for drug smuggling and laundering money that got hidden in shipped goods.

We hoped we could get in at least one interview before calling it a day.

I wanted to talk with Brent Patrick, but we didn't have a business location for him, just an apartment address. With this in mind, we decided to make him our last try for the day.

By now, the sun was setting. We located Brent's apartment in an upper-middle-class area of the Grove. I knocked on his door, but no one answered.

When I peered into his windows, I was surprised to see the apartment empty with not a stick of furniture in sight. I knocked on some other doors in the apartment complex to see if any neighbors knew Brent. Although they had seen him come and go, no one knew any personal information about him.

We tried, but we ended the day with zero interviews.

Eric and I agreed to meet the follow morning at the FDLE offices to prepare for the last interview on our current list—a Miami judge.

The Search for a Murderer

After my regular morning run in Homestead, I drove an hour to the FDLE office.

I used my key code to enter through the front door. Just as I walked into our building, I heard—rather felt—a plane flying overhead. The walls vibrated again, echoing more booms. We had pretty much gotten used to the repercussions of working next to an airport, but we still found ourselves startled every once in a while by the overpowering sounds of a plane coming in or taking off really low.

I hurried upstairs to an empty squad bay. I picked up the room's coffeepot to fill it with water.

When I got into the kitchen, a supervisor was folding up the brown tweed sleeper-sofa. I saw a few clothes spread across the small kitchen table and chairs as if they had been hung out to dry.

Seeing this special agent supervisor under these circumstances took me by surprise. I stopped in my tracks temporarily, feeling as if I was intruding upon his privacy.

When I recovered, I said, "Good morning, Sir."

He looked at me and shook his head back and forth before cocking it to one side. "It's no secret I move in here every time my wife throws me out of the house." He shook his head again. "After she threw me out this time, she had second thoughts. She lay down on the ground behind the back tires of my car as I packed up to leave."

I gave a half-smile and said, "Oh, my." I really didn't know how else to comment and why he even shared his marital challenges with me.

Then I filled the coffee pot with water. As I walked out of the kitchen, I said over my shoulder, "Coffee in the violent crime squad room in a few, and I'll have plenty to share."

Eric arrived a few minutes later, and we began to plan our interview with Judge Hail. Eric was prepared and said he wanted to take this interview.

I said, "No problem. I'll take some notes and interject any questions I feel we need clarification on or if we need more information."

We headed back to the Grove to an elegant condominium building. We knew from our intelligence data that at the very least, the judge associated with Pascal on a social basis. We also knew that the judge ate many meals at Bianchi's and that he and Pascal travelled together to football games. Although his name had come up in the Court Broom case, law enforcement didn't have enough evidence to arrest and charge him.

When we rang the bell, Judge Hail opened the door. He looked like an ordinary man—average height, medium complexion, neatly trimmed graying hair. However, his demeanor was anything but ordinary, starting with our showing him our credentials.

He studied both of our ID cards and glanced back and forth between Eric and me. He furrowed his brows and turned down the corners of his lips.

"What do you want?" he snapped.

Eric said, "We have a few questions for you, Your Honor. May we come inside and talk?"

Judge Hail's eyes narrowed as he looked both of us up and down. He hesitated before stepping aside to let us in.

I said, "Your Honor, we need to talk to you about Pascal Romano. He's a suspect in the murder of a Department of Revenue employee."

The judge didn't blink. I thought he'd make a great poker player.

Eric started asking him questions. The judge sat with his arms crossed. He gave us less-than-enthusiastic answers. "Yes, I have dined at Bianchi's, but I don't know this Pascal," he stated in a bored and tolerant tone.

When pressed about the road trips for the games, he claimed, "A lot of folks go on those same trips. I don't know all of them." He rolled his eyes.

His boredom then turned into a smirk that I wanted to wipe off his face. He was an attorney, and as an attorney, I needed to accept that he wasn't about to incriminate himself or admit to being friends with a murderer.

When we left his condo and got into our car, I said, "I don't believe him. He lied."

Eric nodded his head in agreement.

Next, we made our way to Frank Brown's office. Since we were in the midst of normal business hours, we had hoped we would catch him there, but we didn't. So, we headed to his multimillion-dollar home in the Grove.

While driving down Frank's street, I was able to catch glimpses in between some of the houses of the beautiful, deep, dark turquoise-blue water on Key Biscayne. The large homes looked out of place on their small lawns, but then I figured that the lack of space in the front yards gave the residents more spacious backyards to overlook and appreciate the water view.

We rang Frank's doorbell. A few moments later, he opened the door.

I tried not to show my surprise when I saw him. After being at his business the day before when we encountered his thug employee, I expected him to look like a character on the television series *The Sopranos*.

Instead, Frank turned out to be quite handsome with blonde hair and a fair complexion with freckles. He appeared well-groomed in a casual country-club manner, welcoming us as if we were old friends. He immediately engaged us, offering us a seat and a cool drink.

We all sat in his exquisite living room with floor-to-ceiling windows that looked out to the bay. I spotted a multimillion-dollar boat docked to the north side of his backyard. The other side contained an infinity pool, where the pool water looked as if it continued into the bay. A large covered patio with a full outdoor kitchen sat between the house and pool.

He leaned forward as if he embraced our presence. "Yes," he said, "I know Pascal from the football games. In fact, when Pascal opened Bianchi's, I helped him with a loan of a few hundred thou. Since then, I've eaten at Bianchi's a few times."

At least he admitted to the loan and knowing Pascal, but he wasn't going any further. Of course, he was smart and only admitted to what he knew we could prove. Frank remained calm and smooth and looked me straight in the eye as he spoke.

Although very personable, I suspected he too was lying. No one gives an acquaintance four hundred sixty thousand dollars in cash, especially knowing the recipient was a waiter on a ship and then waited on tables in Miami for just a few years. Furthermore, Pascal had no proven business background. This, along with Frank's business location at the Port and the way his employee treated us the previous day, gave me a sinister feeling of mafia involvement.

However, we definitely had a much more pleasant meeting with Frank than we did with the judge. At the end of the interview, though, we walked out of his utopian home with unanswered questions and not anymore pertinent information than we had when we arrived.

Eric and I agreed that with our gut feelings about some type of mafia connection or criminal activities at the Port, we should keep Frank on our radar.

We then drove to Hilda's house and office, checking on both every day. Finally, the Monday after New Year's, we saw her car parked in the driveway of her home.

We parked our car far enough away so that she wouldn't "make us" but close enough so that we could keep an eye on her car. We decided we'd wait until she left and follow her so that we could get a feel for her before we conducted the interview. Of course, on our wish list with this ploy was that she would lead us to Pascal.

About an hour later, Hilda's front door finally opened. She came outside with her purse and clothes draped over her left forearm and holding the hand of a little girl with her right hand. She put the clothes into the passenger side of the front seat before helping the child into the backseat of her black late-model E-class Mercedes-Benz.

After she pulled out of her driveway, we pulled out of our parking spot, keeping our distance behind her. Thank goodness for the New Year's Eve party hat that sat in the rear window of her car. It acted like a beacon, making it easy to keep an eye on her and follow her for most of the morning.

We watched as Hilda dropped off her child at school, dropped off her clothes at the dry cleaners, and stopped at the post office, returning to her car with a stack of mail. Next was her office.

Eric and I parked nearby. We took an elevator to her beautifully decorated second-floor suite where her staff assistant greeted us. Her long brown hair was pulled off of her face with a red scrunchie.

I pulled out my credentials while simultaneously saying, "I'm Special Agent Turner, and this is Special Agent Pollen. We're here to speak to Hilda Fletcher."

The assistant pursed her lips as she peered over the top rim of her thick glasses to examine our credentials and us. "You need to make an appointment to speak with Miss Fletcher."

Eric and I glanced at each other and then around the empty reception area. We had waited long enough to speak to Hilda, and we weren't going to be put off any longer. We weren't clients wanting to retain her; we were law enforcement needing to solve a murder.

We walked past the gatekeeper, making a beeline to Hilda's office.

I heard the assistant following us, saying, "Excuse me. You need an appointment. You can't go in there."

We just ignored her and kept walking. I opened the only door from the reception area to a large office.

Standing near the window stood a beautiful woman looking down onto the pink sidewalk. She didn't move as a result of our abrupt invasion but kept staring out the window, obviously deep in thought.

I saw from her reflection that her driver's license picture didn't do her justice. Every strand of her shiny black hair seemed to be in place and surrounded a flawless, creamy, and pale complexion. She covered her dark eyes with a heavy flair of makeup. Still, I could see a sadness, which was confirmed by the downturned corners of her perfect rosebud mouth.

Hilda accentuated her black suit with an ivory Chanel silk blouse. She wore a double strand of pearls with a centered larger pearl and a pair of diamond earrings.

Her assistant said, "I'm sorry, Miss Fletcher. I told them they needed to make an appointment."

Hilda stayed in the same position as she had been when we burst into her office. In addition to sad, she looked detached.

She said, "That's okay, Martha. Just close the door behind you."

I looked around at her office and noted how it exhibited her obvious sense of perfection. The slightly modern ambiance in black and muted tones complemented the expensive, sophisticated furnishings. Also, the walls seemed to have an unusual amount of mirrors for an attorney's office.

Eric said, "Miss Fletcher, I'm Special Agent Pollen, and this is Special Agent Turner. We're with the FLDE, and we need to talk to you about Pascal Romano. What's your relationship with him?"

After a few seconds, she turned around to look at us. She took in a big sigh and rolled her eyes. In a bored tone that sounded as if she was reading the same words that she had read a thousand times, she said, "I'm his attorney, and as you know, I can't discuss or reveal any information due to attorney-client privilege."

I thought, *I really need to inject some energy into Miss Fletcher.*

Then I said, "Really? We heard you were having an affair with Pascal."

She looked at me with a steady stare and didn't respond. She remained calm without any facial changes.

Eric said, "We've talked with a lot of people who know you and Pascal. We know you're his mistress, not his lawyer, so cut out the bullshit-client story."

Inwardly, I said, *Thank you, Eric.* This gave me the chance to save Hilda so that we could come to an "understanding." I was about to become Hilda's best friend in this game of good cop, bad cop.

I spoke with compassion and omitted any temptation to judge. "Miss Fletcher, I understand your love for Pascal and feel terrible for what you must be going through."

She turned her attention on me, and her eyes softened. I returned her look with a slight and encouraging smile. "We need to talk, Miss Fletcher," I said. "We suspect Pascal murdered Ronald."

I then gave her the reasons for our suspicions.

She said, "I don't know anything about this murder or Pascal's involvement for that matter."

I was on the fence about whether Hilda knew that Pascal had committed the murder. I reminded myself that he wasn't yet publicly named a suspect.

I said, "I know you and your ex-husband are fighting for custody of your daughter and that he's taking you back to court. That's got to be stressful."

Her eyes opened a bit wider as her head recoiled back a little in surprise. We now had her complete attention.

Eric allowed a nasty exclamation to escape from his lips, and I gave him dirty looks to enforce our mutual disgust. I wanted Hilda to see that I agreed with her about Eric's crude and rude behavior. I wanted to bond with her.

I continued. "Miss Fletcher, I know how hard you've worked to earn your law degree and your estimable standing in the community. You've achieved so much. You'd be foolish to risk everything for a murderer. You're risking your career and custody of your daughter, all for a man. It's too late to help him now anyway."

I leaned forward, closing the gap between us. I spoke a little bit louder than a whisper. "You fell for the wrong guy, and if you try to stick by him, you will lose. We've already subpoenaed all of Pascal's phone records. You would be a fool not to cooperate with us."

A tear slipped down her cheek. Hilda started talking and filling in the blanks about what happened between herself and Pascal on the night of the murder to this morning.

"About eleven that night on Christmas Eve," she said, "Pascal called me." She turned to look back out the window and then back at me. "He told me he had an out-of-state family emergency and was driving to Virginia. I thought it strange because I didn't know he had any relatives in Virginia."

She glanced at Eric but then stared back into my eyes. "I did have one short conversation with Pascal while he was in Virginia. He seemed very upset, but he wouldn't tell me what he was doing there. Then on New Year's Eve, I took my daughter to Disney World."

The tears became sobs, and then they increased in intensity.

"Pascal and I planned the Disney trip together. We were getting engaged over the holidays."

Of course, I wasn't about to mention Pascal's wife while she gave this account of Pascal's activities. Then she told me something that floored me.

"Pascal showed up at my house last night around six. I had just gotten home from Orlando. He told me that he'd come back to tell me goodbye. We had sex and took a shower together. Afterward, I took him to the Miami Airport and dropped him off at the curb about eight. He told me that he needed to leave town and that he was going to Italy."

Now we were getting the information we needed but wished we had obtained yesterday. I asked, "Which airline did you drop him off at?"

"I don't know."

"Did Pascal have his passport when he was at your house?"

"Yes. I saw it when he emptied his pockets before having sex, and then I saw him put it back in his pocket when he got dressed. He took it with him to the airport."

Hilda looked out the window again before giving us an important piece of the puzzle. "On the way to the airport, Pascal pulled out a flat metal box that he had tucked inside his jacket. He then opened the window and threw it out."

I now knew what had happened to the hard drive of Pascal's computer.

Excitement and urgency surged through my body, so I was glad she wasn't looking at me for the moment. I forced myself to keep my voice soft and compassionate. "Can you recall where he may have thrown it out?"

"Somewhere near the airport on Le Jeune Road."

Eric asked, "Did Pascal tell you whether he saw anyone else when he got back to Miami from Virginia?"

Still staring out the window, she responded. "Yes. He went to see his wife and baby, Frank Brown, and his lawyer Howard Goldstein." She sniffled.

I recognized Howard Goldstein's name. He was known as a high-powered defense attorney. He represented one of the judges in the Court Broom case.

I felt sick. Apparently, we had just missed Pascal. I began to wonder if we had gotten to Frank's house a little too late or if they had met someplace else and if Frank had met with Pascal before or after he spoke to us.

I then obtained a detailed description from Hilda of what Pascal wore and what his travel bag looked like.

I asked, "Where is Brent Patrick, and what's his relationship to Pascal?"

"They're friends."

Her reflection in the window revealed that she was still crying, albeit silently. Her shoulders shook slightly from the sobs.

"Does Brent represent Pascal in any legal matters?" I asked.

"No. Just friends. Brent recently moved to San Francisco over the Christmas holidays. He's supposed to be entering a seminary there to become a Catholic priest." She turned around to face me.

We needed to talk to Brent. I asked, "How can we contact Brent?"

"I have his number." She bent over her desk and looked through her rolodex. Evidently she found Brent's number because she stopped and scribbled something on a yellow pad.

I glanced over at Eric.

After ripping off the top sheet of paper, Hilda handed it to me. "Here. This is the only number I have for Brent."

"Thank you," I said and meant it.

Before we left, I said, "Miss Fletcher, you need to contact me immediately me if you hear from Pascal and with any information you have about his whereabouts."

Hilda was now doubled over as she leaned on her desk. She no longer tried to hide her tears. She just nodded in response.

The fact that someone like Hilda would have been so crazy in love with this little creep just astonished me.

About an hour later, Eric and I found ourselves walking along the roadside where Hilda thought she saw Pascal toss out the hard drive. We searched and searched but never located it.

We then stopped at the office before going next door to the airport. We wanted to obtain some color photos from Pascal's driver's license picture. We planned to take them to the international airlines that flew to Italy and show them to the employees.

With copies of Pascal's picture in hand, we stopped by the Miami-Dade County Airport Police substation. Because of their ongoing relationships with airline personnel, we wanted to ask them to help us canvass with his picture.

We notified the NMBPD about our progress and asked if any of them could help look through the airline passenger lists. Hal Cohen agreed to meet us.

We spent hours at the airport. We checked with all of the international airlines and then with the airlines that commute through other international airports. We didn't uncover any records of Pascal on any passenger list, and none of the employees recognized or identified him from our picture.

San Francisco, Here We Come!

The next morning, Eric called Howard Goldstein to set up an appointment for an interview. Howard refused. We weren't surprised.

I then telephoned Brent Patrick in San Francisco. I told him what his friend Pascal had been doing over the holidays.

Brent said, "I can't talk with you about my client Pascal due to attorney-client privilege."

That sounded familiar, and I was getting really tired of that game. "Mr. Patrick, I know you're friends with Pascal and not his lawyer. According to what Hilda told me, you're a friend of Pascal's who *happens to be* a lawyer."

I decided to appeal to Brent's sensitive side. After all, he must have strong values of right, wrong, and justice if he planned to enter a seminary to become a priest. He seemed to soften as I explained how Ronald helped his wife who was ill and in a wheelchair. I felt that I made headway with Brent, but he still didn't believe his friend could commit murder.

I hung up after Brent gave me permission to call again. I also began planning my first trip as a special agent to San Francisco, California. I sensed Brent might have more important information, and I knew I needed to interview him face to face. When I called him again, he agreed to meet with me.

My next step was to call the San Francisco prosecutor's office and request use of their interview room. I thought it would offer us a good, formal setting.

I called Lynn to fill her in on Brent and my plans to visit him. "Wanna take a road trip?" I asked.

"Let's do it!" she said.

Things began to move fast. Just after the murder, we had served Pascal's phone company with a subpoena. Now they finally started producing phone records of his telephone calls, so we were able to identify where he was in Virginia.

I then put out a nationwide BOLO (Be On the Lookout) for Pascal's vehicle. This BOLO improved our luck because within a couple of days of the broadcast, Pascal's car turned up abandoned at a small regional airport near Lynchburg, Virginia.

Eric and Hal drove to Lynchburg to seize the car and bring it back to be processed for evidence. We were learning that Pascal wasn't very adept as a criminal. Eric discovered the Taurus gun, a major piece of evidence, under the front driver's seat of Pascal's Ford station wagon. What were the odds that the gun found would prove to be one-in-the-same gun used in Ronald's murder?

Lynn and I purchased our airline tickets and headed off to San Francisco to interview Brent. My staff assistant had booked our hotel at The Inn at the Opera. Even though it offered the government rate, the accommodations were still outstanding.

Once we landed in San Francisco, I enjoyed the refreshingly cool weather for May. On our first evening there, Lynn and I discovered that the opera was hosting a fundraising event with food and wine tastings. We were able to get tickets and enjoy the delightful atmosphere with great food and drinks.

The next morning, we called a taxi and stepped out into the fog. It began to dissipate during our drive to the prosecutor's office located in the heart of the city.

We walked into the waiting room decorated heavily with wood. After introducing ourselves to the young woman sitting behind a desk, she smiled and said, "Yes. Mr. Patrick's already here and in the interview room waiting for you. Come with me."

We complied and followed the petite receptionist down a short hallway with brown carpet and entered the small conference room. Brent stood and shook both of our hands.

The receptionist asked, "Can I get any of you anything? Coffee? Water?"

Lynn and I answered simultaneously. "No, thank you."

Brent shook his head.

The receptionist left the room and closed the door.

I thought Brent to be a pleasant-looking young man, probably in his early thirties, with an average build, brown hair, and brown eyes that he kept wide open. He didn't smile.

His eyes flickered between looking directly into my eyes to looking into Lynn's eyes and then back to mine as he spoke. "I had already left Miami and was in San Francisco on Christmas Day when Pascal called me. He told me that he had committed a horrible crime and then drove to his Kendall apartment and packed a bag."

He glanced down for a moment before looking back at us. This time his eyes looked somewhat damp. "He told me that he had pried the hard drive out of his computer and then went to Bianchi's and took out all of the cash from that night's transactions. He then headed to Virginia with the cash and hard drive."

His eyes seemed to focus on nothing or no one in particular as if he was deep in thought. He then stared at Lynn with a slight tremor in his frown.

When he spoke again, he sounded a little hoarse. "I didn't know what the crime was, not until you called me and told me about the murder."

He then gazed down at his trembling hands, his eyes narrowing as he studied them. "I asked Pascal why he took the hard drive out of his computer. He said he had written a confession letter on it. He printed it out and took it with him. It explained why he committed the crime. He told me that he didn't want the police to find the hard drive and see the letter."

He looked back up at us. "I told Pascal that he needed to right his wrong and tried to offer him some spiritual guidance. I prayed with him at the end of our conversation."

I believed Brent when he said he didn't know what kind of horrible crime his friend had committed. On the other hand, though, he did withhold information. I was sure he felt that since he was a lawyer, he could claim lawyer-client privilege and that Pascal had told him this information in confidence. Not that this was a legitimate excuse, but I was more interested in Brent's help and a candid interview than trying to prove a case against him.

He turned out to be a really nice guy. After we finished the interview, he asked, "Hey, have you had much of a chance to do some touristy things?"

Lynn and I glanced at each other. We looked back at him and shook our heads.

"Well," Brent continued, "then I suggest taking a trolley to Market Street and having lunch on the wharf."

We did and enjoyed ourselves. At a small restaurant, we sat at a table in the corner to distant ourselves from other diners. We talked about the case over lunch, agreeing that it appeared to be coming together. We also agreed that Pascal was out of the country and hiding in Italy.

Since we had accomplished our goals in San Francisco, we flew back to Miami the next day. The flight was long, and Lynn and I talked very little due to the lack of privacy on the commercial flight. We kept our conversation to generic issues, like agreeing that we both thought Brent was a nice guy. Otherwise, Lynn read a book, and I stared pensively out the plane window, thinking about the case.

When I arrived back to Miami, I took a cab over to the office. I couldn't wait to see Eric so that I could tell him everything that Brent told us.

When I walked into the squad bay at the MROC, Mark pulled me aside. "Let's go across the street to the Cuban coffee window. We need to have a talk."

I didn't like Mark's tone, and my pulse raced a bit. After ordering our jolts of caffeine, Mark said, "Floy, I need to let you know that the Miami SAC [Special Agent in Charge] decided to have Eric take over this case. He says it's because Eric's got more experience working homicides."

My slightly racing pulse turned into a full-throttle as my stomach seemed to sink. To say I didn't like this bit of news would be an understatement.

Some past scenes flashed before me, actions that out of naivety I ignored and wrote off as the behavior of two close friends. I remembered when Eric and Hal were leaving to find the car in Virginia, I caught them huddling together in a hushed conversation and sharing some smirking interactions between them. I wondered if during their trip to Virginia, they had developed a strategy to get Eric catapulted to case agent.

I wanted to get to the bottom of this, but I dared not do or say anything at the time. I was angry, frustrated, disappointed, and confused, and I knew I didn't need to do or say anything I may regret later.

I was also disappointed in Eric, but if truth be told, I guess I wasn't really surprised that he and Hal circumvented me since they had already worked together. I figured they probably had been talking about the case without me and that there were some facts that they had intentionally not disclosed to me.

A few hours later, I managed to calm down. I went to see my immediate supervisor.

I said, "I just found out that Eric's replacing me as case agent."

"Yeah," he said. "I'm sorry about that, but the decision came from the top."

"Well, then, I'd like to speak with the SAC about it."

"Sure," he said. "Go for it."

I walked to the SAC's office and knocked on his closed office door. After I heard a "Come in," I opened the door, walked in, and closed the door behind me.

"Sir," I started. "I understand that I'm being replaced by Agent Pollen as case agent. I don't understand. I've conducted a solid investigation all along the way, and I want to remain case agent."

He looked up at me from the keyboard on his computer. He responded in a matter-of-fact tone. "Eric has twenty years of homicide experience, and this is your first homicide. I want an experienced homicide agent on this case. Too many eyes on it."

"Sir, Eric will always have twenty more years in homicide than me. Will he always be able to take away all my cases? Was there anything I did wrong with this case?"

The SAC's eye opened a bit wider, surprised at my question. He then glared at me. His tone was firm when he said, "That is my decision."

Then he went back to typing on his computer, ignoring me. He had just dismissed me, confirming in no uncertain terms that his decision was not up for discussion. I knew it wasn't in my best interested to try and make my case.

I walked away feeling even more frustrated. I had taken this issue up as far as I could, and it obviously didn't go well.

It was what it was, and there wasn't anything more I could do.

Hilda Pulls Through

Regardless of my "demotion" on the case, I had established a rapport with Hilda. She and I had developed a mutual trust of and respect for each other, and I didn't want that connection to be severed. I wanted to keep an open line of communication with her, something Eric didn't have, just in case Pascal reached out to her.

I felt in my gut that she could very well be the key to finding Pascal, so I continued to check in on her. I was like a dog with a bone. I may not be part of the decision-making process any longer, but Ronald's wife needed to see justice served for her husband.

My frequent attempts paid off. A few months later, I heard from Hilda.

"Pascal called me," she said. "He told me he was in his hometown in Italy."

Interpol had been notified about Pascal fleeing to Italy. They may have previously looked in his hometown, but now with this confirmation, law enforcement could concentrate all of its efforts on looking for him there. Thanks to Hilda, they found him, arrested him, and put him in an Italian jail.

Eric and Hal had already been over in Italy looking for Pascal and interviewing potential witnesses. Once Pascal was apprehended, they stayed a little longer to interview him.

A few months later, my supervisor called. "Floy, I need you to go to Italy with a Marshal to pick up Pascal. Once the extradition process has been finalized, I need you to bring him back to Miami."

He then told me the name of the Marshal who was assigned to go with me. Fortunately, this Marshal happened to be a friend of mine. He also had my Stetson hat from my trooper days in his collection.

Needless to say, I was thrilled and excited about my international trip. I think my immediate supervisor felt bad that I had been removed as case agent on this homicide and wanted to do something nice for me. He knew I had my heart in this case regardless.

So, I did what any special agent would do when presented with a trip to Italy. I went out and bought a wool suit and coat while the Marshal's office purchased our plane tickets.

We were set to go. Two days before our scheduled departure, though, the FBI notified us that the Italian court overruled the extradition due to Florida's death sentence.

I was disappointed and again frustrated. Their intervention made no sense. The Miami-Dade Office of the State Attorney had waived the death penalty on this case for that specific reason. They had gone the extra mile and did whatever was necessary to ensure that Italy complied with the extradition.

Pascal never did come back to Miami, but the Italian court did. Eight jurists, who were all attorneys, and an Italian judge flew to Miami.

I can't fathom how they accomplished trying this case since they didn't have jurisdiction here or over it. The crime was committed in North Miami Beach, but that didn't discourage the Italian Court from being the ones to try it. Apparently, the State Department and the Department of Justice thought this approach was okay too.

They held Pascal's trial in Miami's historical federal courthouse. It was built in 1928, after a horrible hurricane in Key Largo caused a lot of death and destruction. The outside of this legal building was made with reinforced keystone. The courtroom's interior exhibited Mediterranean ornamentation with a Renaissance design. Long wooden benches topped off the very elaborate decor.

The trial was held in two phases. The first phase was in Miami where the Italians didn't ask me any questions except for Pascal's telephone records, which proved he was in Virginia when he called Hilda. Then the state attorney asked me to explain my involvement, so I presented a brief overview. I testified about my investigative activities through an interpreter. I ended up being on the witness stand for only about an hour.

The second phase was in Taranto, Italy, where I didn't testify.

The Italian court did sentence Pascal to twenty-three years in prison and fined him two hundred thousand dollars. He was to serve his sentence in Italy, which doesn't have a death penalty. Prisoners can obtain paroles and pardons much easier in Italy than in the U.S.

I personally felt the trial was a sham.

A lot of questions remain about the outcome of this case. Most of them I can only speculate, such as how Pascal got to Italy. I think Frank Brown might have an idea. I could only guess that Pascal took a cab to the Port of Miami where he jumped on a ship, similar to his jumping off one when he came to Miami years earlier.

What happened to the confession letter that Pascal printed out before destroying the computer? Hilda told me she heard that Pascal's alleged attorney Howard Goldstein burned it in an ashtray in his swank office when Pascal visited him.

We were never able to obtain enough proof to file criminal charges against Frank or Howard for aiding and abetting a fugitive.

After this case, Eric and I remained cordial to each other. We never recouped the camaraderie we had once felt. I preferred not to work with him anymore and kept him at a distance.

As time went by, I discovered that he befriended and consequently burned more agents. I think Eric liked the spotlight. Unfortunately for him, he ended up alienating himself from some of the best people I have ever had the privilege to work with as an agent.

Mrs. Brooks felt that Ronald received justice with Pascal's sentence. I didn't have the heart to tell her my feelings on the matter.

She crocheted THANK YOU in white letters on a red ribbon with a brass ring for me to hang in my office. Every time I looked at her handiwork, I thought of her, and I thought about the senseless loss of her husband and best friend.

I finally closed the door on my first homicide. Although its logistics may not have seemed typical at that time, I would soon learn that when it comes to murder, anything goes.

CHAPTER 3

Drugs, Drugs, and Undercover Stings

I entered my home and found only my Rottweiler Rex waiting to greet me. I stopped in my tracks as I remembered why.

Sure, I had walked into an almost-empty house many times before, but now was different. My husband had just moved out.

As I looked around my bedroom and then my bathroom, I couldn't find any sign of him as if he had never lived here. The lack of his presence felt strange and sad.

His leaving didn't come as a surprise. We had spent years trying to pound the square pegs of our marriage into the round holes of careers and caseloads. No matter how much we tried to force those pegs to fit, we both had come to the mutual agreement that our marriage just wasn't going to work.

I had a difficult time accepting the separation because I didn't want a divorce. So, in May 1994, four months after he moved out, I finally gave in and admitted that I needed some help to deal with the loss. I then made an appointment with my pastor. We talked about the loss of my marriage and discussed how a person of faith moves forward after this happens.

My broken heart needed prayers and guidance as I entered this new phase. Most of my grief came from the realization that I had lost what could have been. Like most of us, I had gotten married with forever in mind, envisioning growing old together and sitting next to each other in rockers reminiscing about all of our yesterdays. Now one of those rockers was empty, and I found myself facing tomorrow and growing old alone. I wasn't afraid of being alone; I was just sad that the door had been slammed and locked on those dreams that had once involved my soon-to-be ex-husband.

I felt so thankful I had a job that I loved where I could maintain my home without changing my lifestyle. The understanding and support that my coworkers gave me while I made the transition to the single life was greatly appreciated.

As I tried to recover from this loss, I got hit hard again. I had heard that God won't give you more than you can handle, but sometimes I must admit I questioned that statement. I noticed that Rex, who had been diagnosed with cancer a few months previously, was getting worse. He moaned and obviously had a difficult time walking. I couldn't get him to eat, and he didn't seem to have any energy.

I tried to think optimistically, that it was just temporary, but I could no longer ignore the signs considering his diagnosis. I loved him so much, and he had been with me through thick and thin, through Hurricane Andrew, through experiencing my daughters leaving the nest, and through my reintroduction into living alone. He had been my emotional anchor when no one else could be.

With Rex, I felt open to share my hurts, frustrations, and pain, and not once did he think of me as weak. Instead, he listened to my venting and then rubbed his head against my legs as if to say, "I understand, and I'm here for you."

I called my veterinarian friend and told him what was happening.

He said, "Floy, I know you don't want to hear this, and I don't want to say it, but for the sake of Rex, I have to. He's suffering, and it's time. The only thing we can do right now is to keep him from suffering anymore."

My throat tightened, and tears filled my eyes. I looked at Rex lying in front of me, his sad eyes pleading with me to take him out of his misery. The tears flowed unabashed until Rex became a blur. I got down on the floor and lay next to him, allowing myself to cry freely. I wrapped my arms around him.

Through my sobs, I whispered close to his ear, "I know, boy, I know. You just want it all to end. I don't want you to leave me, but I've got to make the unselfish decision to let you go so that you don't feel this pain anymore. It's so hard, though, because I love you so much."

I wanted someone to tell me that it was all going to be okay, but I knew it wasn't. I needed someone who understood the depth of my pain. I needed emotional support.

Jacob and Sarge immediately came to mind. When Jacob, Sniffer, and I worked on the FHP's Felony Drug Interdiction Team, we trained under Sarge when he was the direct supervisor over Miami's FHP K-9 squad. They would understand because they too were dog lovers.

I pulled myself onto my feet and called Jacob. Thankfully he answered on the second ring.

"Jacob, this is Floy." My shoulders shuddered as I tried to hold back my sobs.

"What's wrong?" He knew me so well.

"I've gotta...I've gotta take Rex to the vet. Jacob, he's in so much pain, and I've got to end his suffering."

Before I could utter another word, Jacob said, "I'm on my way."

A big sigh of relief escaped me. "Thank you," I managed to say through my silent sobs. "Can...can you call Sarge?"

"Dialing him right now. See you in a few."

I held the phone in my hand, not paying attention to the fact that he had hung up. In a few seconds, I heard the beeping tones coming from the earpiece of the phone notifying me that my caller had long since ended our conversation.

When Sarge, Jacob, and Sniffer walked into my house, they found me lying on the floor with Rex. I was so glad to see the three of them.

Jacob's eyebrows furrowed with concern. Then his eyes softened. "Floy, we'll help you get Rex to the car."

Sarge didn't even try to smile. However, his voice was gentle as he spoke. "Floy, you don't have a choice. He's suffering."

I looked over at Rex and nodded. "I know." A new wave of tears escaped my eyes.

Jacob drove, and I sat in the backseat next to Rex. On the drive over there, I studied my furry best friend. Seeing the pain in his face only confirmed that I was doing the right thing, but oh, how difficult it was.

I reflected back to my time with Rex. Eight years ago after working a Christmas morning shift, I drove to the home of my vet and his wife. They were not only dog breeders, but they were also my friends. I had brought a red ribbon with me and tied it around the neck of the little eight-week-old bear-looking puppy.

When I got out of my car in my driveway, I held this precious puppy against my chest and walked inside my house. My girls, around ten and fifteen years old at the time, were watching a Christmas show on television.

"Hey, girls, look what I forgot to put under the tree," I teased.

Both blonde heads snapped around to see what bonus gift they may be getting for Christmas. When their eyes fell on the puppy, they squealed and giggled with delight.

They ran over to me saying, "Let me hold it. Let me hold it."

I laughed at their obvious joy. "I thought we'd call him Rex. What do you think?" I asked, watching Rex take turns licking their faces.

Throughout the years, Rex had become my constant companion. When I had come home to an empty house, I always had my faithful companion at the door waiting for me.

Then I was jolted out of my memories when I realized we were pulling into the vet's parking lot. I involuntarily let out a groan. I hugged my big boy and held onto him, knowing that my time with him was coming to an end.

Jacob touched my arm. "Let's go, Floy. If you want, Sarge and I can take him in for you."

I was reminded of a similar scene many years earlier with Jacob and another FHP partner named Dean. I had just watched my best friend and mentor Pete succumb to cancer. I didn't want to let go of Pete's hands when he breathed his last breath, so Jacob had to remove them for me.

Although the loss of Pete was much more devastating, and I still feel the pain from it today, in my arms was a different kind of best friend, a dog who was also dying of cancer. At that very moment, though, he still had life in him, but he was suffering.

I shook my head. "No. He needs me there with him."

Jacob carried him inside the vet's office because he was too weak to walk.

I forced my own weak legs to trudge behind them. Each step brought me closer to the end.

I went back with Rex to be with him, to hold him and comfort him. We needed that time together so that we could tell each other our final goodbyes.

When I let him go for the very last time, the only comfort I found was knowing that soon, Rex's pain would end. The anguish I found was knowing that soon, my pain would begin.

The Down and Dirty of Narcotics

A week had gone by since losing Rex, but I still missed him so much. I felt my broken heart would never be the same again.

My youngest daughter Mary Ellen popped in from college with a two-year old Rot named Hardy. I was ecstatic to have such a big, furry gift. Although Hardy could never replace Rex, I felt confident that he would help heal my wounds.

Fortunately, my job allowed me to work through the many stages of grief by helping me take my mind off of the losses. My next assignment was on a narcotics squad. It was short-term and lasted only a few months. I was glad to have Mark working with me again. Although he was no longer my field training agent, I still continued to rely on him for his expertise from time to time.

Late one afternoon, he called me. "Hey, Floy, this is Mark. I need you to meet me at the Sofitel Hotel near the airport. I'll be in Room 809."

A little perplexed and curious, I said, "Okay. What's this about?"

"A narcotics case that we're working on." He then hung up without any further ado.

By the time I entered Room 809 at the Sofitel Hotel, I saw Mark and six DEA agents hovering around one skinny, dark-skinned young man with long black hair.

I looked at Mark and asked, "What's going on?"

Mark walked over to me and began to fill me in on the nasty details of this case. He cocked his head toward the subject of everyone's attention. "Our friend over there arrived here from Colombia early this morning after boarding in Bogotá around midnight last night. U. S. Customs thought the man fit the profile of a drug smuggler and pulled him out of the checkpoint to question him."

I glanced back over to the young man, who was now bent over as if his stomach hurt.

Mark continued. "During their interview, he seemed to be in abdominal distress, so Customs suspected he was a body packer and may have ingested some drugs. They took him to Jackson Hospital to get him x-rayed. And whatta you know, the pictures confirmed that his stomach contained numerous condoms filled with something. Even though those condoms were tied off at the ends, if one of them bursts, that's a horrific death. I'm not quite sure if any amount of money is worth that."

I nodded in understanding. Mules trafficked drugs by packing them in condoms and then swallowing those condoms. This method had become such a trend at the Miami Airport that Jackson Hospital's Ward D expanded a new section reserved for those "body packers" who were ushered over from the airport.

Mark shook his head and rolled his eyes. "This guy admitted to swallowing *eighty* condoms of heroin. So Customs called the DEA, and they went to the hospital and took custody of the smuggler. Then they brought him here and called FDLE."

I nodded again, knowing that the DEA and FDLE had been working closely together on these types of cases. They wanted to garner the benefits of sharing resources and manpower.

I said, "By the looks of him, I assume the hospital gave him some laxatives."

"Yep, and we're ready for them to do their job. One of the agents already placed a strainer over the toilet. All we have to do now is wait for him to expel the heroin."

I gave an involuntary shiver. "Expel" was a nice way to put what was about to happen. Now I understood why they called this squad short-term. Who could make a career of this?

At this moment in my job, heck, in my life, I was grateful for two things. First, I was the only female in this group. I would be relieved—no pun intended—from watching the heroin reappear.

Secondly, our large suite included two bathrooms. I didn't have to share a bathroom with the mule.

The meds were obviously working. The mule moaned as his dark skin turned a horrid shade of green. I knew I wasn't paid enough to endure this glamorous and exciting side to my profession.

My partners prepared themselves to greet the packages. They had gathered plenty of newspapers to cover the fold-up table they brought for the heroin birthing. Then they laid a plastic yellow blanket over the paper.

The DEA agents came to the unanimous decision that only one person would handle the condoms—the mule—but under their strict supervision. They were considerate enough to offer him lots of disposable gloves to wear as he unwrapped each condom.

After our smuggler removed the heroin from the condoms and placed it on the plastic blanket, he then put on a new and clean pair of gloves. He repackaged the drugs in a bundle, wrapping it in heavy-duty brown paper that also had a plastic lining. I realized that if I had known my assignment prior to my arrival, I would have brought room freshener.

Next, we planned our controlled delivery to the owner, which was a tactic used when law enforcement had acquired illegal narcotics, and the smugglers cooperated, like in this case. Police could then control telephone calls between the smuggler and the buyer and thus the delivery of the narcotics.

Both the calls and the delivery would provide evidence that the buyer was involved in this drug-distribution network. Then we would work our way up the food chain to dismantle criminal enterprises and keep drugs off the streets.

We needed to get our doper feeling better for his next assignment, though. By the time we had to leave, our mule still looked a little green although most of his natural coloring had returned.

When all was said and done, we were in that hotel room for over twenty-four hours. None of us had ordered room service throughout this operation for obvious reasons. Going without food for so long had put me in a foul mood for the next transaction.

We had already worked out the details of the handoff that was to take place in a seedy shopping center where all the shoppers spoke Spanish. A DEA agent named Jim Winters and I were assigned to the takedown. Once we saw the handoff, we would jump out of our parked cars and chase after the receiver as he walked away with the package.

With our plan in place, the nine of us drove to the shopping center around noon. One by one, our six unmarked cars trickled into the shopping center to wait for the transfer to take place.

Our mule got out of one of the cars and walked to a nearby bench. I was alone in my car, and because women are not usually considered to be cops, I was able to get closer to the sidewalk. My clear line of vision allowed me to see the approach of a clean-cut Hispanic male wearing a golf shirt and Bermuda shorts. He looked calm, but the numerous visual sweeps he kept performing on the parking lot made me think he was the buyer.

Then bingo! I was right. Bermuda shorts walked by the bench and without slowing down his pace, nonchalantly grabbed the handle of the bag and kept walking.

Jim and I jumped out of our cars. The receiver had his back to us, so he couldn't see us. He continued to stroll down an interior sidewalk tucked in between the buildings for access to the rear of some of the stores.

When I got about fifteen feet away from the receiver, I drew my gun. Then just before I reached him, I yelled, "Police! Get down!"

The guy didn't even turn around to see who or what was yelling or even if who or what was yelling at *him*. Instead, he erred on the side of caution and sped up, and I followed suit and ran after him. Thank God for all of my morning runs throughout the years.

When I got within arm's reach, I grabbed him from behind. With Jim's help, we secured him in handcuffs. I gave him to Jim since the DEA would be the ones to prosecute him in federal court. As far as I was concerned, my job was done, unless of course this case went to trial.

Mark and I went back to our offices for a couple of hours to finish our paperwork. Undoubtedly, this was a gruesome operation and one I didn't look forward to repeating.

The whole time I worked, all I could envision was driving home pedal to the metal to take a long hot shower.

An Undercover Drug Sting

Thankfully, the FDLE narcotics squad had more going for it than the pooper detail. Like any job, it had those tasks—like the one we just completed—that made one question why he or she ever considered working in that profession, let alone choosing that career path.

Then there were those tasks that made it all worthwhile. For instance, we had been conducting a lot of surveillance in the west end of Kendall, which is a suburb located southwest of Miami. Surveillance operations usually required half a dozen undercover agents.

We had been watching one guy on and off for a couple of months. Losing him at this point was no big deal because we always knew where we could find him. He happened to like afternoon movie matinees and then afterward, he ate at a great Cuban restaurant.

The squad flipped coins to become one of the two agents lucky enough to keep eyes on him while he was in the theater, which of course meant those agents had to watch the movie too. It definitely was a step up when you went from the pooper detail to the movie detail.

Unfortunately, movie theaters were rare when working in narcotics. A lot of drug activity took place in hotel rooms. One challenge we faced when conducting narcotic deals in those types of settings was acquiring eyewitness evidence. To solve this dilemma, the technical agents provided a regular-looking table lamp to the squad. However, it was anything but regular. Embedded within its ceramic base was a hidden video camera.

We put this lamp to the test in a motel located off I-95 in Hollywood. During this particular operation, our agents planned to purchase one kilo of cocaine for twelve thousand dollars.

Mark and I went to the bank and withdrew the funds from the FDLE undercover account. We then placed the money in an olive-green duffle bag.

Afterward, we met the rest of the team at the FDLE office to again go over the plans and last-minute details. We also agreed to the code phrase of "Looks like the real stuff" to signal to the takedown team to make the arrest. We felt comfort in knowing that the surveillance teams would keep us in their sights and cover us from the time we left the office to the conclusion of this deal.

These situations constituted some of the most dangerous we faced. For one, during the exchange of drugs and money, we never knew if more bad guys were going to show up than anticipated. We just knew to expect the unexpected and be prepared.

Also, when the dopers examined the money or drugs, they were known to initiate "rips," which was slang for ripping off each other. Of course, this possibility put us on edge too. After all, since all of their activities were illegal, who was going to call the police to file a complaint?

Even worse than getting ripped-off was knowing that they placed little to no value on human life. Sometimes dopers just shot each other, especially if they thought they were dealing with other bad guys. Then if they knew we were cops, they might have been quicker to pull the trigger.

During this particular operation, we played the role of buyer, so hopefully they were on edge as well. Mark and I helped set up the room for the drug deal the day before the scheduled takedown. The transfer of the drugs would take place there and the payment in the parking lot. We never wanted to make it easy for the bad guys to rip us off by having both the product and money together.

Our supervisor, who stayed in a room adjoined to the takedown room, assigned Mark and me to be in the money car, which was a white convertible that was seized in a previous drug deal. I would sit in the car while Mark showed the money to the seller in the hotel's parking lot. Other agents would watch us in case the bad guys decided to steal our money and take off with it.

Mark would then give the car keys to the seller to instill confidence that he had possession of the money. Once Mark approved the drugs, the seller believed that he and Mark would walk back to the car together. He would then take the money and give the keys back to Mark. Of course, it would never get to this point because we planned to arrest him beforehand.

When the time came to conduct this operation, Mark and I drove up in the seized convertible. Some of our undercover team members sat in a van with a sign saying, "Jerry's Pest Control Takes Care of Bugs."

Our cell phone rang, and Mark answered it. He listened for a few minutes before saying, "Okay. Got it."

Mark panned the parking lot. "That was our team in the van. They said the seller was in a silver Mercedes parked in the side parking lot. They also saw another Latino-looking man wearing a red shirt and Panama hat get out of the car and walk around to the front doors of the hotel."

I looked toward the hotel's front and saw a man smoking a cigar who fit their description. "I see the guy," I said.

Mark didn't respond, but I saw that his eyes were also directed toward the same spot. "I'm calling the seller now."

He pushed some numbers on the cell phone. "Yeah, it's me. We're in the front parking lot in a white convertible backed up into a parking space next to the shrubbery, so come on and take a look at the money."

He terminated the call. "Okay, he's on the way. Wearing a green silk shirt with palm trees."

A couple of moments later, we saw a tall and slim Latino man, probably in his mid-twenties, wearing a green silk shirt with palm trees, dress pants, and alligator loafers without socks. He seemed to be covered with gold from the chains around his neck to the bracelets wrapped around his wrists. He also wore a solid gold Rolex, which was the watch of choice by drug dealers. He possessed the complete *Miami Vice* look. He kept his eyes on our car and made a beeline to us.

"Showtime," Mark said and got out of the car.

Before our new friend got any closer, Mark tilted his head toward the trunk, signaling to go there. I tried to keep an eye on what was occurring through the rearview and side mirrors.

Mark opened our trunk that held the money. The raised trunk door prevented me from seeing anything through the rearview mirror, but since the convertible top was down, I was able to hear the conversation.

Mark said, "There it all is. Go ahead and look."

I didn't hear anything for a couple of moments and assumed the seller was inspecting the cash.

I thought about how happy I would be when this operation was over, and we could put the money back in the bank. That would signify that we were successful and hopefully, no one got hurt.

My heart pounded as I waited for the okay to move forward with the deal. The moments seemed like hours before the seller said in a slight Hispanic accent, "Twelve thou. Hmm. Okay."

The trunk door slammed shut. Mark handed the seller the keys to the car and said, "Room 305."

Mark and the seller split up. Mark walked to the hotel and subsequently to the hotel room. The seller went to get his dope. The cigar smoker stayed near the hotel entrance to ensure I didn't take off with the car and rip them off before they could take possession of the cash. He was the eyes and ears for the other bad guy. At the time, I had no way of knowing whether or not he was armed.

My earpiece allowed me to hear everything going on with Mark and the seller. A few minutes later I heard a knock on the hotel room door.

Mark whispered, "Here we go."

The door opened and then slammed.

The same slight Hispanic voice I had heard at our trunk said, "Here. Take a look, my friend."

Next, I heard the unzipping of a bag and the rustling of paper. I envisioned Mark taking out a package and cutting a very small triangle, or "window pocket," into the plastic bag with a small pocket knife.

I knew that agents in the adjoining room were getting ready for the takedown. They were watching everything that occurred on the monitor.

Mark then gave the code phrase: "Looks like the real stuff. Let's go get your money from my car."

I heard the room door slam as I assumed Mark and the seller entered into the hallway. Then it got real exciting. Several people yelled, "Police! Get down!"

Obviously, the takedown team had descended upon the seller with guns drawn. They arrested him and seized the cocaine. Unfortunately for him, our handy-dandy lamp would provide us with an excellent video recording for the jury.

One of the takedown members notified the surveillance team in the van that the seller had been apprehended. That was their cue to move in on the cigar smoker in front of the hotel. They swooped him up, cuffed him, and stuffed "the pest" into Jerry's Pest Control van.

I was now happy. The operation was over, and I was able to put the money back into the bank. Most importantly, no one had gotten hurt.

I had to fill out a Cash Transaction Report (CTR) for the bank to receive the twelve thousand dollars in cash. I always worried that the IRS might not believe I transferred funds for government business, but they never audited me.

Future Israeli Prime Minister Ariel Sharon

At times, our governor, governors of other states, and dignitaries visited our area and thus needed protective services. Mark and I were assigned to this team called POS, or Protective Operation Services.

In late summer 1994, I got assigned to respond to the Fontainebleau Hotel on Miami Beach to be the driver for a protective detail for then-General Ariel Sharon. Years later, in 2001, he would be elected prime minister of Israel.

Sharon was staying in South Florida for fundraising events, but there were a lot of concerns about his safety. After the 1993 bombing of the World Trade Center in New York City, we had received intelligence information from the FBI that the "Blind Sheikh" had made threats to Israel, placing Sharon at risk.

Earlier, someone had murdered a well-known rabbi in New York City. A lot of speculation exists that this killer was now believed to have had links to Osama bin Laden's network. Some historical researchers felt this murder victim became the first Al-Qaeda murder in the U.S.

I drove to Sharon's hotel in a torrential downpour. I arrived early, and since I had expensive equipment and extra guns in my car, I never used a valet service for security reasons. Instead, I parked the car as close as I could get to the hotel's main entrance and ran inside.

Before I could reach the door, the skies seemed to open wide as the rain began to fall harder and faster. I got drenched.

I then rushed to the basement laundry where a sweet lady dried and pressed my suit. I probably should have incorporated the hotel's beauty shop into my final preparations, but time prohibited it. In the meantime, I used a towel from the laundry room to dry it as best as I could, but I'd have to live with the frizz.

I re-entered the marble-and-gilded-mirrored hotel lobby from the basement stairs. I felt much better wearing dry clothes.

The elevator doors opened, and I stepped inside to go to the penthouse floor. When I knocked on Sharon's door, a very muscular, clean-cut young man greeted me. His bulk and muscles made his neck seem short.

I presented my credentials, including my badge while announcing, "Hello. I'm Special Agent Turner with the Florida Department of Law Enforcement. I'm assigned to be your protective-operations driver."

This Israeli Army officer looked less-than impressed. In fact, his lowered eyebrows and frown spoke volumes—evidently my being there annoyed him. My guess was that he was the macho-warrior type.

Sharon, on the other hand, seemed much more personable than his security guard. When I entered into his suite, he walked over to greet me. His eyes were soft, and his smile was genuine.

He grabbed my hand and shook it. "Hi, I'm Ariel Sharon," he said, as if there was any question. Very rarely did I get such a warm welcome from those I protected.

I used the Protective Operation Services vehicle to drive Sharon to a Miami Beach private home belonging to a very wealthy Jewish man involved in fundraising for Israel. Afterward I drove him to a kosher county club in Hollywood, Florida.

We were escorted to his table. Mr. Sharon sat down and looked around. His eyes landed on me standing off to the side.

He said, "Agent Turner, come join me. Sit. Eat."

When I hesitated, he said, "I will not take no for an answer. I insist. Come sit at my table and eat with me." He pointed to a chair.

I thought, *Well, why not.* After all, I was hungry.

So I sat, and I ate! Who was I to let Mr. Sharon down?

After dinner, he called me over for a photo shoot. Having escorted many dignitaries, Sharon's cordiality impressed me, and I always considered him to be a gentleman.

Sharon stayed safe during his visit to Miami. However, I wouldn't learn about Osama bin Laden and Al-Qaeda until years later.

Spies and Lies—All in a Day's Work

On a nice and slightly cool winter day in late 1994, my supervisor sent me to the Hyatt Hotel located on the Miami River. I met with a wealthy woman who was married to a high-ranking Cuban official.

This particular woman had approached the FDLE in the past regarding narcotics cases. My supervisor had wanted me to talk with her to see what kind of criminal information she wanted to bring us.

We sat in the elegant hotel lobby in expensive floral-covered chairs separated by a small round coffee table. She leaned forward in her seat, trying to close the gap between us.

When interviewing a potential informant, policy required us to have witnesses; we were never to meet one-on-one. So, Mark and a few other agents covered my meeting to ensure it didn't have any countersurveillance. While some agents walked around the lobby, others sat in nearby chairs, and one sat on a sofa pretending to read the newspaper.

I studied the informant as we talked. Her red hair hung loosely, and its color complimented her fair skin. She wore expensive clothes and dripped in gold and gems. Gold bracelets, a gold necklace, and gold earrings accessorized their respective places. Long red nails extended her already-long fingers. What appeared to be a five-carat ring encircled the ring finger on her right hand. A very large emerald ring enclosed a finger on the other hand.

She shared her concern for her safety, and rightfully so. She claimed to have information on Cuban officials who were involved in the drug trade taking place in Florida. She also alleged that they were spying on U.S. officials. Since her husband was an official in the Cuban government, she stated that she had obtained a lot of her information through her husband's colleagues. She knew that coming to us and passing on what she had heard bordered on espionage.

Her husband still lived in Cuba, and she didn't share his surname or his residence. In fact, she lived in a very expensive waterfront condo on Miami Beach, which was part of a very expensive lifestyle that she had developed as a paid informant. Although her "job" was dangerous, she was obviously willing to take the risks. To maintain her lifestyle, she needed a lot of financial assistance for her information.

The more we talked, the more she convinced me that she had valid information about the importation of illegal drugs into the U.S. I thought that we would probably lose her to the feds due to her Cuban connections, and her information would better serve them anyway. Plus, they were in a better position to pay her more money.

After I finished my interview, I said, "Okay. I'll call you or stop by your condo in a few days to let you know what my supervisor decides."

We ended up losing her to the feds. The last I heard, she struck a deal to become an informant for a federal agency. They agreed to supplement her income with four thousand dollars per month.

As I walked out of the hotel after that initial conversation, I received a call from a friend of mine who was a detective with the South Miami Police Department. Some thieves had stolen some expensive, modern-art paintings from an art gallery. Some of the paintings were valued as high as thirty thousand dollars.

The burglar had approached the detective's informant to help fence the merchandise. Of course, he didn't know that the informant worked both ends. For a price, the informant told the detective he would broker a deal to sell the painting to an undercover officer.

After explaining the operation to me, the detective said, "Floy, I don't think they'll suspect a woman as a UC, and I need someone with this kind of experience. Would you mind going undercover on this? I'll put together the takedown team."

"Sure. Let me run it by my supervisor."

After my supervisor approved the operation, he assigned Mark to work the case with me.

Then the detective had his informant schedule a meeting between the seller and me at a popular hamburger eatery near the airport. This all went pretty fast. I didn't even have time to get back to my office before my friend called back and told me that the deal was going down within a couple of hours.

We arranged to first meet in a strip mall about two blocks away from the eatery to finalize our surveillance and meeting plans. The detective gave me a wire, and he kept the recording device. I put it in my purse and walked away so that we could test it. I kept talking about how I sure could use a strong cup of Cuban coffee. I looked over at my friend who gave me the thumbs up.

I then drove to the hamburger restaurant and pulled into its parking lot. I figured that I probably needed to tweak my attire and look more casual. Before getting out of my car, I took off my suit jacket, rolled up my sleeves, and untucked my shirt from my pants.

I walked into one of the stalls in the bathroom and taped the wire in my bra. Then I walked out into the dining area.

I'm not a great fan of fast-food restaurants and wished we could have selected another venue. My seating choices were slim to none—either we could sit in a greasy booth, or we could sit at a greasy table. I chose the booth to wait for the seller.

I thought about how crazy this day was and would be glad to go home and relax.

A few minutes later, I saw a white-paneled van pull into the lot and park. A short guy wearing a dirty T-shirt, sunglasses, and jeans walked into the restaurant.

Instead of going to the counter to order food, he looked around as if searching for someone. I figured he was my subject and that he was looking for me.

He spotted me immediately since I was the only pale-skinned person in the place. He sat down, and we began discussing his merchandise. I told him I needed to view it.

We walked to the van. He opened the backdoor to reveal about fifteen paintings.

I gave the predesignated signal of "Looks good to me."

I immediately heard sirens yelping, tires squealing, and brakes screeching as unmarked police cars came from out of nowhere. Mark, my detective friend, and four uniformed police officers from the South Miami Police Department jumped out of their vehicles. The detective grabbed the seller and handcuffed him.

I turned and walked away. I didn't want to be part of the takedown.

I was tired, and as far as I was concerned, this was just another busy day of working undercover and busting criminals in the land of sun and fun.

CHAPTER 4

The Glades Prison Escape

I had received my final divorce decree. Although I had already grieved the loss of my marriage, seeing it in black and white gave me the closure I needed to move on.

Mentally, I tried to adjust to the single life, and dating seemed scary. I waited a bit before entering that world, and when I did, I had no idea of the challenges I would face.

For instance, I went out with a good friend who happened to be a businessman. I soon discovered that my lifestyle wasn't compatible with his. Whereas he was an avid golfer, enjoying the weekend country-club life, I worked late many nights and was constantly called out to work on the weekends.

The fact of the matter was, criminals weren't always so obliging to my love life. I didn't take it personally. I had long realized that they didn't keep normal business hours, choosing instead to schedule most of their unlawful activities beyond the nine to five on weekdays.

I dated a few other men as well. Some had issues with my carrying a gun while others were bothered by my taking phone calls from work while on dates. In all fairness to me, I had warned them beforehand that I kept a gun on me at all times and that I was on call twenty-four-seven with the FDLE. In the beginning, they said, "No problem." Their tones seemed to change, though, when the possibilities became realities, and they had to wait while I was on the phone for half an hour or so, or if we had to cut our date short.

A great example of how my work intruded into my potential for finding "love" happened on a Monday evening on January 2, 1995. My date and I had just sat down to a pleasant dinner when I got a call. My cellular phone had a push-to-talk radio channel, and when I heard the chirping sound, I knew the call was work-related.

"Excuse me," I said, rising from my chair with my phone in my hand.

My date raised his right eyebrow as his chin tucked back in surprise. He then gave a brief nod, which I took as his understanding I would need to take the call in private. I walked outside of the noisy restaurant to answer my phone.

After depressing the speak button, I said, "Agent Turner."

My supervisor responded, "Hey, Turner. We've got six inmates who've just escaped from the Glades Correctional Institution." He proceeded to brief me on the details.

According to my supervisor's report, the escapees had all been in prison for murder, which made their escapes that much more dangerous to the public. As with many criminals, they were resourceful and applied their skills, temperaments, and determination to get out of jail for free. They had managed to dig an eight-foot-deep tunnel for their escape route. After lowering themselves into this tunnel, they wiggled inside the two-foot-wide space for forty-five feet before emerging into freedom.

My supervisor continued. "A corrections officer noticed them fleeing and fired two shots. They don't believe any of them were hit. One of the inmates, Felix Carbonell, was immediately apprehended by correction officers outside the prison fence, but the others escaped through a field. Now we've got five more dangerous felons out there, and they all have ties to the Miami area.

"The helicopters are already conducting searches as we speak. It's late, and we can't do much right now. Let's get some sleep so that we can be wide awake and alert tomorrow. We're holding a five-a.m. meeting at the MROC, and I need you to be there."

We hung up from each other, and I stood contemplating the situation. My supervisor was right—we couldn't do anything more tonight.

I rejoined my date. Although he greeted me with a smile, I sensed it was forced. I sat down and picked up the menu.

"Everything okay?" he asked, his eyes intently watching my face for my expression.

"Yeah, sure," I answered with a shrug, not wanting to discuss the call with him. I changed the subject by talking about the menu.

For the rest of the evening, which wasn't long, things between my date and me were stiff. Obviously, that phone call had put a damper on our possible blooming relationship. We parted after dinner, and that was the last I saw of him.

When the time for the meeting arrived the next morning, I showed up at the office before sunrise. The room was full with close to twenty plainclothes agents, detectives, and cops from several other agencies, including the FBI, U.S. Marshals Fugitive Task Force, Miami-Dade Police Department, and the Miami Police Department.

Six thick manila folders sat on the table, including one of the captured prisoner. We wanted to learn about his family and associates as well as his connections with the five who were still on the lam.

We broke up into six groups so that we could take turns studying each of the six folders with the escapees' mug shots and records. We looked through each prisoner's past and their approved and denied visitor requests. For sure, these were some very bad boys.

We compiled lists of places to search for them. Our FDLE analysts ran computer checks on the prisoners' families and known associates to gather more detailed information.

I was assigned to partner with an FBI special agent named Terry Rhodes. His attire amazed me. His worn blue jeans, ratty, soiled, and faded yellowish T-shirt, and his cowboy boots contradicted the appropriate FBI attire of dark suits, white shirts, and ties. He didn't even come close to meeting the FBI's dress code for tactical operations, which consisted of a navy-blue golf shirt with the embroidered FBI logo, starched 511-tactical pants, beige hiking boots, and a nylon FBI raid jacket.

He complemented his independent fashion statement with the most intriguing accessory—a bandolier slung across one shoulder with shotgun shells loaded into the ammunition pockets. He made his final declaration with a black bandana covering his head.

I guessed Terry filled the role of the FBI's problem child—unconventional, stubborn, and perhaps a bit rebellious. I must admit he impressed me with his obvious disregard for fitting into the mold. I didn't understand how he was accepted as an FBI agent, though. I could totally see Terry with the DEA or Customs, but the FBI? No way.

We walked outside. The sun was starting to rise, and the sky looked like a beautiful painting with swirls of orange, red, and blue. I appreciated the cool weather accentuated by a moderate breeze.

I asked Terry, "Whose car should we take?"

He said, "Need to take mine cause I picked up a zone deer on the way here, and he's in my car. I need to drop him off at my place." (Cops refer to dogs in the hood as zone deer.)

I walked over to his car and looked into his backseat. Lying curled up on the floor was a sleeping black shaggy puppy.

I thought, *I'm glad it's winter if the puppy's got to stay in the car.* Then I thought about the FBI's strict limitations they placed on agents using their official bureau vehicles for personal business. This guy really broke the rules as I understood them.

That night, the task-force members searched all of the homeless encampments in Miami. We knew that a Latin escapee could easily enter and blend into these encampments without its inhabitants noticing him, let alone questioning him.

Frankly I never knew about most of these encampments prior to that day. In one large section under the interstate ramps, families lived in cardboard boxes, tents, and lean-tos, which were basically a structure made of plywood or something similar propped up against a tree or light pole. Residents cooked in front of these dwellings.

Since no plumbing existed in the encampments, the inhabitants urinated and defecated in the open next to where they lived. My heart broke for these people, especially for the children.

For the rest of that first week, the task force members searched all of the known areas associated with the escapees, and we expanded our search to include overgrown fields, under bridges, next to railroad tracks, in abandoned warehouse-like structures, in old apartment buildings that had become empty shells, and in the Everglades.

After covering much of the city and coming up empty-handed, we utilized the National Guard and their Humvees. They drove their military trucks into the woods and Everglade areas surrounding Miami and traversed over rough terrain.

These soldiers delighted in taking any small hill or dirt mound at full speed and then bottoming out to prove how tough their Humvees were. My back surely felt the consequences of being thrown around inside the vehicle, not that the seating offered any comfort with its thin padding. The only thing I had to show for our efforts was a painful back because we didn't spot any signs of the escapees.

By the first of the following week, two transients walked into the highway patrol station and gave us our first break. They had spent the night in an encampment a few miles west of the station, and they reported seeing some of the escapees living there. Evidently when they had gone into a large store to bathe in the restrooms, they had glimpsed some television coverage of the prison break and recognized the mug shots.

Since the FDLE and the Florida Highway Patrol were both part of the state system, we requested a couple of the FHP K-9 units. Their dogs were trained trackers and good at their jobs.

By now, our group had grown to about thirty agents, detectives, and troopers. The supervisor in charge called the entire task force, including the support staff, into a shift briefing at the MROC just before sunset so he could give us our assignments.

A lot of manpower was assigned to the search. For the entry into the wooded encampment, the FDLE supervisors divided us into six teams comprised of agents and detectives, and some had K-9s. We also utilized a lot of SWAT members to help search the inner perimeters, and additional teams were assigned to cover the outer perimeters.

Because of my experience in working with the K-9 squad as a FHP trooper, I volunteered to ride with my former partners Jacob and his K-9 Sniffer. The FDLE agreed that this would be a good pairing.

Of course, I was ecstatic. Not only had Jacob and I remained very close friends since I left the FHP, but our years of working together had enabled us to trust each other's abilities in dangerous situations.

I rode with Jacob and Sniffer in his marked patrol car to the highway patrol station. Since it was within a few miles of the encampment, my supervisor thought the FHP station would be the perfect place for everyone to regroup, recheck weapons, plan our entry caravan into the woods where the escapees had been seen, and basically make sure everyone was on the same page. We hoped the other escapees were also hiding in the same place as their colleagues.

I checked all of my equipment to ensure that I was ready to face these dangerous fugitives. I had been wearing tactical gear all week, and I kept two handguns and two flashlights with batteries on me continuously. I also wore black-leather gloves minus the fingers.

For my last-minute preparation, I imitated Terry and donned a black bandana. I wanted to darken my profile by covering my blonde hair.

Jacob, Sniffer, and I then rode together to the encampment. Jacob told me that he and Sniffer were assigned to stay close to his car in case they were needed for a chase.

Just when we arrived inside the compound, I heard gunfire. I jumped out of the car and into the dark of night, leaving Jacob and Sniffer behind. I figured these felons could be armed, so I was pretty sure someone was in trouble.

Terry caught up to me and yelled, "Come on."

As Terry and I ran toward the gunfire, we came across a small wooden structure with a piece of plywood propped over the front entrance. Terry started walking past the structure, but my gut told me to hold up. I didn't ever want to have my back to a structure that had not been searched.

I yelled, "Wait! We need to clear this in case it's occupied."

Terry turned to me and said, "Okay. You go first, and I'll cover you."

I knew this could be a very dangerous situation, so I knew I needed to apply caution to the nth degree. These escapees were murderers, and I had to assume they didn't believe they had anything to lose if they got caught.

I drew my gun and held it in my right hand in the ready position. My left hand held my flashlight under my gun hand. Terry held his shotgun to his shoulder, ready to shoot if necessary.

I could feel my heart pounding hard in my chest as adrenaline surged throughout my body. I kicked a four-by-eight sheet of plywood to the side and entered the shack. I swept the small room with my light and gun and realized that it was large enough to hold only the twin-size mattress covering the floor.

Then something caught my attention. I couldn't believe it. Underneath the mattress were two feet sticking out of the end.

I motioned to Terry. He came up beside me, his shotgun still poised for action.

I fell into survival mode. My vision was focused, and I heard every sound in the shack. I felt eerily calm, confident with my tactical training and knowing that my partner Terry stood next to me ready to take matters into his hands should the situation require it.

I kicked the mattress off the hump huddled underneath it. I saw a man lying on the floor.

I stuck my 9mm Beretta very close to his head and calmly stated, "If you move one muscle, you're dead."

Terry then came closer to also cover the man's head with his shotgun. I holstered my gun, took out my handcuffs, and cuffed the suspect. He didn't resist, and for that, I was relieved.

At that moment, we weren't a hundred-percent sure he was one of the escapees, but the fact that he was hiding from us in such a manner told us that he was guilty of something. However, with our attention on the escapees, we knew the possibility existed he was one of them, and we weren't taking any chances.

He got to his feet. In the dim light of Terry's flashlight, I could see that he was Hispanic and very dirty. He looked down and away from the light.

I asked, "Cómo te llamas?" In English, that means *what's your name?*

He looked back up at me, his eyes narrowed, and his chin jutted forward in defiance. "Alvarez."

His answer took me by surprise. One of the escapees was named Alvarez.

I said, "No way."

He said, "Yes, I am. My prison ID's in my pocket." Evidently, he spoke English.

Thank goodness Terry and I had searched this structure.

I radioed our apprehension and arrest to my supervisor, and then we walked back to the cars with Alvarez. My supervisor stood on a gravel clearing waiting for us.

I said, "Here's Alvarez."

Mark walked up with another FDLE agent. Both had been assigned to the Marshal's Fugitive Task Force.

My supervisor said, "Hand over Alvarez to Mark."

Mark shrugged and raised the inside of his eyebrows. I could tell he felt like the guilty cat that swallowed the canary. He probably knew I wasn't happy with this arrangement. Nevertheless, I was pretty sure he was happy to be on the receiving end of getting all of the credit.

I watched with frustration and disappointment as Mark and the other agent whisked Alvarez away. They had their pictures taken with their trophy while Alvarez wore my handcuffs!

I was miffed that Terry and I didn't get a photo shoot or any recognition whatsoever for that matter. After all, we're the ones who risked our lives by approaching a very dangerous felon, not knowing if he was armed and waiting to shoot us, yet we and our efforts were pushed aside. However, at that end of the day (or operation), I was really glad I caught a really bad guy.

My supervisor decided to reward me by assigning me to secure the shooting scene where another escapee lay dead in the woods. This violent criminal had been the one involved in that exchange of gunfire that had transpired when Jacob and I had first arrived at the encampment. Evidently, the escapee lost.

I got some crime scene tape from Jacob, trudged over to the body, and surrounded the area with the yellow tape. This dead body looked like Swiss cheese from being shot about six to eight times. I stayed with the body for hours until the Medical Examiner came and removed it.

Not exactly what I had expected or wanted for a job well-done.

A Good Shoot

A Miami Police Department (MPD) detective came forward immediately to report that he had shot the escapee.

Still the FDLE called in a Miami-Dade homicide squad to investigate the police shooting. The lead detective summoned all of those who had participated in this operation and were on the scene of the shooting. He needed to debrief them to ensure that no one else had discharged their weapons into this escapee.

Since I was on the scene and secured the scene *and* watched the body for hours, I was on his list. He didn't waste any time getting down to business. As soon as the body was removed, I had to report to the command post where the detective and stenographer waited for me.

He said, "You understand that I need to interview you and check your gun." His soft-spoken tone had a firmness and professionalism to it.

He maintained this tone throughout the interview while he grilled me. He asked me over and over, "Did you ever shoot your gun?"

Over and over I answered, "No."

Ignoring my answers, he asked, "How many bullets do you keep in your gun? Do you keep one in the chamber?"

Undoubtedly, he intended to be thorough, and thorough he was.

I said, "I have one round in the chamber and fifteen in the magazine."

"I'm going to need you to hand over your gun for inspection."

I complied and handed him my gun. He checked it and then handed it back to me.

He asked. "Any backup weapons?"

"Yes." I reached down and pulled out my five-shot .38 revolver from my ankle holster. I handed it to him with the grip facing him and the barrel facing downward.

He then checked that gun and handed it back to me.

I and both of my guns were cleared.

After this case, I ran across this homicide detective many times. We became friends.

As the investigation concluded, it revealed that this was the MPD detective's fourth fatal shooting in the line of duty. I passed him when I left the building after my debriefing, and his demeanor created compassion within me. His shoulders were slumped over, and his arms, hands, and legs visibly trembled. His eyes didn't focus on anything but instead darted back and forth. The stress of killing another human being had definitely taken its toll on him, even if he had no other choice, and even if the person he shot and killed was a dangerous murderer. As a colleague in law enforcement, I recognized his primary goal was to make sure that he and his fellow task force members would be safe and going home at the end of the day.

I'm sure he didn't lightly make the decision to fire his weapon into the escaped prisoner. He knew every decision he made would be put under a microscope and examined by those responsible for ensuring it was a "good shoot," a term used for those police shootings deemed justified.

We all knew that the previous shootings in which he had been involved had been initiated by fugitives and drug dealers. Still, the detective had been placed on administrative duty while each of the shootings had been investigated. The results proved that all of the incidents had been justified, and the detective had been cleared. Now he faced a final burial in an administrative position, possibly for the rest of his career.

It was a well-known fact that for those cops involved in more than one shooting, their agencies buried them in paperwork positions. The decision was actually for the cop's protection, even if the shootings had been justified. Multiple shootings might give the public the perception that this officer was "trigger happy."

I walked outside of the command post and called Jacob for a ride back to the homeless compound. Although three escapees were now out of the equation, we still had three more fugitives out there.

Fortunately, within the next few days, two of those three fugitives were apprehended and arrested separately in the inner city of Miami. One of them brazenly walked in front of a police car, and the vigilant cop recognized him from the BOLO mug shot. Then someone had seen the fourth escapee posted on television and subsequently spotted him walking along a sidewalk in Little Havana, and he called in the tip.

We had also received national attention on the case when the television show *America's Most Wanted (AMW)* aired the pictures of all of the escapees. *AMW* host John Walsh continued to feature the mug shots until all of them were captured.

It paid off. A tipster from South Florida had seen the last escapee's picture on *AMW*. Then this tipster happened to be in Mexico at the same time the escapee was there and being arrested for shooting someone during a burglary. The tipster took the escapee's picture and used the Internet to identify him. He then contacted U.S. authorities. The FBI agents and Marshals flew to Mexico, extradited the escapee to the U.S., and promptly placed him right back in prison.

This prison escape turned out to be one of the largest in Florida.

When the dust settled, the task force members chipped in money for lunch at the famous Miami Beach restaurant Joe's Stone Crab. Politicians, actors, athletes, and cops were known to dine there. However, that's not why we went. We just liked the food and ambiance that Joe's offered.

We took our to-go lunches out the back door to a pavilion in a beach park. We then feasted upon stone crabs while enjoying the camaraderie of each other and basking in our victory of taking five murderers off the streets.

I ran into Terry about six months later. He still refused to wear the FBI's uniform of the day. Instead he chose a well-worn pair of jeans and black T-shirt with a flannel shirt as a jacket. Of course, I had to ask about the zone deer he had had in the back of his car.

At the mention of that shaggy dog, his eyes lit up as he gave me a crooked smile. "Yep, still got it, and I added a few more to my pack."

CHAPTER 5

The Fugitive Task Force

fter the Belle Glade escape from the Glades Correctional Institution, the state of Florida decided to monitor prison escapees and fugitives. As a result, in the spring of 1995, the FDLE announced the implementation of a fugitive task force at the MROC, the largest and busiest of all seven FDLE regions.

I learned about this task force as soon as the openings hit the FDLE circuit. My friend and colleague Milton Drew always seemed to have his ear close to the ground when it came to FDLE news, many times before it was even announced.

I got his call one night after coming home from work. When I saw his name on the caller ID, I felt a tinge of excitement, certain that whatever he had to say would be interesting.

After giving me the inside scoop, he said, "I'm applying to it, Floy. You should think about applying too. It's really a dream gig. Lots of perks. We'll get new cars, new equipment, and lots of overtime."

If Milton called about an opportunity, especially one to which he was applying, I listened. I trusted him on a lot of different levels and always respected any advice he offered me. Not only was he highly intelligent with a law degree from a prestigious Washington DC university, but I knew he looked after my best interest. In fact, when he had been in charge of the MROC, and

I worked as a trooper with the FHP, he recruited me to the FDLE. So far that recommendation was working out just fine.

"Sounds good to me, Milton," I said.

After gathering more information about the detail, I applied.

I was excited to learn that Mark had also applied for one of the slots as well. I hoped we would both be selected because we had always worked very well together. I didn't blame him for taking credit for the Belle Glade escapee I had apprehended. After all, he didn't have any control over the supervisor assigning my arrestee to him. We had experienced too much good together to allow that to come between us. I had moved on and looked forward to this great opportunity.

As it turned out, Mark, Milton, two other FDLE agents, and I got assigned to the new squad. The task force supervisor knew I had captured the Belle Glade fugitive, and I think choosing me was his way of acknowledging that I was well-qualified for this position.

The FDLE decided to keep the other two agents with the U.S. Marshals Fugitive Task Force since they had already been assigned to them anyway. As a result, Mark, Milton, and I were left to work together, and the three of us rapidly evolved into a small, cohesive team.

We made an interesting squad. My tall and thin physique and fair coloring contrasted Milton's short stature and slight frame. His tortoiseshell glasses made him look more like a lawyer than a cop. Regardless, he had the reputation of being one of the best shots in the FDLE. He could handle any weapon with expertise. This skill provided common ground with Mark, who was a FDLE SWAT agent.

On the other hand, Milton differed from Mark and me in that he loved the night action and partying. He enjoyed barhopping with the Miami homicide cops and prosecutors from the state attorney's office.

He was part of the in-crowd who worked hard and played hard. Unfortunately, a lot of these cops spent most of their time off either working or clubbing. The fallout was a very high divorce rate.

From time to time, our trio found ourselves looking for fugitives in the same areas as RID. We dressed for the streets with jeans, FDLE-collared T-shirts clearly identifying us as police officers, and running shoes.

Unfortunately, this forced me to push my new and more professional suits to the back of my closet. At least I wasn't exactly wearing tactical clothing like I had worn with the highway patrol. I was merely dressing down from the professional attire.

Wearing more feminine clothes and feeling like a girl was good while it lasted. For now, though, my attire was secondary to my mission, and with my new partners, I knew I was destined to have fun and action.

Armed Robbery at the Taco Hut

One of our first assignments on the Fugitive Task Force brought us to an armed robbery that occurred at the Taco Hut in Fort Lauderdale.

The Hut participated in a work-release program for state prisoners close to their release dates. Those who got accepted into this program had to have shown themselves as ideal prisoners while serving time. By this point in their prison terms, they were assigned to a minimum-security facility, similar to a halfway house, where they were trusted with coming and going from jobs and necessary appointments.

Businesses participating in the program hired them. Prisoners benefited because they would leave the state system with some money to begin a new life on the outside.

So on a clear night with a bright full moon and as the Hut was closing, a robber wearing a balaclava mask walked into the unlocked restaurant. The employees didn't notice the interloper because they were too busy cleaning so that they could go home for the night.

The robber spotted the manager in the dining area and rushed over to him. Now he had at least the manager's attention as he pointed a gun at him and demanded the evening's cash.

The mask covered every feature of the robber's face except for his eyes and mouth. However, the manager thought he recognized the voice, build, and mannerisms as belonging to one of his work-release employees named Dell.

After handing over the money, the manager and his employees ran outside the restaurant. The manager looked back inside. He saw the robber remove the mask and then saw his face, confirming his suspicions that the perpetrator was indeed Dell.

The manager called the police on his cell phone and reported a robbery in progress. The Fort Lauderdale police arrived at the site within a few minutes.

Because the manager didn't see the robber leave the Hut, the police couldn't be sure if he was still inside, so they called for SWAT. They responded.

The police spent the next forty-five minutes interviewing the manager and other employees, who ensured them that no customers were in the store when the robber approached. SWAT proceeded to shoot gas into the restaurant.

When they went inside, they didn't find the robber. They did find his mask near the backdoor behind some bushes.

In addition to the manager's affirmation that Dell was the armed robber, we now possessed the mask that contained the suspect's DNA. Since Dell was a felon and in the state's DNA system, we were sure that the mask's DNA would match Dell's. The only lacking component was Dell himself. That's where we came in as the Fugitive Task Force.

By midmorning the next day, Milton, Mark, and I arrived at the Hut to speak with the manager. As we pulled up, we observed a decontamination company working in the restaurant.

We learned that every item in the store needed professional care because of the gas discharged by SWAT. All of the food, drinks, paper products, and condiments needed to be destroyed. The tables, chairs, counters, and all appliances needed to be decontaminated to the tune of over thirty thousand dollars. Taco Hut got the bill for this service. Soon afterward, the well-intentioned restaurant dropped out of the work-release program nationwide.

We started a check of Dell's approved visitors and his recorded telephone calls from his time in prison. We discovered that his visitor list included a female cousin. After interviewing authentic relatives, we learned that this cousin was actually his girlfriend.

Since all approved visitors were required to provide identification, we were able to grab her address from the prison's visitor log. The three of us drove to the girlfriend's house to begin surveillance. Before sunset, we saw Dell walking out the front door and strolling on the sidewalk. We swooped down, grabbed Dell, handcuffed him, and took him back to jail where we charged him with escape and booked him.

Unlike what you see on TV, the DNA results from the mask took about eight months to come back. It confirmed that Dell was the robber and our strong case had just solidified.

As a result, we added a few more charges—aggravated assault and robbery. He would now have about twenty more years before participating in his next work-release program.

Let's hope he learned something.

Murderer on the Run

As time permitted, I searched about six weeks on and off for a fugitive wanted for murder. We had gone to areas where he lived and frequented, and we interviewed numerous people, including relatives, friends, and neighbors. Many of them reported seeing him in Overtown, a neighborhood in northwest Miami.

During our investigative efforts, I learned that this murderer had a girlfriend who lived in Overtown. We watched her apartment from time to time but couldn't devote enough hours to a constant surveillance. Plus, we stood out in the inner city. We didn't want to get identified as the "PoPo," an endearing name given us by those who lived in the hood.

We knew this girlfriend was seeing him, but we didn't know how or where they were meeting, so I decided to approach her and interview her. I had a strategy. I figured her man would mess up with this relationship sooner or later, and I wanted to be waiting when he did. If she got mad enough, I would get a call. This method had worked well for me in the past. In fact, I had nabbed more than one fugitive from a vengeful girlfriend.

One evening, I saw her walking toward the local grocery store, also referred to as "the-stop-and-rob." We gave this moniker to these quick-type stores because they frequently got robbed.

I walked up to her on the sidewalk and handed her my undercover name and cell phone number on a plain piece of paper. I didn't want to give her my business card in case the bad guy found it.

I knew that if and when this call came, I needed to get to the location ASAP. I couldn't waste time just in case they kissed and made up.

In a low tone, I asked, "Did you know your boyfriend's a fugitive? If you ever need some money, I'll pay you for information leading to his arrest."

She turned around to see who spoke to her, her eyebrows furrowed in confusion. I kept walking as I placed the paper in her hand. Out of the corner of my eye, I saw her glancing between the paper and me, and her face never did register comprehension.

The girlfriend must have figured out what the paper meant and who I was because within a couple of weeks, she called me. She told me that he had taken all of her cash out of her house and that her friends had seen him with another woman.

She said, "I know where she lives."

Oooh, I could hear the delight in her voice mixed with a heavy dose of pissed off.

Mark, Milton, and I drove to the "other woman's" two-story pink apartment complex decorated by trash strewn throughout the courtyard. We pulled our unmarked vehicle far enough away so that we wouldn't be noticed but close enough to watch the comings and goings of the complex's residents and visitors.

After sitting there for several hours, the fugitive walked out of the apartment building and walked in the other direction of our car. We drove up behind him. While Mark and I jumped out of the car and grabbed him from behind, Milton steered the car in front of us and stopped in case our felon friend tried to run. We had him blocked in from all sides to ensure apprehension.

We then called for a marked police car from the Miami-Dade Police Department to take him to the warrant division located in their main police headquarters. We followed them and verified his identity and wanted status.

I always gave credit where credit was due. I recognized that if not for these fugitives' infidelities, I probably wouldn't have caught as many of them as I did.

William Congreve was right. "Hell hath no fury like a woman scorned."

No Honor among Thieves

On one hot summer day in Kendall, we looked for a young man wanted for armed robbery.

We had hit the streets in the areas where the wanted man was known to live, work, and frequent. We talked with some of his known associates and friends, and we left our business cards with each one of them. This tried-and-proven approach had almost always given us a lot of information in the past, so we used it over and over again, and this time around, this method didn't disappoint.

A friend of the robber had heard through our efforts that the police were looking for his buddy. Since he needed money, it only made sense that he would call us to sell out his friend's freedom to meet his financial "needs," demonstrating that there is no honor among thieves.

This "friend" told us that our fugitive might be at his mother's apartment for Mother's Day. We knew this tip might be reliable since Mother's Day was known to be an excellent holiday to locate and arrest fugitives. Despite their crimes and sins, most of them still loved and respected their moms.

Milton, Mark, and I drove in Milton's car to the mother's apartment unit where she lived on the fourth floor. Since we had a tip, we decided to knock on her door to see if our fugitive was there. Upon exiting our unmarked vehicle, we silently counted up four floors, and lo and behold, there stood our robber on a balcony seemingly taking in some fresh air.

We knew we needed to take advantage of this opportunity to apprehend him. We ran to the stairs, taking them two at a time. Our adrenaline worked overtime as our human physical bodies strived to pull more air into our lungs.

Just as we got to our destination, our fugitive jumped off his mama's fourth-floor balcony to the ground. He landed like a cat and took off running.

I was astonished. I thought, *This guy must be crazy and obviously didn't care about breaking a leg or getting another type of injury*. After all, who jumps four stories? Two stories, I could see. Three stories were pushing it, but four stories? No way! Not too many people would do that, so I figured he really didn't want to go to jail.

The three of us headed back down the stairs. We thought he must have run between the apartment buildings, out of the complex, and into a parking lot. We searched all of the bushes and shrubs, but we lost him. Obviously, he hadn't been hurt too badly or hurt at all, which amazed me further. How could someone jump four stories and then get up and run?

For the next few months, we remained at a standstill. We seemed to keep hitting brick wall after brick wall in trying to locate our fugitive.

Then we got the break we needed. That same "friend" needed more money. He had kept my card and called my cell phone.

He asked, "Agent Turner, you still wanting to arrest my buddy?"

My heart raced at his inference that he knew where we could find his buddy. Still, I forced myself not to respond directly to his question. I needed to verify the legitimacy of his information.

I asked, "You know where he is?"

"I can tell you where he works if you're willing to pay me for my information."

I thought, *Who needs enemies when they have friends like you*.

However, his willingness to betray his pal in return for his thirty pieces of silver worked in our favor. Sometimes when it comes to money, a friend has to do what a friend has to do.

After agreeing to pay for the location of the robber, our informant said, "Yeah, well, he paints cars."

He then gave me the name of the car repair shop and its address. Again, his information turned out to be very credible.

My two partners and I drove to our fugitive's job. When he saw us, he frowned and gave a big sigh. He didn't even look around for an escape route. I think he knew he was cornered and that his stretch of freedom was up. He turned around and put his hands behind his back, anticipating our handcuffing him.

As we walked toward our car with our robber, he said, "You know that day I got away when I jumped off the balcony? Well, I climbed a tree and watched while you looked for me. I had to make myself get up that tree cause when I jumped, I sprained both of my ankles and couldn't run."

Still, he was able to climb a tree and hide in the branches. His remarkable feat definitely broadened my perspective of what some of these perps could and would do when determined to escape jail.

After that, we always looked up into the trees when searching for anyone who ran.

Hurricane Opal

In 1995, as September evolved into October, a hurricane named Opal threatened the Florida Panhandle.

Due to the slow police response to Hurricane Andrew in 1992, state authorities realized that immediate response from outside the hurricane area needed to be in place and ready before the hurricane hit. That reaction time was critical for restoring the infrastructures for public safety, such as the roads, bridges, telecommunication systems, and electricity. It was also important for restoring a police presence since many times law enforcement living in the area have damage to their homes, vehicles, and stationhouses.

Based on these needs, the FDLE established a new set of response procedures for its agents. From then on, if any state emergency cropped up, we were required to pick up and take action at a moment's notice.

The powers that be expected extra focus on preparations throughout the entire hurricane season, which ran from June 1 through November 30. The FDLE gave us sleeping bags, tactical gear, MREs (Meals Ready to Eat), cans of Fix-A-Flat, rain suits, rubber boots, and a black nylon duffle bag with large yellow letters that read "FDLE Police." I kept all of these items, along with my personal underwear, toiletries, and necessary lipstick and mascara, in the trunk of my car.

The MROC supervisors assigned Milton, Mark, and me to be members of the Hurricane Opal response detail. The day before Opal was anticipated to hit, the three of us drove each of our FDLE vehicles from Miami to meet agents from the Fort Meyers Operational Center in Gainesville. We figured that people from the beaches and low-lying areas where the hurricane was slated to make landfall needed to evacuate. They probably would travel east on I-10 and fill up the hotel rooms in Tallahassee, so Gainesville would have more available rooms.

Plus, Gainesville was only about a hundred and fifty miles away. We spent the night there in the same Holiday Inn where I had stayed while working as an undercover trooper for the Rest Area Comprehensive Enforcement task force a lifetime ago.

The morning after our arrival, we drove to the FDLE training center in Tallahassee for a briefing and assignments. I saw the agents from the Palm Beach field office there also.

Mark got assigned to Panama City and Milton and I to Pensacola. Mark came up after the meeting and asked if I would switch with him. He was married to a cute female agent from the Fort Lauderdale Office who had been assigned to Pensacola during the hurricane. He wanted to be near his sweetheart.

I agreed to take Panama City. Then Mark obtained permission from our supervisor for the switch.

I found out that the Palm Beach agents were also assigned to Panama City. Since I was the only Miami agent going with these guys, I felt like the odd person out.

By now, the hurricane had already hit and was devastating Panama City and Pensacola. All of the responding agents had no choice but to wait it out in Tallahassee for the hurricane winds to die down before going into the impacted area.

When we were cleared to leave, the agents assigned to Panama City drove our cars and followed behind the supervisor to our designated hotel. By the time we arrived, the roads were full of debris from the high-speed winds.

I entered the dimly lit lobby. The thing about hurricanes was that you could always count on the winds for knocking out the electricity. Obviously, the hotel used a generator to give it some light.

My supervisor said, "I need everyone to check with the hotel clerk and get your room numbers."

I did as instructed and was able to see enough to walk over to the check-in desk. A small, thin man stood behind the dark counter.

He smiled and greeted me in return. "Welcome," he offered.

"Thank you. I'm FDLE Special Agent Floy Turner. I understand you have my room for me."

"Right, Agent Turner. I apologize, but our phones and computers are out. We're having to use the old-fashion method of assigning rooms." He opened a large green book and then turned to grab a key from a metal box hanging on the wall.

"Here you go, Agent Turner. We have your room on the fifth floor." He wrote down my information and handed me a gold key with a green plastic rectangle attached. "Unfortunately, I'm sure you can understand that our elevators aren't working. The stairs are through that door over there."

He pointed to a light-colored steel door that I assumed led to the stairs.

Great, I thought. *Elevators are out, so I'm going to have to climb up five flights of stairs with all of my gear.*

Complaining wasn't going to do any good, so I accepted my fate. "Thank you," I said, took the key, and walked over to the designated door. I pulled out my flashlight and entered the darkened stairwell. I knew my room and bathroom would also be void of light, so I hoped my eyes got used to the dark really quick.

I trudged up the stairs, trying hard not to huff and puff as I finally made it to my floor. I used my flashlight to find my room number. Finally, at the end of the hallway was my room.

I opened my door and dropped my gear on the floor. It was dark, hot, and stuffy due to the lack of air conditioning.

I had nothing to keep me in my room. I needed to go downstairs anyway for a scheduled briefing with the FDLE supervisor, so I headed on back down those stairs to the lobby for our meeting.

I saw my supervisor and six agents from Fort Lauderdale and West Palm Beach. They were all talking among themselves. They briefly glanced over at me as I approached them and then resumed their conversations.

Now that we were all present and accounted for, my supervisor said, "Okay, listen up." He then proceeded to give us updates of the storm and thus our assignments, including partners.

When he called out my name with the name of Gary Carmichael, I looked around to see who would be my new partner. A very tall, broad-shouldered handsome man gave me a slight smile and half wave, signaling that he was Gary Carmichael.

I was captivated by his salt-and-pepper hair, expressive green eyes, and great smile. In fact, he took my breath away. I smiled in return, hoping it didn't give away my racing pulse.

I had worked hurricanes before and actually lived through Hurricane Andrew. This one, though, just got very interesting. From what I was seeing…literally…I knew I was going to love working it.

However, Gary gives a somewhat different version. He says that since most of the Palm Beach agents didn't know me, and I was the only female, they drew straws to see who would be my partner. He lost. Of course, he can't tell this rendition without a smile on his face.

Gary and I were assigned to the midnight shift from seven at night to seven in the morning. Like most cops, he wanted to drive. I wasn't about to argue with this good-looking man, so I agreed.

We climbed in his gray Monte Carlo. Gary did a great job driving through the downpour and maneuvering on the washed-out roads.

Since we didn't know the local geography, and all of the road signs and traffic lights were down, we used standing landmarks to determine our location. The big eighteen-foot concrete monkey that towered from the goofy golf course on Highway 98 served as a navigation landmark and meeting place since the monkey could easily be identified from the road.

Looking at the destruction in the area, I thought it looked like a war zone. It reminded me of my hometown of Homestead after Hurricane Andrew barreled through a little over three years ago. The only difference was that with Hurricane Andrew, what got hit were my city, my community, and my own home. That was much more emotional than what we drove through now.

Speaking of emotions, I knew I needed to grab hold of mine. Gary and I hit it off as friends, partners, and colleagues, but I realized I was starting to possess a physical attraction to him. I also realized that for now, I needed to push that attraction aside and apply caution. After all, I really didn't know much about him. Furthermore, I had long ago developed a self-imposed rule to never get romantically involved with a coworker. I saw the damage it could cause if it went awry. This rule didn't stop me from feeling relieved upon learning about his single status.

My emotions felt like they were the ball in a ping-pong game, going from heart to head and head to heart. As it turned out, emotions beat logic.

Keeping my attraction for him at bay was more challenging than I had expected, and being alone with him in a car for twelve hours a day didn't help. In fact, it allowed us to learn more about each other. The more I got to know him, the more I really liked him.

At first we treaded carefully, only sharing our professional history. Gary told me he had moved from a FDLE office located in the center of the state to the Palm Beach office. Before the FDLE hired him, he had served as a city police officer for Delray Beach. His extensive resume of working long-term high-profile undercover narcotics investigations with the FDLE and the Delray Police Department and federal cases with the FBI and DEA impressed me.

The more he talked, the more I became attracted to him beyond the physical. I respected his investigative knowledge, but I was especially drawn to his even-tempered, intelligent demeanor.

Nevertheless, I understood that we could experience consequences if we became involved. I didn't want to be the center of jokes and rumors that cops love to make.

For all I knew, Gary could go back to Palm Beach and forget all about me. Geographically, getting involved with him was not the most desirable kind of relationship since we lived and worked a hundred miles from each other.

With all of my reluctance, I still threw caution to the wind. By our second night together, we ended in an embrace with a long and delicious kiss.

I learned later on that Gary had been telling the rest of the squad members how much fun he had working with me. They then all asked Gary to let them work a shift with me. Gary's response was, "No way!"

We ended our week and hugged and kissed each other goodbye. I didn't know where this was going or if it was the end. However, I knew where I wanted it to go. I knew that if given a little more time, I could be head over heels with this man, something I had never felt to this degree. I knew that I felt close to falling in love.

I drove back to Miami, and I couldn't get Gary off my mind. I kept telling myself to stop, but the heart wants what the heart wants, and I knew my time with Gary had changed mine forever.

Within a few days of returning to Miami, Gary called me on my office phone. He wanted to say hi and check in.

Admittedly, I was a tad bit surprised, but the exhilaration of hearing his voice caused a warm sensation to envelope me. After all, he called! Yay, he called! Maybe, just maybe he felt the same about me.

I couldn't hide the large grin that erupted on my face. Sitting at my desk in a large squad bay, I regretted the lack of privacy. Pulling in my lips to control my smile, I looked around at the other seven desks all lined up in sets of four and placed against the outer walls.

Milton's desk sat to the left of mine, and Mark's desk sat in front of me. At the moment, both were way too close. I didn't want them to know who was on the phone; I didn't want them to know my heart was leaping with wonderful feelings that very well could involve love. Quite frankly, none of this was their business.

I pressed the phone hard against my ear almost to the point of pain, I guess in an effort to subconsciously keep them out of my conversation. I whispered so they couldn't hear me and so that I didn't give away the purpose of this call.

My two partners became very quiet. I knew they were trying to eavesdrop. We worked so close together that they knew most of what I was always doing.

Striving to keep secrets from these two created a problem of sorts. At this point, I think they believed nothing was off limits. I couldn't even make an appointment with the gynecologist without these guys listening to my conversation. Of course, I knew all of their secrets too.

Now was different. They knew I didn't want them to know the identity of the person I was speaking to on the phone. So as investigators, they gathered their intel through observations, casual questions, and of course, eavesdropping. My attempts at secrecy must have raised some red flags. I knew they would be looking for clues and delving into my personal life.

I didn't begrudge them their curiosity, which at times bordered on obsessive. Milton and Mark were the best partners I could have ever had. They watched my back, and I watched theirs, just like Jacob and I had done when we worked together as troopers on the Felony Drug Interdiction Team.

The phone calls with Gary became more frequent, and soon he started calling me at home. At least there, I didn't have Mark and Milton straining to overhear my conversations.

Then Gary and I began to date and see each other more, and we took advantage of opportunities that placed us close to each other. For example, I had volunteered for a night's assignment on a joint fugitive operation with his former department in Palm Beach County. Since he still lived there, I was able to see him before and after work.

But our relationship was never one way, and I appreciated his willingness to give. I appreciated how he too made an effort to spend time with me and how on many weekends, Gary could be found visiting me in Homestead.

As a result, our dating life flourished.

The Hunt for a Serial Killer

While I was in Tallahassee dealing with Hurricane Opal, a serial killer was murdering prostitutes in or near the expansive ten-acre Miami City Cemetery located in Overtown and Liberty City. In fact, his killing spree had been going on since August 1995. He had killed all four of his victims by hitting them in the head with objects he had found along railroads or unkempt roadways. He then undressed them and used a gasoline accelerant to burn them postmortem.

After the third murder took place in the early part of 1996, a task force was formed that included the FDLE and the Miami Police Department (MPD). While Mark was involved in another case, Milton and I were assigned to the midnight shift on this task force. Our duties included talking with the prostitutes and street people to develop leads, patrolling in an unmarked car, watching for and monitoring suspicious activity, and surveillance.

I was glad to hear that the FDLE deployed Gary to the day shift. He was also assigned to follow up on leads and identify possible suspects.

Having a serial killer on the loose created an intense, high-anxiety situation in what was now considered an economically destitute area. Ever since Interstate 95 and the Dolphin Expressway were built over it in the 1960s, Overtown had been overwhelmed with constant traffic noise. Add to that the riots in the eighties, and it just didn't have a chance to recover.

As a result, Overtown was aesthetically dilapidated. The two- and three-story concrete apartment buildings were rundown with faded, cracked, and dirty paint covering its exterior walls. Brown dirt replaced the green grass. Alleys smelled like urine. Trash littered streets and sidewalks. Bars had been installed onto the front of the mom-and-pop grocery stores. The only sign of life and beauty were the grand palm trees that continued to sway their fronds as the wind blew.

The vicinity became a haven for drug dealers, drug users, pimps, prostitutes, and street people who idly hung out. When marked police units patrolled the area, kids ran up and down the streets yelling, "Five-O, Five-O" as a warning to the dope peddlers standing on every corner.

We hit the streets hard, talking with the folks, conducting interviews, and neighbor canvassing. Within a few weeks, word on the street reached us quickly that allegedly, someone by the name of Dread could be the one committing these gruesome murders. In fact, the murders were so ghastly that many of the Cuban, Puerto Rican, and Caribbean officers from the MPD called the killer the *Chupacabra*. This translated into a monstrous "goat sucker."

DNA tests had become the standard practice for the investigative purposes of identifying or ruling out suspects. Blood samples would have been preferred, but everyone knew that collecting blood from these street people would not be easy. The FDLE state forensic laboratories settled on buccal swabs and gave us the DNA swab kits to conduct our mission.

When we came across someone who could fit the profile of our murderer, I asked, "Hey, I'm trying to eliminate suspects on a serial homicide. A quick way we can do this is by letting us swab the inside of your mouth for a DNA test. Can we swab your mouth?"

Every once in a while, some suspects refused. When that happened, I asked for their identification. When they couldn't produce anything, I took their pictures and asked for their names.

Fortunately, though, most of them complied. Once I got their permission, I donned my protective gloves and opened a brown paper envelope from the FDLE lab that contained two buccal swabs. One at a time, I rubbed the long swabs along the inside of the cheek of the mouth to collect the cells.

Those running the actual DNA tests could then obtain a large database that eliminated and identified suspects. Law enforcement liked this investigative tool because of how easy it was to ship the swabs to the lab. Furthermore, subjects found this technique noninvasive and painless. It was a win-win for all, except for those who were guilty.

Some of these victims visited homeless areas. Consequently, Milton and I returned to several of the same homeless encampments in downtown Miami that I had visited during the Belle Glade escape.

We then went to Sheldon House, a large homeless shelter in Miami's city limits. I had become very familiar with this shelter when I attended Barry University as a student. I had pitched in when one of our professors, a Catholic priest, encouraged us to help prepare and serve meals there.

We requested DNA samples from the men loitering on the sidewalk outside the building. We came across numerous males who cross-dressed as females. Some of the detectives took pictures of them for the photo board they kept in the homicide office. They could put these pictures in their database and use them to help in the identification process in case the killer mistook them as women, and they became his victims.

During the long nights, Milton and I backed my blue Monte Carlo into an alley. The tinted windows kept us hidden from anyone who wondered into the alley, and it gave us the opportunity to play one of our favorite games: monitoring how many men peed on the outer sides of the green dumpsters every night.

I could enjoy our game from this vantage point, but I recalled the times I was given the pleasurable task of searching a dumpster. This was just another example that showed how my job wasn't always so glamorous and sometimes got downright nasty. From time to time during the course of my duties, I had to search dumpsters because lots of bad people liked to dump evidence in these large trash containers of sorts. Although definitely not a fun part of crime investigations, things could get fun really quick whenever we found something incriminating.

We also drove around and spoke with the "working" girls, a word we used for prostitutes. I felt a connection to these women from my days of working undercover as a prostitute with the highway patrol.

Not all working girls in this area were girls, though. Cross-dressing males also worked as prostitutes. Seeing them dressed in extremely provocative clothing that exposed a lot of skin or perhaps thigh-high boots was not uncommon. They complemented their attire by wearing lots of makeup and teasing their hair to make it voluminous. Some of the johns who purchased their services never knew they were males.

I enjoyed talking with the prostitutes, regardless of their true gender because they were always quick to provide me with intel. I also realized they were subjected to violence and often the victims of beating and abuse.

One night, an older working lady gave me information about Dread. I radioed everything she conveyed to me to one of the lead investigators.

He said, "I may have talked to her already. What does she look like?"

"Well," I said, "she only has one eye."

The detective said, "I need more of a description than that. We've got about half a dozen working girls with only one eye."

When we got together later that night, the detective explained that the pimps punished their property for a perceived misdeed by knifing them in an eye. Prostitution was a dangerous line of work as these women faced potential peril from both their customers and from their pimps. Now, though, they were terrified because they knew other prostitutes were being targeted and murdered.

I was enraged to learn of this monstrous method of maiming human beings. In an effort to enforce power and control, the pimps resorted to using violent mutilation. Today I know that many of these women were victims of sex trafficking, but in 1996, we didn't recognize or use the term "human trafficking" for modern-day slavery.

These women were mere slaves and suffered severe injustice. They were deprived of their basic human right to be free. I wanted to find these pimps and make them pay for their despicable behavior. I kept interviewing these street women, but none gave me any information about their pimps.

I couldn't keep pursuing this undertaking. My focus needed to remain on my other assignment of finding a murderer before he struck again.

Then on one sweltering night, we caught a break. A Miami police officer announced over the radio that a prostitute had flagged him down. She told him that she had been beaten by a man a few months ago, but she had struggled free and ran away. Now, she had just seen that same man riding a bicycle.

Milton and I had been sitting in our car a couple of blocks away from the reported incident. We knew that all of the murdered prostitutes had been beaten before they had been killed.

We looked at each other, our eyebrows raised. Now we had a lead on a man who had beaten a prostitute. Although the beating of prostitutes was common, we couldn't ignore the similar M.O. We wanted to locate him to check him out.

I said, "Let's go. That could be our guy. He shouldn't be hard to find since not many people are riding bicycles in this area late at night."

Within seconds, one of our FDLE task force units saw a man riding a bicycle and stopped him. Milton and I drove to the scene. When we arrived, we saw a very dirty, thin, small, and balding man sitting on the curb. Two FDLE agents stood over him.

The first item about him that caught my attention was his boots. The tread looked exactly like the ones in the blood that was discovered inside an abandoned gas station where the monster had killed his third victim.

Also at the gas station crime scene, the murderer had left burned stick matches, an unusual item. I asked this man to empty his pockets. He complied, withdrawing a few unused stick matches.

I then noticed a plastic gray grocery bag tied to his handle bars. Inside was a small baby-food jar that contained an amber liquid.

I thought, *Well, there's the gasoline he could have used to ignite the fires to burn the dead bodies.*

We read him his Miranda Rights.

I asked, "What's that liquid you have in the jar?"

He replied, "Gas."

I knew we had located our killer.

I managed not to react, kept my posture still, and maintained a poker face. The euphoria was overwhelming, though, and I wondered for a moment if this was what an out-of-body experience felt like. I couldn't help but wonder if this was really happening. Most cops work an entire career and never have a case come together and end like this.

We notified the Miami homicide detectives. They came and took him to the station to begin a series of interviews. I was again assigned the fun task of going dumpster diving, and this time behind his apartment building. Of course, I couldn't help but think of Milton and our game.

Milton and I drove to the dumpster. I suited up in a white "bunny suit," donned two pairs of latex glove, and was already sweating like a pig when I entered the green bin. Fortunately, the moon provided some light.

My first thought was *How many men had peed* inside *this dumpster?* Milton and my dumpster games had only taken into account those who peed on the *outside*.

I searched through spoiled chicken, used baby diapers, and every other gross item that you could imagine. Welcome to the world of homicide investigations. Unfortunately, my efforts delivered nothing of value.

Within a couple of hours of the arrest, our FDLE analyst ran an analytic check. We discovered that our serial killer Francis DeJuan had entered Florida during the 1980 Mariel boatlift when Castro emptied his jails and mental wards. DeJuan had been living in Miami since then. Through talking with his neighbors and the working girls, we learned that he frequently purchased sex from street prostitutes.

We had gathered a great amount of evidence against him, such as shoe prints that matched the ones found at the murder sites, the stick matches, the gasoline, and the prostitute's complaint that he had attacked her. Still, a confession would seal the deal because this was really all circumstantial.

We knew that the DNA lab results could take months, so the detectives allowed DeJuan to go home later that night. They wanted to build a more solid case, so while there, he let them search his second-floor apartment in Little Havana, not too far from the Overtown area. They also continued interviewing him but stopped when he got tired.

After I cleaned up from the dumpster at the MPD, Milton and I drove back to DeJuan's apartment about three in the morning. We parked to the side and sat in one car while four other task force members sat in two other unmarked cars close by. He didn't have any curtains, so we could see him meticulously wiping and cleaning his apartment until sunrise.

We would need to watch him like this until we could obtain his confession. Until then, we couldn't leave this assignment, so we took turns sleeping. I caught some sleep before DeJuan left his home at noon for his job as a dishwasher. He worked for a restaurant in Coconut Grove that was owned by a famous Miami Dolphin football player.

Milton and I ate lunch at DeJuan's workplace while we watched him wash dishes. I don't think he recognized us and probably thought we were just more customers.

Toward the end of his shift, two Miami homicide detectives arrived and waited while DeJuan finished cleaning all of the dishes at the restaurant. They then whisked him away to a beach park on Key Biscayne that overlooked the beautiful turquoise water.

Milton and I followed behind them. The detectives took DeJuan out of their car and walked with him on the beach. They wanted us to stay in our car so that we wouldn't interrupt their progress with DeJuan. We complied and kept an eye on them in case they needed back up.

We saw the detectives offer DeJuan a Burger King sandwich. All Miami homicide detectives swore BKs had magical powers for obtaining confessions.

Once DeJuan finished his meal, the detectives radioed us and told us that he confessed to the murders. One of the detectives reported, "He said that the voices told him to kill those women."

After the confession, we followed behind them as they drove him to all of the crime sites where his victims were murdered. The detectives once again asked us to keep an eye on them from our car, and once again we complied.

However, their plans soon changed when DeJuan told them, "The voices are now telling me to kill you." Now the detectives wanted us to interrupt, and so they summoned us to move in closer.

Milton and I got out of the car and walked at a fairly fast pace to where the detectives stood with a handcuffed DeJuan between them.

The next day after DeJuan had been safely tucked away in a protected cell at the Miami-Dade Jail, the celebrations began. We arrived at the Miami Fraternal Order of Police (FOP) lodge building about two o'clock for a party. Only three females attended the festivities: the FDLE Criminal Profiler Lee, the MPD Crime Scene Technician Vivien, and me.

Gary came to the party too. We talked over a few drinks and danced together. We strived to keep our demeanors very casual, even though we had been seeing each other once in a while between shift changes. We didn't want our colleagues to know we were dating.

As the party rocked with a shortage of women, the guys started dancing together. This group turned out to be crazy and wild.

We enjoyed our adrenalin high from arresting a serial murderer. Most police officers will never investigate a serial homicide, let alone solve one.

Experts believe that the survival statistics for street prostitutes is forty times lower than women not involved in prostitution. Prostitutes are easy targets for serial killers.

Years after I retired and worked as a consultant for the Office of Justice Programs, I attended a national homicide conference. An FBI Behavioral Analyst from Quantico presented a case study on our serial homicide. He had profiled the case during the investigation. I knew he had studied the perpetrator's profile through his expertise and had used the police reports, autopsy results, and periods between the murders to give the task force a time sequence of when he felt the perp might strike again.

I still think about the woman whose pimp butchered her with a knife and gouged out her eye. After talking with her that one night, I never saw her again. I looked for her whenever I found myself in Overtown.

I fear she is dead by now. I wish I could have helped her.

This case opened my eyes wider to a dark world that most people preferred to ignore, and I couldn't help but think, *If not for the grace of God go I.* For many of these women, this destructive and dehumanizing journey started out as a means for survival, not as a career choice.

I guess seeing the gouged eye hit me harder than I cared to admit. Although we considered this to be harsh and unusual punishment, prostitutes came to think of it as their norm. To me, that wasn't even close to being okay.

CHAPTER 6

The Crash of ValuJet
Flight 592 into the Everglades

I got settled back into the fugitive task force after experiencing the exciting culmination and closure of the serial-killer task force.

The date was May 11, 1996, and I was finishing up some weekend yard chores. I wiped the sweat from my forehead. We hadn't even hit summer, yet the weather was already brutally hot.

I looked around at my progress and accomplishments. *Yep, just a few more weeds to pull and then time for a cool shower.*

The ringing of my home phone interrupted my thoughts. I rushed through the sliding glass door off my patio and stepped into my wonderfully cooled home.

I picked up the phone and heard Mark's voice on the other end. Since Mark usually didn't call me during the weekends for casual conversation, I knew his call didn't come with good tidings.

"Floy," he said, "a commercial airplane has supposedly crashed into the Everglades."

I tried to comprehend what he said. All I could initially grasp was "plane" and "crash" and "Everglades." Then my body froze as my mind finally put those words together.

I closed my eyes. I was afraid to ask how many people were injured. I was afraid to ask if there were any survivors.

127

"Where exactly?" I managed to get out, even though it was almost a whisper.

I thought, *Dear God, what are we facing here? Fire? Hazardous material? Broken metal or metal shredded into dangerous objects?*

"In the East Everglades off Tamiami Trail about twenty miles east of Miami. I'm headed there now."

"I'm on my way too, Mark."

I knew this area well from my drug-interdiction days with the Florida Highway Patrol. I had also used the canals in this area to bass fish a few times.

I took in a deep breath and wondered just what we were about to get ourselves into and what we were about to find. I shook my head as if to shake the terrible visions from my mind. At the moment, I couldn't allow myself the luxury of pondering the possibilities.

I quickly changed clothes. I then grabbed some equipment out of my garage that I thought might be useful for this specific job, such as heavy-duty work gloves, boots, and rope. I jumped in my FDLE car and drove a few blocks to the west. Then I turned onto Krome Avenue, which would lead me to Tamiami Trail. I turned onto the road that ran next to a canal leading to the levee.

I drove for about fifty minutes before seeing several marked units from the Miami-Dade Police Department parked on the side of a dirt road. Their overhead lights flashed like a neon sign yelling, "Over here. Over here."

My heart raced. I remembered troopers telling me stories about the Eastern Airlines crash in the Everglades in December 1972. One hundred and one people were killed in that crash, but they pulled seventy-five survivors out of the shallow water. I prayed for survivors on this flight as well.

I stopped and looked around the area and became confused. I only saw Everglades sawgrass and a section of water that looked darker than the rest. The serene picture before me appeared as if nothing had happened, as if nature had been left alone to flourish without interruption.

I asked the officers standing nearby, "Where's the plane crash?"

One pointed toward the water with his hand and said, "You're looking at it."

My eyes narrowed as I tried to understand this situation. "What? This can't be where a large DC-9 plane crashed."

I just couldn't believe that I couldn't see anything. It felt like such a strange sensation. How could I be looking at the shallow waters of the Glades and not see a plane?

Surreality overwhelmed me. I expected to see survivors. I hoped for survivors. I wanted survivors. Instead I saw nothing, not even a pile of mutilated steel.

I asked, "How many on the plane?

"Over a hundred souls. All gone," another officer said, shaking his head.

My knees weakened as his report devastated me.

Later on, one of the rescue workers dubbed what I viewed in front of me as the "black hole." The massively eerie sight was filled with jet fuel. Those who saw it from the air said the hole was about the size of the airplane fuselage, maybe twenty-five feet across, but it was more deep than wide. The plane's nose diving into the lush terrain of sawgrass created a thirty-foot crater in an area that was normally three to four feet deep. However, none of this could be seen from the ground. Everything merely looked normal.

I stood on the canal bank and felt a presence join me. I looked out of the corner of my eye and saw Mark. His pale face and gaping jaw told me that he felt the same way as me—disbelief.

I kept on repeating in my mind, *Where's the plane? This can't be the site.*

I stood there looking at nothing but Everglades and a canal for over an hour. I finally headed home with a heavy heart. I just couldn't figure out how this plane and all of its one hundred ten passengers could just disappear.

Mission: Search and Recovery

The crash site was deemed manpower-intensive and dangerous. In addition to the twisted metal hiding in the water, alligators and snakes presented a problem. Consequently, almost all of the SWAT members from the surrounding agencies were assigned to work in the water. Since Mark was on the FDLE SWAT, he too was assigned to the crash site.

The FDLE still needed more agents to recover human remains, so I volunteered. My supervisor thanked me and told me not to wear contacts to the crash site because they could become contaminated. As a result, I decided to replace my contacts with my military glasses so that I could still see. They weren't my first choice in eyewear, though. Truth be told, they were ugly. Although the rubberized straps made them functional, they made me look like a freak when they were on my face. Wearing them was definitely a test in humility, and as far as I was concerned, I passed with flying colors.

Two days after the crash, Mark and I were ordered to return to the area to start our assignment. I met Mark at the Broward County's Holiday Park, which is a tourist attraction for airboat rides and alligator exhibits. The owners had offered their assistance in the recovery and investigation of the crash by allowing the police to use their boat ramps and large parking lot for their cars and equipment.

Their gratis proposition came in handy because the crash site was only about twenty minutes away from Holiday Park. Not only did it offer better access for police boats, but their airboats could cut through the sawgrass at top speeds, making the trip to the site much quicker. Plus, its parking lot could accommodate more equipment than parking at a nearby canal bank.

Once I arrived at Holiday Park, I boarded one of the police boats. The airboats were being used to take food and supplies to the site. I then embarked on the ride to the crash site where the recovery efforts were taking place.

The intense sun made the atmosphere blistering hot. I knew my morning runs had gotten me impervious to the heat, but my fair skin was still vulnerable to a burn.

An army reserve soldier rode on the boat with me. I learned that he too was working at the crash site but as a liaison in case we needed equipment or supplies. He gave me his army camouflage hat, saying, "Here, so your face doesn't get sunburned."

I smiled and thanked him, truly appreciative of his generosity and important contribution to the protection of my head from the glaring sun. A National Traffic Safety Board (NTSB) Investigator then gave me a token in the form of small gold pin to place on the hat.

We pulled up to the bank of the water. I was amazed to see that since I had left, the crash site had been turned into a small city in the middle of the swamp. So much equipment had arrived in just two short days.

For instance, the fire department had set up two large tents. I learned that one of the tents held food and rows of cots for us to recover and relax after our shift in the water. The second tent had been set up for work areas and for the storage of equipment.

As everyone exited the boat, the command staff directed us to attend a briefing that would include a safety presentation, the operational plan, and any important updates.

All members of law enforcement were assigned to the recovery of remains; that was our first priority. Of course, we all were on the lookout for the black box, which was the flight recorder, and singed or blackened instruments from the cockpit. We were referred to as "divers," although we didn't actually *dive*. Our job was to search the water by wading through it.

A member of the Miami-Dade Police Department (MDPD) psychological services spoke during the last part of the briefing. He talked about dealing with the feelings and emotions we might experience from encountering so much death and destruction.

Lastly, one of the speakers told us to rehydrate continually throughout the day with water and power drinks. Then someone told us to go to the supply tent where we would be issued our protective gear.

Once inside this tent, I walked through the rows of tables, picking up a white disposable crime scene suit, a pair of rubber waders, two sets of latex gloves, and a pair of heavy work gloves. I pulled the suit over my clothes and then put the latex gloves on my hands, one on top of the other, topping them off with the work gloves. I taped the area from the cuff of the gloves to the end of the sleeves near the wrist. That way, I would prevent any contaminated water from leaking beneath the gloves and onto my skin. Finally, I selected a surgical mask and a pair of eye goggles to place over my military glasses.

Mark and I began to assist each other in suiting up. Thankfully, my height and slender build granted me the ability to fit easily into the suit. My long legs and large-enough feet allowed me to be comfortable in the waders. Because of the tedious procedures required, each of us took about fifteen to twenty minutes to complete the process of getting dressed to go into the water.

We exited the tent. The coordinator, who was an incident commander from Miami-Dade Fire Rescue, told us that our shift in the water started in twenty minutes. We stood near the bank and waited for our "ride." None of us talked. I imagined we all dreaded what lay ahead.

The airboat returned from a stint in the water. Six SWAT members from the MDPD jumped out and waded to the bank, each wearing a frown and not speaking a word. Two Miami-Dade detectives stayed on the boat along with an FDLE SWAT sharpshooter. He sat on top of its platform to protect the divers in the water from alligators and poisonous snakes.

I slid down the embankment to make my way to the airboat. I couldn't help but question whether I possessed enough physical strength to pull myself up into the boat while wearing the heavy waders.

At that time, I was the only woman performing these duties, and I needed to prove that I could handle them. The fact is that most women don't have as much upper-body strength as men, and I was no exception in that department. Although running had given my legs a lot of strength, it did nothing for my arms. The whole time I prayed for the ability to endure this strenuous undertaking.

I got into the water, which came up to my waist, and waded to the rear of the boat. When it was my turn, I heaved myself aboard. Once I realized I had succeeded, I emitted an audible sigh of relief (or was it a sigh of surprise) for completing the first step.

Our team of six FDLE agents had all managed to board the boat. During the short ride to our assigned grid, the detectives handed us nets and gaffs, which were large iron hooks attached to poles or handles. They were normally used to land large fish, except we weren't searching for fish.

When we arrived, we saw a MDPD diver suited up in his scuba gear and tank. We watched him dive into the water and into the black hole. When he rose back out of the water, he shook his head.

He came over to the boat where the detectives sat. "I couldn't see anything. The water's too murky. I was only able to feel the small metal parts."

I wasn't encouraged by his report, which motivated me that much more to work hard to find *something*. I got out of the boat, stepped into three feet of muck, and found myself in a marshland surrounded by six- to twelve-foot-high sawgrass. The soft mud encased my feet, and I felt the need to constantly shift my weight from side to side. I worried that if I stayed still in one spot too long, I might become stuck in this sucking sludge.

A lot of environmental hazards filled the area, including the aircraft's jet fuel and fluids and decaying flesh. I didn't see any signs of wildlife or even insects.

A plastic flag hanging off a long dowel rod was used to identify the spot where the last team left off in their search and the new team was to begin. To make sure we kept our search in straight lines, we used long ropes to guide us.

I did my twenty minutes in the water that morning, and I felt like it was the longest twenty minutes of my life. We had to fight the challenges that nature unmercifully threw at us. In addition to the intense heat, all of that heavy protective gear we wore made wading through the water difficult. The muck sucked our boots into its soft floor, so lifting our feet out of it took strength.

I managed to get through this ordeal better than most of the guys because I was thin and my runner legs were more conditioned. No wonder they broke up the "diving" time into twenty-minute segments; it turned out to be the hardest task I have ever experienced in my career. We needed to push ourselves to not only endure but to work though the discomfort when our bodies screamed they couldn't take anymore.

Once we filled our nets, we left our lines and waded over to the boat and gave them to the detectives. They logged the location of the search grid and went through the contents. In addition to taking pictures of our findings, one detective placed a numbered metal identification tag in the net. Then the other detective logged the information.

They placed the human remains in a decontamination bag with another metal tag. Out of respect for the victims' families, I won't go into detail about our discoveries. Even the most seasoned police officers found the sights traumatic. Many of them couldn't return back to the crash site after their first recovery attempt due to the physical and emotional stress.

After emptying our nets, we trudged back to our line to continue the search. By the time we finished our time in the water, we all had to pull ourselves aboard the boat. I did it, but doing so was even more challenging than when we first embarked upon this trip because I had become extremely fatigued.

The exhaustion went beyond physical, though. We were all mentally and emotionally spent as well. Our twenty minutes in that water had taken its toll. To succeed at this horrific assignment, we needed to compartmentalize what we saw.

On the boat ride back, no one spoke a word. I glanced around at the group, and everyone's face appeared pensive. We all stared out into the Glades as the wind from the ride acted like a giant fan, cooling us off from the glaring sun's heat.

I imagined none of us paid attention to the scenery. I imagined we all had the same thoughts going through our minds—the horrid sights, the tragedy, and the senseless deaths, while probably feeling a smidgeon of guilt that we were glad to be out of there. Yes, we had a lot to think about although we preferred not to have to think about any of what we saw.

Once the boat brought us back to the crash site, some firefighters helped us up the embankment. One of them said, "Go directly to the decontamination area now."

My exhaustion caused me to feel so heavy climbing up the bank. Knowing we hadn't even scratched the surface, I realized that I would need to go through this same process over and over again day after day for God only knew how long.

A detective took all of our collected evidence to the appropriate tent areas. The metal pieces of the plane were taken to one tent while the human remains were taken to another. The body bags were moved nightly to the Miami Medical Examiner's Office where the contents would be examined and possibly identified from the DNA collected from family members.

I entered the decontamination area manned by fire rescue. They gave me instructions on what to do. I was glad someone was there to assist me with the process because by now, I really didn't want to try to figure it out on my own.

First, a firefighter showed me where to stand on a walkway of plastic sheeting. He made sure I was steady on my feet as I raised them up one at a time to step into a short metal tub, which would be used to sanitize the bottoms of my waders from all of the toxins in the water. He held a spray hose connected to a container of disinfecting chemicals and sprayed them onto my waders and then hosed them off with water.

We then entered a rinse station containing bleach and a hose that sprayed a water solution onto my waders to remove the sanitizing chemicals. The firefighter then placed the waders on a drying rack.

Next, a team of firefighters removed my other protective clothes in a methodical manner, peeling them off and placing them in a marked biohazard bag. When they got to my hands, I noticed that pools of sweat had gathered in the tips of each finger of the latex gloves.

Last but not least, I came to a row of metal chairs. I sat on one of them and cleaned my face, making sure I targeted the areas that might have been exposed.

Complete fatigue overtook me when I walked into the tent with the makeshift beds. I climbed on top of a cot and relaxed for about ninety minutes before I had to return to the crash site.

I had only undergone one mission, and I still had two or three more to go before the end of the day. I drank a power drink and water. I felt like I needed to eat, but I hesitated to put any food in my stomach. I didn't know if it could tolerate anything solid.

Fortunately, every trip into the water became easier than the previous one. That didn't mean that I wasn't getting worn out from exerting myself time and time again. By the time I got on the boat ride to go home that night, I was glad I was done for the day. I had to get away from this environment because physically and emotionally, I didn't think I could take anymore.

The garage to my house in Homestead held my washer and dryer. I hated doing laundry in a hot garage and had always wanted the convenience of having my washer and dryer in the home. However, their location now made me thankful. I didn't need to worry about contaminating my house with anything from the crash site.

After closing my garage door, I stripped out of all my clothes and placed them directly in the washing machine with bleach. I didn't have to worry about privacy since I lived by myself. Both of my daughters had moved away to live their own lives.

My youngest daughter called me that night. She happened to be a flight attendant at that time, so making that connection brought about a bit of alarm.

She asked, "How was it today, Mom? What did you see at the crash site?"

I didn't want to talk about what I had found because doing so would force me to think about it. I just couldn't be brought back into that world and back into my experiences of that horrible day.

"You don't want to know," I said. "I love you."

I then hung up.

We were given a day off before going back to the site. The time went quickly. I ensured I stayed in shape by running in the morning; I ensured I stayed hydrated by drinking plenty of fluids; and I ensured I stayed rested by, well, resting. I also made sure I was prepared for the following day by getting my clothes ready.

During those down times, I tried to get my mind off the crash. I didn't want to make it tougher by allowing myself to focus on all of the sadness and loss of life. I knew I had to put that off until after I had finished this mission.

When the time approached for another harsh shift, I worried that I wouldn't be able to persevere, stay strong, and get through the day without getting sick from any of the contaminants. I learned that a lot of the team members had become ill from stomach issues and high fevers. Some even ended up in the hospital for a few days.

Every time I returned to the site, the "City in the Glades" had grown. By the time I arrived there for my second day, more tents had been added to store food and drinks and to store more equipment, such as building supplies. Sadly, we needed more room to store body parts too, so a refrigerated trailer sat over to the side to do just that.

The firefighters had built steps on the embankment and a small dock for us to walk out and board the boat. They had also built sidewalks for us to walk on when it rained so that we didn't have to trudge, slip, and slide through the slick mud.

A stationary, air-conditioned bus was now on the premises. It provided us with a cool and comfortable area to rest. I think we all appreciated it more when wearing all of that heavy gear that made the Miami heat even hotter. The bus also provided protection from the afternoon storms.

I tried to take every precaution I could, but during one of our searches, the agent next to me lost his footing in the water as he stepped into an unexpected deep hole. He came down hard, causing the water to splash up and outward. Wouldn't you know, but on that particular day, all of the smaller goggles had been taken. I had to instead wear a pair of larger goggles that didn't fit close to my cheeks. The looseness allowed an opening at the bottom so that water was able to splash into my lower left eye.

However, as serious as this could have been, I couldn't leave until we finished our grid search and got back into the boat to return to the site.

After going through the decontamination, the firefighter put a soft contact lens into my eye. He then ran a solution through a tube attached to the lens to flush it out.

One of the firefighters said, "If your eye itches, burns, or feels irritated at any time during the night, then go to the Bascom-Palmer Eye Institute immediately."

Great.

Finding Strength in Love

The recovery detail had a high turnover rate. Several of those who worked it got replaced for a variety of reasons. Some got sick in that environment and couldn't return. Some were summoned to court, and others had cases that required their attention.

Gary Carmichael got assigned to the detail about a week after it started. He drove from Palm Beach to my house in Homestead several days a week since it was closer to the crash site. We worked and travelled back and forth together.

I enjoyed having him close. We were both sickened by what we saw. In our line of work, though, we had learned not to dwell on our feelings but to shake them off and continue on with the mission. On the outside, we looked and acted normal, although we both lost weight due to our lack of appetites. We only ate enough to fuel us.

The rare times we talked, I felt like I could share my feelings without ridicule. His emotional support helped get me through this grueling assignment. We always seemed to draw strength from each other.

The times he stayed at my house gave us the chance to get to know each other better. We learned that we possessed the same life values, the same religious faith, and the same on-the-job experiences and life expectations.

We got along so well together. It didn't matter what we did; in fact, sometimes we were just content to be with each other without the need to talk, let alone do anything. We just truly enjoyed being together, whatever it was.

Closure

About five weeks after the plane crash, a MDPD police officer finally located the black box.

With this discovery and the recovery and collection of as many human remains as possible, instruments from the burnt cockpit, and the remaining parts of the aircraft, we could do no more, so the detail ended.

Toward the end of our time in the Glades, the wildlife began to reappear. I first noticed a small frog on a leaf while in the water. Next, someone discovered a large alligator sunning itself on the canal bank. A wildlife officer, who had been assigned to the crash site for possible gators and snakes, grabbed it from behind. He managed to hold its mouth closed while someone taped it shut so that it couldn't bite anyone. He and a couple of officers then carried the gator to the bed of his truck for relocation.

Our last day was brutally hot, almost like a force of nature pushing us away and saying, "No more. Let the dead rest in peace now."

I stood on the canal bank and talked to some of the other police officers and firefighters. The incident commander walked over to us.

He said, "Heads up. A bus will be here soon with the family members. They want to see the area."

His news saddened me, but perhaps seeing where their loved ones died might bring some kind of closure to them. I hoped that the DNA testing would provide the identity they needed to bury them and complete the closure process.

When we saw the bus driving up on the hard-packed dirt and gravel berm in our make-shift temporary village, we lined up and bowed our heads in respect.

I lifted my head and watched as they got off the bus, their eyes searching the site. If we thought working this crash site was tough, seeing the faces and grief of the family members turned out to be even more difficult. Then most of them bent their heads in prayer.

I don't think a dry eye existed in the line of rough-and-tumble law enforcement and firefighters.

After the families left, we gave each other hugs, making typical cop talk like, "Stay safe out there"; "Been great working with you"; and "Let's meet again for a drink."

For a five-week period, my team worked from sunrise to sunset every other day. I was so proud of being part of a group like this, regular folks who did the difficult and dirty jobs that others could only imagine. All of us who worked this terrible event are bonded forever.

Although many folks have forgotten about this crash, and some have never heard of it, I knew the memories of it would never leave me, nor would I ever forget them. As soon as the search mission ended, I finally allowed myself to focus on the sadness. I finally allowed myself to reflect on the tragedy and the senseless loss of so many lives. I finally allowed all of my pent-up emotions to escape. Now I finally allowed myself to cry, and cry I did.

Afterward, the Miami-Dade Police Department presented all of us with an award. Everyone who searched the water received the Silver Medal of Valor Award, the highest honor given to a nonmember of their police department.

The investigation ultimately showed that the crash was caused by the improper loading and storage of oxygen canisters in the cargo area that erupted in fire and caused the crash. As a result, one hundred and ten souls were no more in this world.

CHAPTER 7

Modern-Day Slavery 101

etective Scott Adams called me at my office early one bright and warm winter day in January 1997. I knew him from when I was a trooper with the Florida Highway Patrol, and we had worked together on narcotics cases and stings.

"Hey, Floy," Scott said. "I've got a case that I'd like the FDLE to investigate."

"Okay. What's it about?"

"I've got a male subject here who I arrested at a low-rent brothel in Homestead. He claims to have information about a large-scale Mexican brothel operation involving young teenage girls. Floy, this case could extend throughout Florida and even into other states. I've gotta give this investigation off to an agency with statewide jurisdiction."

My stomach twisted into a thousand knots at the thought of perverted men victimizing these children. I couldn't help but think of my two daughters. I had to—no—I must find these young girls and rescue them.

I felt I needed to act on Scott's intel immediately, but at the time I was still assigned to the fugitive task force

"Let me see what I can do, Scott. I'll get back to you ASAP."

I left my desk and walked to my supervisor's office, my feet feeling heavy with every step, not because I dreaded talking to him but because Scott's report grieved me. My supervisor's door was open, and he was obviously absorbed in some papers he was reading on his desk.

After knocking on his open door, he lifted his head and smiled when he saw me. "Come on in, Floy, and have a seat," he offered using his hand to point to the two empty black chairs in front of his desk.

I sat down and got right to the chase. "Sir, I just had a detective from the Homestead Police Department call."

I proceeded to repeat Scott's report. "I need to look into the possibility that children are being victimized. I'm requesting permission to look into the case."

I then held my breath as I waited for his response.

His eyebrows furrowed in concern. "You're right," he said. "Since children are involved, you need to move quickly."

I thanked him and hurried back to my office to call Scott. "Hey, I'm on my way to your office to meet with your informant."

An hour later, Scott and I sat in HPD's interview room with a wormy, small Colombian informant who went by the name of Tito. He worked in the tomato fields in Homestead, so I imagined he earned his swarthy complexion from working outside in the Miami sun twelve hours a day, six or seven days a week. He appeared calm as he told us some alarming information about young Mexican girls who were forced to work as prostitutes.

He claimed to know about the Cadenas, a wealthy Mexican family who lived in Lake Worth. They smuggled twelve- to thirteen-year-old girls into the United States from Mexico. Then they forced them to work as sex slaves in brothels located throughout Florida and as far north as South Carolina.

I asked Tito, "How do you know this?"

"I hang out in the Mexican communities in Lake Worth. I hear things."

Tito wasn't coming forth with this information because he was a fine citizen reporting a crime or wrongdoing. He faced some legal issues of his own and needed to cut a deal. When the detectives raided a brothel, they found him standing just inside the brothel's front door waiting his turn.

They proceeded to frisk him and found a few grams of cocaine in a baggie on his person. They couldn't charge him with soliciting prostitution because he wasn't doing anything at that time but standing in the front room. Fortunately, though, all of the prostitutes turned out to be over the age of eighteen.

I said, "Once I verify your information, Tito, I'll submit my recommendation to the state attorney."

Police commonly use this tactic on those who find themselves facing criminal charges. In return for their cooperation, they'll make a recommendation to the prosecutor to reduce or dismiss charges.

After we debriefed or questioned Tito, I realized this investigation needed to start in Palm Beach County, about ninety miles and two counties north of Homestead and where Lake Worth was located.

Because protocol prohibited an agent to be one-on-one with an informant, I asked my partner Mark to drive down and meet me at the HPD. When he arrived, we took Tito back to the FDLE offices. We wanted to interview him more in depth so that we could establish his credibility.

We found an empty interview room and initiated the process. We took statements from him about his past, current, and ongoing criminal activities as well as what information he possessed regarding the Cadenas and their illegal operations. We then needed to document Tito as a cooperating informant, which required fingerprinting him, taking his picture, having the analyst run his criminal history, and checking on known associates.

Tito told us about several brothels in Palm Beach County, so we began identifying and mapping out their locations. We also began verifying information about the Lake Worth family.

I contacted the Immigration and Naturalization Service (INS) to ask for their assistance since they were all bilingual and had jurisdiction over undocumented aliens. They jumped onboard once they heard about the possibility of exploited children working in brothels, so I set up a meeting with them.

Mark and I then left to drop Tito off at a Spanish restaurant.

Mark said, "Tito, be a good boy, and stay here until we come back to get you."

Tito nodded in understanding, and we drove to the INS Miami office.

When we got out of my car, Haitian pedestrians dressed in customary vibrant colors blocked the streets and jammed the sidewalk, protesting against what they perceived to be unequal immigration practice. They felt that the U.S. government gave Cubans, who had fled to escape Castro's inhumane treatment and communist regime, better treatment than them because of the Wet-Foot-Dry-Foot policy. This meant that if Cubans made physical contact with American soil, they could stay here. However, none of the Haitians who crossed the ocean and made it to America were allowed to stay if they didn't have a visa.

These protests by the Haitian community became a common practice. The fact that the immigration office was located in the heart of Little Haiti made these protests convenient.

Mark and I elbowed our way through the crowded sidewalk and walked through the barricades. I heard Creole chanting and saw that many in the group carried posters making statements such as how they want an American life and that they should be able to flee Haiti and stay in the U.S.

I made my way toward the front door of the old two-story INS building. I tried to sidestep the discarded chewing gum and nasty cigarette butts that seemed to fill the sidewalk.

This 1960s structure showed its age, looking outdated, weathered, and dirty. Faded gold hurricane shutters ran from top to bottom and around all four sides of its dingy off-white exterior walls. I believed this to be the most neglected federal building I had ever seen.

Visiting immigrants stood in line in front of this building for long hours. Apparently, its appearance didn't deter them from their goal: to obtain green cards or seek political asylum.

Once inside, the interior didn't change my opinion regarding the years of disregard. Its stained walls badly needed a coat or two of paint. The furniture looked like it came with the building. The chairs' steel frames were riddled with dents, and the seats' vinyl upholstery contained rips.

We showed our credentials to a guard and circumvented the metal detector. We filled out the visitor log with the receptionist.

She smiled and gave each of us a clip-on visitor's tag. She then picked up her green phone and pressed three numbers on her green dial pad. "Agents Harper and Turner are here."

She placed the receiver into its cradle and looked back up at us. "Someone will be here in a moment to take you on up."

We thanked her and stepped to the side to wait for our "guide."

A few moments later, a slim man dressed in jeans and a blue golf shirt exited the elevator and walked over to us. He held his hand out and said, "Hi, I'm Agent Sims. You can follow me upstairs."

We took the elevator to the second floor where we were led to an open squad bay with about ten desks that were lined up in two rows. I turned to thank Agent Sims, but he had already left the room.

A young and handsome man rose out of his seat to greet us. "Hi, Agents Turner and Harper. I'm Agent Tim Booker. Thanks for calling us."

He led us to a desk where an older and slightly overweight man with thinning hair sat. "And this is Agent Glen O'Neil. Please, have a seat."

We did and then proceeded to methodically go through all of our information

Agent O'Neil said, "I know a Border Patrol agent in Palm Beach. I'll call him now and set up a meeting."

Once he got his friend on the phone, he described the situation. He put his hand over the receiver and looked over at Mark and me. "Hey, he's very interested and wants to meet ASAP at his office. You okay with that?"

We nodded.

Mark said, "We need to make a few stops along the way, and then we'll meet you all there."

Agent O'Neil then spoke back into the phone. "Okay. Eight o'clock?" He looked over at Mark and me with raised eyebrows and a thumbs-up gesture.

Both Mark and I gave a single nod of agreement.

On the way to the meeting, Mark and I wanted to go by a couple of the brothels, so we went back to the Spanish restaurant to pick up Tito. He climbed in the backseat and directed us to a desolate field off of U.S. 441. This road ran the north-south length of western Palm Beach County. He told us about a single-wide mobile home in a wooded area located off this road and at the end of a small trail.

When we first glimpsed the single wide at a distance, we didn't see any vehicles or people. We decided we'd return that night when more activity may be present.

Tito then directed us to a house in Boynton Beach. It had that unoccupied appearance with the lack of window coverings. Plus, a handwritten "For Rent" sign was posted in the front yard.

Tito said, "I swear that's all I know. I'll speak to some of my contacts to see if I can get more information about other brothels. So can you take me home now? I hadn't been home in a couple of days, and my wife's going to be mad."

"Sure," I said.

Now that he was a documented informant, he was no longer in custody. He had already provided us with a lot of information, so we wanted to be nice to our informant. I had learned from experience that we'll get more from these snitches if we act like we want to be their buddies and help them. We didn't need Tito with us since he had confirmed where the traffickers lived.

We drove Tito to West Palm Beach where he lived with his wife and baby. We parked in front of a one-story building on the corner of Southern Boulevard and Military Trail and followed him into a rundown one-room apartment.

The interior consisted of dirty walls. A pot of black beans and a pan of rice sat on top of a well-used stove, which appeared to have never been cleaned. A wrinkled and cheap cotton throw covered the sofa next to a small wooden table. Cheap plastic blinds covered a large picture window. Some of the slats were crooked or missing, giving us a good peek out over the sidewalk. The baby's crib sat next to the television and a highchair stood near the small kitchen. Both the crib and highchair needed a good scrubbing.

Tito's wife was small in stature, and her dark hair reached halfway down her back. She wore a very tight-fitting top, jeans, and large gold-hoop earrings. The baby looked cared for and well-fed.

Tito introduced us to his wife. "Baby, I got into some trouble in Homestead, so they're here to help me with my problems."

She seemed fine with the situation, which wasn't surprising. I suspected she knew he was involved in illegal activities.

Before leaving, I explained the facts of life to Tito. I ended our talk by saying, "Tito, I am now your new best friend."

He didn't flinch. In fact, he didn't give away any emotions. He wore a blank expression on his face as if I told him it was raining outside.

I continued. "You're going to need to call me and check in daily. I'll be expecting your information about the brothel locations. Otherwise, you'll be cribbing with the roaches and rats in the Dade County Jail."

Tito gave one nod. His face still showed no emotions.

At that point, Tito was all we had. I knew time was not on our side. Those girls needed us, and they needed us yesterday.

A Race to Save the Children

Mark and I arrived about eight o'clock that night at the Border Patrol office. It was located at the west end of the Palm Beach International Airport.

We pulled into the parking lot and saw INS Agents O'Neil and Booker getting out of their cars. We greeted them, and I said, "Glad to have you work this case with us."

They smiled and agreed. We all walked to the old, metal World War II Quonset hut that had been renovated into offices. Before entering, we heard the familiar sounds of jet engines thrusting and revving up as they took off and landed.

The window in the metal door allowed us to show our badges to the gatekeeper, who sat at a small metal desk inside the lobby. He gave a quick nod and buzzed the door to unlock it.

The four of us entered into an office where two Border Patrol agents and a short, beefy, and balding captain greeted us. He led us into a small conference room. Four other people wearing the dark olive-green Border Patrol uniforms sat at the table waiting on us. Everyone in the room introduced themselves.

I shared the information we had gathered on the Lake Worth Cadena family. "We believe they're involved in the recruitment of juvenile females from Mexico. Some of these girls are possibly being held as sex slaves in some of their alleged brothels in Palm Beach County."

I spoke about the location of the trailer and the house that appeared abandoned in Boynton Beach. Everyone agreed about the urgency of getting out to that trailer. Not only did we desperately need to rescue the girls, but we knew the likelihood existed that they could be moved to another location at any moment.

The captain and I devised an operational plan while assessing the risk. We decided to enter the woods from the roadway so that we could observe the area for any activity. Then we would conduct a knock-and-talk interview at the trailer.

I took a few extra minutes to notify my supervisor in Miami. I told him about our information-hunting expedition to verify Tito's story and more importantly, to rescue the girls.

However, investigating the activities at the trailer fell to the Border Patrol because they and the INS had jurisdiction over the undocumented aliens. Additionally, Border Patrol agents were required to be fluent in Spanish, so they would be greatly needed since the girls were from Mexico and probably only spoke Spanish. The agents' ability to communicate in the girls' language could further this investigation.

Mark ended up getting called to another investigation involving a fugitive, so I was left as the only FDLE agent. This made me a little apprehensive. I knew Mark, but I didn't know these agents. I had never worked with the Border Patrol and was unfamiliar with the extent of their training. Ultimately, I needed to rely on my confidence in my abilities and my own training.

I told them that Tito thought some of the brothel enforcers were armed. I was certainly used to armed encounters with bad guys from working the drug-interdiction task force as a trooper, but in the back of my mind, I always played the what-if game.

About nine-thirty that night, the two INS agents, the Border Patrol captain, two Border Patrol agents, and I drove our respective vehicles to an area near the single-wide trailer. Once we arrived, we left our cars near the highway.

The sky was cloudy, so when we entered the dark wooded area on foot, we could hardly see the path. Fortunately, I saw a very dim light coming from the trailer.

We couldn't use our flashlights, so we travelled slowly through the woods. We needed to surprise anyone we may encounter.

We literally crept down a dirt-covered path surrounded by trees and foliage. We were sensitive to every twig breaking and the rustle of every leaf we stepped on. To me, the sounds were magnified as if a microphone picked up on each and every one of them and blasted them throughout the atmosphere. However, I knew I was being oversensitive.

When we got close to the old, rusted, and battered trailer, we didn't see the expected line of men waiting outside the door. Initially, I felt disappointed and worried that this brothel may have closed and that we might have missed an opportunity to locate the girls. I hoped the situation was merely that the brothel had yet to open for business.

Upon approaching the trailer, I breathed a sigh of relief as I saw some movement within it. My adrenaline surged more as I realized we could save these girls while putting away some monsters in the process.

The captain told one of his men to knock on the door. We all unholstered our guns and kept them at the low, ready, tactical position. Although our intention was a mere knock-and-talk method, we knew the possibility existed that there may be an exchange of gunfire.

We all stood on both sides of the door, flattening ourselves against the outer wall. The Border Patrol agent reached out his arm to the side and knocked. Police officers knew never to stand in front of a door in case the occupant decides to shoot through it from the inside, which they have done too many times in the past.

A Hispanic male who looked to be about fifty opened the door. His furrowed brow and frown revealed that he wasn't happy for whatever reason. When he saw us, he squinted his eyes. If looks could kill, he would have killed us right then and there.

The agent spoke to him in Spanish.

The other Border Patrol agent leaned his head close to mine. "He's telling the guy we want to search the trailer, and...he's agreeing to let us come in and look around."

His consent didn't mean that nothing illegal was happening inside. Most of the time these bad guys were usually illegal immigrants, so they didn't stop law enforcement even though they knew they would be caught red-handed participating in criminal activities.

The Border Patrol agent went in first, and I rushed in behind him. As soon as he got out of my line of fire, I held my gun in a tactical position, ready to fire if necessary. At this point I didn't know what might be waiting for us.

The only thing that greeted me was a grimy kitchen that smelled of garbage. Out of the corner of my eye, I saw the agent handcuffing the perp.

I didn't see anyone else, so I yelled, "Kitchen is clear."

The captain came into the trailer along with the rest of the team. Then that Border Patrol agent and Agent Booker took the handcuffed occupant/gatekeeper out of the trailer. At this point, they were detaining him to find out his status and if he was in the country illegally or not.

Before I could start walking down the short hallway, another male of medium height and with a dark complexion, moustache, and long, pointed nose exited from the first door. His mouth was slightly opened, and his eyebrows were pulled down in the middle. He appeared curious as to what the commotion was.

I pointed my .40-caliber Glock toward him. His mouth closed, and he showed no more emotion on his face.

I yelled in English, "Put your hands in the air where I can see them."

I performed a quick scan down his body, and it paid off. I saw a handgun grip sticking out of the waist of the front of the man's pants.

I yelled, "Gun!"

The captain sprinted from behind me. I kept my gun trained on the perp as the captain ordered him in Spanish to place his hands on his head, turn around, and kneel on the floor. He handcuffed him and removed the loaded gun. He then handed him off to Agent O'Neil.

"Get him out of here," the captain ordered.

I decided to check the first room, and the captain and his other agent checked the other two rooms, which I assumed was a bathroom and another bedroom. Upon entering that first bedroom, I saw two single mattresses on the floor and a young girl, who looked to be around twelve or thirteen, lying naked in a fetal position. Several crumpled used condoms covered the floor. The sight sickened me.

The room stunk of stale body odor and urine. All sorts of unknown stains covered the sheetless mattresses. The room was void of any other furniture.

This poor young girl looked filthy. She turned and looked up at me. Tears pooled in her brown eyes and streaked down her face. As she raised her arm to wipe her face, she shivered from head to toe.

I began to look for something to wrap her in or some clothes. Since it was winter, I thought she might not only be trembling from fright, but also from the cool temperature in the trailer.

The captain and agent had cleared the other two rooms and were standing outside my doorway. I wanted to prevent any further embarrassment for her, so I turned and told them to back up and that I would get her dressed.

I found some of her clothes in a pile in a corner. I handed her some dirty underpants, a sleeveless top, a pair of worn jeans, and a pair of sneakers. I took off my raid jacket and draped it over her shoulders.

She obviously didn't understand English, and I was limited in my Spanish. We managed to connect anyway through a series of motions and movements.

This small, fragile child hung her head down and wouldn't look me in the eyes. Her shoulders were slumped. She seemed very passive, which I attributed to her ongoing torture.

I was concerned she would be afraid of me because I thought that people in her country may be afraid of the police. Also, her captors might have told her that the police would punish her.

If I had known then what I know today, I would have had a Spanish-speaking victim's advocate nearby to help with this child's rescue. She needed the immediate comfort that an advocate could have provided. I wore a gun, handcuffs, and tactical police gear. I knew the possibility existed that my appearance could further traumatize her.

I tossed the authoritarian police officer role aside and approached her in a nurturing, motherly manner. After all, I am a mother, and she was a child in need of safety.

When I came out of the bedroom, I glanced into the second doorway and saw that it held the bathroom. The captain or agent had left the door open upon his search, and an unbearable stench filled the hallway. I wanted to throw up. The plumbing must not have been working, or the holding tank must have overflowed.

I walked the girl outside. I wanted to get her out of that nightmare, and I also wanted to breathe in some fresh air.

One of the Border Patrol agents, who had been watching our perps, said, "Hey, our guy over here admitted to being in the U.S. illegally."

I gave a quick nod to acknowledge his statement.

We then waited while the rest of the agents searched the premises. One found a loaded, small, six-shot revolver and a box of ammunition in a kitchen cabinet.

After we were satisfied with our search, we closed the unlocked door to the trailer and left. The captain deployed Agents Booker and O'Neil to the house in Boynton Beach to determine if it was empty while he and I took the victim to his office since this was a federal case.

We planned to conduct interviews as well as wait to hear from the agents. If they found activity in the Boynton Beach house, then we'd need to re-strategize and gather together more agents to search it.

The captain interrogated the arrestees. They didn't provide any statements. All were eventually transported to the Krome Detention Center to await a trial or possible deportation back to Mexico.

The officers reported back that the Boynton Beach residence was abandoned.

I sat in on the captain's interview of the victim. Because she didn't speak English, the captain had to translate my questions into Spanish and her answers into English.

I learned that she was only fifteen years old and from Veracruz, Mexico. She said that other young girls had been in the trailer, but they were taken away a few days before we arrived. Since then, she had been the only girl with multiple adult men. I could only imagine what she must have endured in her young life.

We notified the Mexican Consulate that we had rescued a Mexican national youth who was the victim of sex crimes. We also called for a Spanish-speaking female victim advocate and requested that she bring some clean clothes and toiletries.

We couldn't clean up the girl until after she met with the sexual assault investigative team, though. Once the advocate and team were in place, I began my two-hour drive home.

I felt like I had done all I could for that evening. Tomorrow I planned to resume my investigation to locate the other girls.

On the way to my office the next morning, I couldn't get the girls off my mind. I worried about them; they were still mere children.

I called my FDLE analyst and requested he identify the owners of the two properties. I then decided to pay Tito a visit to pressure him. I needed to find the rest of these girls.

Before I had the chance to drive to his apartment, my supervisor directed me to another assignment. He told me to help Mark and Milton with an investigation that the Georgia Bureau of Investigation (GBI) was conducting. One of their special agents was in town looking for an escaped prisoner.

The three of us were interviewing the escapee's family and friends when Tito called halfway through the morning. He told me that he had talked with some of his friends and associates and that he was meeting with someone later on that day who might know the location of a new brothel in Lake Worth.

I let out a sigh of relief, excited with Tito's news. I told my supervisor about Tito's call.

He said, "Go. Take care of it."

I then let out another sigh of relief now that I had his blessing to pursue this lead.

I checked with INS Agents Booker and O'Neil. They informed me that they had been watching the Cadena's Lake Worth home since we started this investigation.

I relayed to them Tito's report. "I need you guys to meet me at Tito's."

I then quickly drove up to Tito's place. The agents were already there waiting for me, so the three of us and Tito piled into my car. He directed us to a small, yellow stucco house located down the street from the Lake Worth Police Department (LWPD) and identified it as the brothel.

We drove back to Tito's apartment where I dropped him off. We then drove to the LWPD where we met the Border Patrol captain, Detectives Dave Henry and Jack Fields, and Mark to discuss the most recent intel and strategies.

When I told them about the brothel in Lake Worth, Detective Henry called in one of their undercover officers (UC). He entered their office wearing a long-sleeve shirt and blue jeans on his five-foot-five-inch frame. A baseball cap covered his dark hair that surrounded his dark, round face. I noted how well he would fit into the migrant field-worker environment. As a result, his Peruvian attributes and attire were perfect for getting into the brothel.

We developed an operational plan. We would send the UC to the door of the brothel where he would make the purchase for sex. Then when he entered a room for the encounter, we would raid the house.

Detective Fields said he would notify SWAT for the entry into the brothel. They could wait in an unmarked van down the street until needed.

I contacted a Spanish-speaking victim advocate and instructed her to also wait down the street until we needed her. I wanted to be better prepared this time around.

The detectives wired the UC with a small recording device, taping it onto his inner thigh so that his pants covered it. They would monitor it from a nearby car. The UC would use the word "verde," which meant green, as the code for us to enter the brothel. The entire conversation would also be recorded for evidence to be used in court.

The Border Patrol captain took his car and rode alone because he needed to be able to respond to another situation that was also pending. Mark volunteered to drive his car. The two INS agents and I decided to ride with him. Since the UC was small and would be getting out in a few blocks anyway, he got in the car with us as well.

We dropped the UC off a couple of blocks away from the brothel. Mark then drove down a side street and parked about half a football field away but close enough to see the front door. We all sat in the car and anxiously watched through heavy-tinted windows as the UC walked to the stucco house.

A few other men stood on a small front stoop. They appeared to be agricultural workers and wore the same type of clothes as the UC.

I felt on edge, worrying about locating these children.

We watched the UC walk into the suspect house, and I heard a conversation taking place in Spanish through his hidden microphone. I could only understand "veintidós."

I knew the UC was repeating twenty-two. I hoped this was the price, and the deal was being made.

I didn't dare interrupt the INS agents as they listened to the conversation. They didn't need to be distracted. This didn't mean that I wasn't chomping at the bit to know what was being said. Good thing I didn't bite my nails because they would have been bitten down to the bone while waiting.

I just knew that the stakes were extremely high on so many levels. I worried about the UC's safety. From the information I had gathered, this officer was in the middle of a ruthless criminal enterprise. An undercover officer always faced danger when involved with criminals in their territory anyway, so this part of the operation was always tense. If the bad guys discovered his true identity, the UC would be at their mercy while we rushed to the scene. That could take a few minutes.

I listened intently to the conversation even though I didn't understand most of it, but I did know how brothels worked. However, I later learned that these brothels had their own operational procedures. Here, the sex sold for twenty dollars and the condom for two dollars, so johns could purchase a "package deal" for twenty-two dollars.

After the customer paid the seller, he received some type of token representing money. It could be a marble, playing card, poker chip, or any other small item established by the seller. This was what the john gave to the girl before receiving the service or sex act. The bad guys preferred this payment method to keep the money out of the hands of the girls. Otherwise, the girls might steal some of it.

My heart began to pound as I finally heard the UC say, "Verde." From the front passenger seat, I opened my door and rushed out. I grabbed the handle of my gun and pulled it out of my holster. I put it in the ready position while I ran toward the house, my heart racing faster.

The SWAT officers got there first, injecting a surge of confidence in me. I entered the brothel behind a couple of them. I saw more SWAT officers handcuffing two men on the floor near the door. I bolted by them to the back hallway where the UC stood in front of an open doorway.

I walked by him into a bedroom with two almost-naked girls huddled together on a mattress on the floor. They hugged each other in fear as demonstrated by the wide-eyed looks of terror on their faces. They appeared to be around thirteen or fourteen years old.

A wire cord crossed the top of the room with two sheets hanging from them. The sheets acted as a curtain to partition off each mattress into a small compartment.

I noticed numerous used condoms scattered about the room like I saw in the trailer. Condom wrappers and crumpled paper towels also littered the floor.

A small nightstand sat in the corner. On top of it laid a little stuffed bear, a bottle of lubricant, and some black marbles. I suspected the marbles were the tokens.

After all of the arrests were made, and the house was secured, I contacted the victim's advocate. She arrived a few moments later with some light blankets for the girls.

I felt sad to learn that these young girls, fourteen and sixteen years old, had been forced into this horrific life. I felt an overwhelming need to understand and know how this sickening injustice was happening in modern America.

Realizing that Tito had provided accurate information again surprised me. He had never earned my complete trust.

After those rescues, Tito took me to a few other locations, but we came up empty-handed. He said, "I think they must have moved the brothels to Central Florida and South Carolina."

With another state now in the picture and the trafficking of these girls across state lines, I knew the time had come to get the FBI involved. They could help with locating and rescuing these girls.

I called the Palm Beach FBI field office and scheduled a meeting. The Border Patrol captain and the INS agents said they preferred I attend the meeting since I had organized it. Tito, Agent Booker, and I went there the day after the Lake Worth operation.

We arrived at the upper floors of a large bank building overlooking the beautiful Intercoastal Waterway. A tall, nice-looking blonde agent named Fred Coates greeted us. He told me he had recently joined the Bureau after being a sheriff's deputy in North Florida.

I introduced him to Tito. Agent Coates ushered Tito into a conference room with Agent Booker and me following behind them.

Agent Coates turned and smiled. "Agents Turner and Booker, Agent Sims will stay here with Tito because I need to have a private conversation with you in my office. Come with me please."

He led us to a door at the end of the hall. We entered the small room, and Agent Booker and I sat down in the two seats by the door.

Agent Coates faced us from across his desk. "We've already been investigating the Cadena family." He paused for a moment before continuing. "Several months ago, some of the girls they had forced into prostitution had escaped and ran to the police, and they called us.

"The Cadena family matriarch does the recruiting. She drives a large, new, decked-out dually pickup truck into Veracruz, Mexico, where she visits poor families with teenage daughters. She wears expensive suits with lots of gold jewelry. Señora Cadena tells the parents that their daughters can make a lot of money in the U.S. as nannies, waitresses, or maids. She promises to look after them. She then assures the families that the girls will send money home to support them."

I thought about the girls we rescued and how they and their families had probably been excited about the opportunities presented to them. This evil woman deceptively lured them to the U.S. with the promise of jobs that didn't exist, and these poor villagers entrusted their daughters to her.

Agent Coates said, "The Cadena family makes about two and a half million dollars a year from selling women and children over and over again. They force them to serve as sex slaves for twenty-five to thirty men a day, and they move them weekly throughout Florida and South Carolina."

I thought I was going to be sick. Instead I involuntarily swallowed hard as I thought about how women and children were beaten, tormented, repetitively raped, and confined to trailers and houses.

"If the girls become pregnant," Agent Coates said, "then they're forced to have abortions. These girls are treated worse than cattle. They're denied food and medical treatment and made to exist in uninhabitable conditions."

I appreciated Agent Coates sharing this information with us. It explained a lot.

Since I was still assigned to another task force in Miami, I knew I had taken this case as far as I could. Plus, my supervisor was already on thin ice for letting me work the case for as long as I did. The FBI had the multi-state jurisdiction, so I felt good about handing my informant and the results of my investigation over to them.

The most important aspect now was saving these innocent girls and bringing the evil Cadenas to justice.

Human Trafficking 101

In the course of the Cadena investigation, over twenty girls and women were rescued. Janet Reno was the U.S. Attorney General at the time. She coined this crime *modern-day slavery*. We now recognize it as human trafficking.

When the Cadena case was prosecuted and sentenced in federal court, the current human-trafficking laws had yet to be written. Since it was the first case on record in modern times, it was prosecuted in federal court using very outdated slavery laws.

Victims of human trafficking are young children, teenagers, men, and women. Force, fraud, or coercion is used to subject them to sexual exploitation, such as prostitution or the sex-entertainment industry. It could also subject victims to labor exploitation, such as domestic servitude, restaurant work, janitorial work, sweatshop factory work, and migrant agricultural work.

After drug dealing, human trafficking is tied with arms dealing as being the second largest criminal industry in the world. It's also the fastest growing.

The approach to investigating human trafficking must be victim-centered and multi-disciplined so that the victim can begin to heal in a safe and secure environment. Once a victim is rescued, the road to recovery is often long and hard because the trafficker has stolen his or her self-worth and dignity. Providing protective services for these victims is as important as the investigation and prosecution.

I was blessed to have been able to make a difference in the lives of three of these girls. I will always remember the injustices they endured in the land of the free.

As a result of the Cadena case, I made a commitment to champion for those who were enslaved. I have been blessed with many opportunities to share my passion for fighting such evil.

We as a society need to hold everyone accountable who's involved in the human-trafficking chain, from the recruitment to the harboring to the transportation to the provision to the purchasing of services.

I never heard from FBI Special Agent Fred Coates again. My supervisor understood my frustration because I wanted to be kept in the loop and see the case finalized. It wasn't about me or gathering kudos for my efforts, but this case was about saving more girls and punishing those responsible.

About a year after the Cadena trial, a friend of mine who was a supervisor at the State Department called me at home early one morning. I was just about to grab a cup of coffee before heading off to work.

"Floy, I have someone named Tito in my office. Appears he's under arrest for passport fraud. Turns out Tito provided your name and said he worked for you."

I had never trusted Tito; I never trusted most of my informants. Now Tito was trying to use my name to get him out of trouble. Tito deserved to be arrested, so I liked this turn of events.

My friend asked, "Is Tito your informant?"

"No. Tell that little worm Tito to call his friends at the FBI."

"Okey-dokey," he responded in a slight uplifting tone, "I'll most certainly do that."

"Hey," I said, "gotta go."

Then I hung up.

I later learned that Tito wanted to take down the Cadena family because he wanted to start his own network for human trafficking.

I hope Tito is still sitting in a prison somewhere.

CHAPTER 8

The Murder of Gianni Versace

My relationship with Gary continued to grow. He told me he loved me and wanted to spend the rest of his life with me. So in February 1997, after a romantic candlelight dinner, he opened a bottle of champagne. I watched the flame flicker across his green eyes. At that moment, I truly didn't think I could be any happier

Well, I couldn't be more wrong.

As we toasted each other, he asked, "Floy, will you marry me?"

His proposal took my breath away, and my heart fluttered with excitement. I didn't hesitate to respond. "Yes!"

He pulled out a beautiful diamond and platinum forever ring from his pocket. "I designed it myself," he said as he slipped it onto my finger.

I marveled at the intricacies of my new ring, knowing that he had planned every detail with me in mind. We then sealed our new engagement with a long kiss.

To say I was absolutely thrilled would be an understatement because I had developed a deep love for Gary. He turned out to be the man of my dreams (and still is). He had proven that real men could be romantic, thoughtful, and loving. I appreciated all of the things he did for me, especially the little things, like dropping notes in the top of my dresser drawers and leaving candies for me in my car.

We then proceeded to plan the start of our life together. We scheduled our wedding for New Year's Day 1998, thinking that a new marriage would be a good way to begin a new year. Although we both should be off on that holiday, the possibility still loomed over us that we might be called in to work some kind of emergency.

Another challenge we faced, and it was a rather large one, was how to address and overcome the logistics of my assignment in Miami and his in West Palm Beach. At that time, FDLE policy mandated agents to reside within thirty miles of their assigned offices.

We lived a hundred miles apart, so we made a mutual decision for me to sell my home. We then purchased a house together further north in Boynton Beach so that Gary could be near his school-age children.

The closest FDLE office was in Fort Lauderdale, about twenty-five miles away, so I applied for a transfer to that field office. I learned that I was the next agent on the list for the transfer. Until it took place, I needed to commute about one to two hours one way depending on traffic from our new home to the Miami field office.

For some folks, that drive might have been overwhelming, but for me, it was all worth it.

Was It a Mob Hit?

About ten o'clock on July 15, 1997, while driving from Boynton Beach to Miami, my dispatcher instructed me to respond to the Gianni Versace mansion located at the 1100 block of Ocean Drive in Miami Beach.

Breena the dispatcher said, "Versace's been shot."

This might seem strange, but I had never heard of Versace. Whoever he was, he probably was important and/or well-off because his address was in the heart of trendy South Beach where models and actors frequented.

I didn't want to come across brainless over the radio because of my ignorance, so I called Breena on my cell phone.

After she answered, I asked, "Breena, who is Versace?"

She gave a small yet audible gasp. "Mama, you don't know who Versace is? He's a world-famous designer for clothes."

Breena always called me "Mama." From the tone in her voice, I gathered she must have thought I just crawled out from under a whiskey barrel to ask such an "unintelligent" question.

The truth was I didn't have a clue about most high-end designer clothes. Ralph Lauren's name was printed on the labels of my most expensive suits. I considered them sufficient enough when wanting to look professional as a FDLE agent.

I headed to the crime scene. On the way, I thought about where I would park. I was familiar with Miami Beach from my days on the RID task force when we sometimes worked in the area for a few special occasions. Also after catching the last prison escapee from the Glades Correctional Institution, the task force came here to celebrate at Joe's Stone Crab.

Miami Beach was always very crowded, especially in the South Beach area on the ocean. The sidewalks were always filled with tourists, and finding a place to park, even for a cop car, was impossible.

I recalled that the Miami Beach Police Station was located close to the crime scene. I decided to head over there since their parking lot always seemed to have available spaces for law enforcement vehicles.

After pulling into one of their empty spots, I stepped into the intense heat from the Miami sun and walked on the sidewalk toward the mansion. I crossed Collins Avenue and saw the familiar corner grocery store that housed a well-known Cuban coffee window where cops grabbed a quick cup of their great java. I normally made a point to visit it when in Miami Beach so that I could enjoy a dose of its high-test Coffee Cubano. Today, though, I needed to walk past it since I had a murder waiting on me.

When I turned the next corner, I saw a long strand of yellow crime scene tape in front of a large Spanish villa. People had gathered outside of the roped-off area, and numerous uniformed members from the Miami Beach Police Department (MBPD) stood guard in front of the tape.

I displayed my FDLE credentials to one of the officers. He wrote my name, badge number, and arrival time into the crime scene log. He then held up the tape for me to cross under.

Although Versace's body had already been taken to the medical examiner's office, I had no doubt as to where the murder had taken place. A blue plastic blanket splattered with blood, which I knew had been used to shield the body from the public, laid next to the front steps right off the sidewalk. These steps led to a tall black iron gate that opened up to a fenced-off lawn.

I walked up the handful of sand-colored steps, tiptoeing around the pools of blood dripping down the stairs. The ocean breeze slightly lifted the outer edges of the lightweight blanket, exposing more blood. The crime scene technicians had dispersed the small black portable easel markers to note where the body and two bullet casings had been discovered. In my experience, chalk has never been used to mark the outline of a body like it is on television.

I walked through the gate that opened up into a courtyard and sidewalk that led to the villa. A man wearing a royal-blue short-sleeve shirt and a blue-and-black-striped tie coordinated with dark pants was writing in a small black notebook. I glimpsed down and saw a badge displayed on the right side of his black belt near his holstered gun.

I pulled out my credentials, which consisted of my badge and FDLE identification card. "Excuse me. I'm Special Agent Turner from FDLE."

The man glanced up from his notebook to greet me. "Hi, I'm Detective Jim Sharkey with the MBPD. Come with me." He then closed his notebook and started walking toward the villa's front door.

I followed behind Jim. He ushered me into one of the most beautiful rooms I have ever seen with colorful mosaic tile, exceptionally high ceilings, and gilded, silk-covered antique chairs. The carefully arranged fixtures not only complemented the airy South Beach ambiance, but it also confirmed the room's vast feeling.

I saw a few other detectives and FDLE agents in the room. Since Versace was a well-known international celebrity (well, well-known to everyone but me), this case required all hands on deck.

Jim briefed us about the developments that had occurred before we arrived. "This morning, Gianni Versace ate breakfast a few blocks away at the News Café. He then walked home about nine o'clock. While he unlocked his gate, an unknown male walked up and shot him twice in the back of the head, leading us to believe the murder was a mob-style execution. Witnesses state they saw the shooter fleeing north on foot.

"The shooting was reported to the MBPD, and units were dispatched to the scene where they established a wide perimeter. Our quick response makes me believe that the shooter is still in Miami Beach.

"A Miami-Dade County K-9 handler and her bloodhound are trying to track the shooter as we speak."

Once the briefing concluded, Jim walked over to me and asked, "Anything you need, Agent Turner? I'm going to go ahead and leave so that I can catch up with the K-9 handler and see if the dog's been able to follow the scent track where the shooter's been seen running away."

I answered, "No, I'm fine. Thanks. Who's the handler?"

"Janice Hardy."

I knew Janice, and I knew her beautiful red bloodhound Biscuit. Bloodhounds have been considered the best tracking dogs. They could track a scent for long distances and for long periods of time.

Jim left, and I walked back to the front of the villa. Seeing the vast number of media trucks surprised me. Crowds of sightseers were herded across the street on the beach sidewalk. To me it seemed like people came from everywhere.

A new FDLE agent by the name of Anne Estevez walked up to the villa and greeted me. I knew her from MROC where she had previously been an analyst.

She looked professional in a suit with a slim skirt and high heels. Her beautiful, curly brown hair touched her shoulders. Upon seeing her attire, I couldn't help but hope and wonder if she kept some tactical gear in her car's trunk. If not, I feared she would become miserable from the pain of walking in those heels, and I knew this was going to be a long day.

Anne asked, "Mind if I tag along?"

I smiled. "Sure."

Anne and I walked to the sidewalk to join Jim, Janice, and Biscuit. We followed next to them as Biscuit pushed his nose down on the sidewalk. His long ears flapped in rhythm with the ocean breeze that travelled from the Atlantic Ocean to our direction. We began to head north and west. Within a couple of blocks, we found ourselves in front of a parking garage.

When we approached the garage entrance, a radio transmission happened to come over the air with some pertinent information. The dispatcher reported that witnesses had told detectives that they had seen a man in a garage located at this same address earlier. They said they saw him on an upper level changing clothes near a parked red Chevy pickup truck, and then he ran out of the garage.

We were now even more curious, and so was the bloodhound. He kept going, and we kept following behind him. We climbed the stairs to the reported level. Sure enough, the bloodhound led us to a pile of clothes and the red Chevy with a South Carolina license plate.

Jim called the dispatcher on his radio and asked for a license check of the plate. After the information was run through the national computer system known as NCIC, or National Crime Information Center, dispatch came back and told Jim that the plate had been stolen.

I said, "Hey Jim, this truck reminds me of a case in New Jersey that was connected to a serial killer. I saw it on *America's Most Wanted*. From what I remember, a caretaker at a New Jersey cemetery was murdered, and his red pickup truck was stolen. The police thought the murderer killed him for his ride."

Jim's eyes remained fixed as he stared at me. I figured he was processing what I had told him.

I continued. "This killing spree's been in the national news since April. This guy's suspected of murdering four people."

As if someone had slapped him in the face to bring him to his senses, Jim broke his focused stare. "Got it," he said. "Let me grab the VIN, and I'll run it through NCIC to see if there's a match with our New Jersey victim."

I anxiously waited for the results. I wanted to pace to get some of this nervous energy out of me, but I thought doing so may be distracting to everyone, especially Biscuit. If Jim's check came back positive, then I knew we had a serial killer on our hands.

We finally got the answer. NCIC confirmed that the red truck was indeed from the homicide in New Jersey.

I called our supervisor over my FDLE radio to report our findings. He assigned Anne to stand watch over the pickup and discarded clothes. These items were considered important evidence.

He said, "We need them to remain preserved in the same state they were found."

After talking to my supervisor, I looked over at Anne. My feet ached just watching her standing there in those shoes on the unmercifully hard concrete.

"Hey, Anne," I said, "I'll stand watch if you want to go to your car and change out of your suit and heels."

Much to my surprise, she declined.

A Serial Killer Indeed

The murder of Gianni Versace began one of the most interesting and diverse investigations with which I had ever gotten involved. On that hot July morning, I could not have envisioned what I would see over the next eight days.

My supervisor, a retired NYPD detective and one of the best street cops I had ever known, assigned me to the News Café to locate any potential witnesses. This was the last place Versace had visited before the murder. I walked south a few blocks and entered the café.

I spoke with the owner, waiters, and patrons. All of them had already heard about the murder. They were shaken, sad, and distraught that the renowned Gianni Versace was gone.

I obtained statements that basically confirmed Versace's status as a regular customer when he stayed in Miami. I then started walking to the MBPD to give them my report. Every place

I went that morning conveniently turned out to be within walking distance of where I had parked my car.

Once I arrived at the station, a MBPD officer stopped tapping his pencil on the small reception desk to speak to me. "Ma'am, did you park your car in our parking lot?"

"Yes," I answered, cocking my head slightly to the side in confusion.

"Well, you may want to move your car into the police garage," he said, pointing toward the parking lot with his pencil-turned-drumstick, "The lot where you're parked is in the process of being barricaded and turned into a media staging area."

I looked out the window and saw large media trucks replacing the smaller news vans and SUVs. I thanked the officer and rushed outside to move my car.

By the time I returned to the station and walked to the third-floor homicide area, I saw a flutter of activity. Supervisors from the FDLE, FBI, and MBPD staked out their respective territories in the large conference room. Analysts from both the state and federal levels carried and wheeled in their computers onto the room's plush green carpet. The technical support services from all three agencies draped wires all over the conference room.

The cushy chairs with attached rollers were being taken on a first-come-first-serve basis. The large dark-wood table acted as the room's centerpiece and magnet, drawing everyone to it. We all waited eagerly to hear the pending briefing and learn how the case would be organized.

I peered out a series of windows on the south side of the conference room that overlooked 11th Street and noticed a traffic jam of trucks. Each of them contained local logos of the news networks. I guess the commandeered police parking lot was on a first-come-first-serve basis too and that it didn't have enough room to hold all of the news vehicles. We all knew this was going to be a huge media event, but seeing the magnitude took me a bit by surprise.

The front or north side of the conference room contained the squad bay. Here the department downgraded the quality of its flooring to a low-grade industrial-beige carpet. Gray modules encapsulated each detective's workspace. They adorned their desks with all of the appropriate knickknacks and working case files.

The quickly formed task force hijacked the MBPD detectives' desks, and so began the process of removing all of their personal treasures of pictures, souvenirs, and police paraphernalia. Their sacrificial gestures contributed to helping the task force take shape.

State analysts handwrote sturdy paper placards with black Sharpie pens. They printed labels such as "Leads to Follow," "Incomplete Leads," and "Completed Leads." They then attached them to large inboxes and outboxes and placed them on the desktops in the squad bay.

I asked one of the detectives standing nearby, "Why are the feds involved?"

He looked around before answering. "The focus has shifted. We no longer think it was a mob hit. We reached out to the FBI and found out that some of their field offices had already been working on some cases against a suspect named Andrew Cunanan. He's been wanted for four recent murders with the most recent one tied to a red pickup truck that was found in a parking garage."

I tried not to smile, knowing that he didn't realize I was one of the cops who found the pickup truck and made the connection to the murder spree.

He continued. "Plus, witnesses who saw someone running from the crime scene gave descriptions that matched Cunanan. Because he's the number-one suspect in this murder, the FBI is now in the house."

What we now knew was that Cunanan had connections with the two homicide victims in Minneapolis, and he killed his third victim in Chicago before stealing his car. Then less than a week later, he killed his fourth victim, the owner of the red truck, and drove to Miami.

Furthermore, the first two victims had been tied to the gay community, and Versace was known to be gay. In fact, Versace's longtime partner had been inside the mansion at the time of his murder.

Under the direction of a supervisor, our FDLE analyst made flyers with the image of twenty-seven-year-old Andrew Cunanan pictured on the front. We received the flyers to use on the street and gave some to the television networks to show to the public. Cunanan was considered very dangerous, so we wanted to ensure that everyone who saw it would be able to recognize the prime suspect should they come across him.

As the day wore on, we uncovered more information about the suspect. As a gay man, he had developed links to gay societies in major cities throughout the U.S., and his reputation put him as a person moving in the same crowds as jetsetters. He sought out wealthy men to support his expensive lifestyle of dining, drinks, and travel.

Since Cunanan loved the limelight and was known to party and frequent gay bars, Milton and I decided to visit a gay nightclub in Fort Lauderdale, one that had yet to be visited by other investigators. We needed to see if we could spot Cunanan.

I had seen a lot of gay activity during my time as a trooper when I portrayed a prostitute, so I didn't feel uneasy about being there in the least bit. Since I wore "plain clothes," I hoped no one would identify me as a law enforcement officer.

Around ten thirty, the club had just begun the night's activities. I soon became immersed in a sea of tight leather jeans, chest-exposing leather vests, and spikes—spiked-up hairstyles, spiked necklaces, and spiked cuffs that adorned some of the patrons. I saw a couple of young men wearing dog collars. The "dominant" men led them around on a leash.

Our plain-clothes attire was probably too plain. We wore jeans, and of course we had to wear jackets to hide our guns. Also, we combed our hair into normal styles. I got the feeling that Milton and I still stood out in this crowd.

We watched the entrance for the next several hours, hoping to see Cunanan. He never did show, so about five in the morning as the club was closing, we pulled out the flyer with Cunanan's image. We spoke to some of the stragglers and showed them the flyer to learn if they had ever seen him in the club.

Some ignored us, but most of the guys responded to our questions politely. They expressed their sympathy about Versace's homicide. None had seen Cunanan at the club or anywhere else for that matter.

When I finally arrived home, I hadn't slept for about twenty hours. I showered and then fell fast asleep for about six hours. After waking up, I got dressed and headed back to Miami Beach.

As I approached 11th Street, I saw the media circus circling their wagons around two sides of the police department. They took over the plaza leading to the station's front doors. Well-dressed reporters stood in front of cameras and spoke into their handheld microphones.

After parking my car in the police garage, I spotted Anne getting out of her car. We waved at each other, and I stopped and waited for her to catch up to me. As she approached, my eyes did a quick scan of her clothing. She looked much more comfortable in her casual top and slacks than in the suit she wore the previous day. My eyes stopped at her feet as I tried to determine if she had ditched the heels.

Anne caught my eyes on her shoes and smiled.

With finality in her voice, she said, "I'll never wear heels to work again."

Media Frenzy

My supervisor teamed Anne and I together. We followed our assigned leads compiled from a combination of public tips, those developed from investigators' canvasses, and some developed by the analytic staff through data checks on Versace's known associates and places he visited.

The media surprised us at how they got to a lot of our leads before we did. For instance, we had received a tip from a pizza shop employee who called into the designated hotline. He saw Cunanan in his pizzeria while working one of his shifts. When we walked into that restaurant, a reporter and cameraman were already interviewing the caller.

The command staff began to suspect the media of utilizing high-tech listening devices. These electronic tools picked up conversations near the windows. If they resorted to these measures, then they probably heard the details discussed during our meetings in the conference room.

By the second day, the supervisors instructed investigators to use only radio channels that were encrypted. The command staff wanted to ensure the media couldn't monitor the police radio traffic.

The situation with the media got so out of hand that all of the investigating agencies used decoys to throw them off. One such ploy was having two detectives rush out the front of the stationhouse with folders. They ran as if on an important mission and jumped into their cars, taking lots of turns and ending up in the drive-through lane of a fast-food restaurant. As expected, the media followed them on this wild goose chase. This gave the investigating detectives, who were actually following a real hot lead, the opportunity to slowly slip out the rear of the station unnoticed.

Monster Sightings

Right after the shooting of Versace, the police had shut down traffic near the crime scene and quickly blocked all of the roads that left Miami Beach. They defined a border by surrounding the area and established a visual by monitoring all intersections and outbound roadways. All beach leads were considered to be a priority. Their rapid response time led most of the investigators to feel that Cunanan was still on Miami Beach.

A few days into the investigation, Anne and I followed some leads that our FDLE supervisor gave us. The manager of a low-rent pink stucco hotel in the seedy north end of the beach community had called the MBPD to report seeing Cunanan. The lead was passed onto us.

We arrived at the three-story motel. I noted that Cunanan seemed to have stepped down a few notches in his lifestyle. The motel obviously needed some rehabilitation. We walked into the small lobby and identified ourselves to the manager.

He said, "Yeah, that Cunanan guy? Well, he rented a room here the night before the murder for thirty-six dollars. I hadn't seen him since then, though."

My heart skipped a beat. Actually, hearing him confirm this report was the best news I had heard all day.

I asked, "Can we see the room that he rented?"

"Yeah." He walked from behind the counter. "Follow me."

The manager escorted us up a weathered narrow stairwell that smelled musty. We then walked through a long narrow hallway with dingy and dirty walls and into a shabby-looking room with cheap, dark furniture that had been scarred from many years of use. Its flowered, threadbare carpet contained holes, and the gray bedspread was old and rumpled. The brown shades covered white peeling paint on the window frames.

I then called in the results of this lead. We preserved security of it until the crime scene units could respond, which didn't take long. Within minutes, the area lit up with numerous MBPD detectives, FBI agents, and crime scene technicians.

We left the hotel to follow our next lead. A woman who had been shopping at a grocery store a few blocks from the hotel called into the Miami Beach Police tip line with a report. She stated that she saw a man looking like Cunanan watching her as she shopped.

Upon buying her groceries, she realized that the cash in her purse was missing. She believed the man had taken the money while she had her back turned from her cart for just a couple of moments. So, when she saw a picture of Cunanan on the nightly news, she phoned in her information.

Two days later, our FDLE supervisor assigned Anne and me to follow up with another lead called in by a sailboat owner. He reported that someone had broken into his boat. The break-in contained some strange characteristics. The intruder had eaten some of the food stored onboard, and then he cleaned the galley when done. The owner also thought the culprit had read one of his books while inside the boat because it had been removed from his shelf and left open on a table.

After our supervisor told us the details of this tip, Anne and I looked at each other and smiled. Our intel reported that Cunanan had a reputation of being a voracious reader and a neat freak.

We agreed that this burglary wasn't normal. We both thought Cunanan had stayed on this boat.

Anne and I walked to the marina since it happened to be in the same area as the hotel. We found the caller's boat and entered its unlocked hatch with our guns drawn.

We yelled, "Police! Anyone here? Hello?"

The silence was deafening. At this point, we didn't know if the boat was empty or if someone was hiding and hoping his or her silence would cause us to go away. Going away was not an option.

We methodically and carefully searched the boat. If Cunanan was still onboard, I didn't doubt he would shoot it out with the police if caught since he probably felt he had nothing to lose.

As it turned out, we didn't find anyone. I called my supervisor and requested the crime scene unit respond and process it for evidence. We placed crime scene tape over the opening hatch and taped business cards near the doors on the cabin so that other law enforcement and the owner would know we had been there.

The likelihood that Cunanan had moved to another boat seemed logical. Consequently, Anne and I made our way down the dock and began to knock on the hulls of the boats or on those windows that we could reach from the dock. No one responded, so we boarded a few larger boats and looked in from the decks, or if the boat was smaller, we bent down to try and peek inside. We made our way from boat to boat to see if Cunanan might be aboard one of them.

We weren't able to check all of the boats because we were called to respond to yet another priority lead. Two maids at the Miami Airport Hilton had called 911 and reported seeing Cunanan in their hotel.

Because the FBI and FDLE had already interviewed them and deemed both very credible, our supervisor told Anne and me to report to the Hilton ASAP for the manhunt. We terminated our self-initiated process of examining all of the boats and drove across the causeway to the Airport Hilton.

Finding this fugitive in a fully booked hotel proved to be a manpower-intensive function. Anne and I were split up. I saw Milton and learned that he and I would work together for this assignment.

Milton and I reported to a briefing with MBPD detectives, the FBI, and the FDLE agents in a conference room off the lobby. We were given the vast undertaking of inspecting every guest room in this massive hotel. This event required organizing and assigning search teams for every floor and then protecting the floor afterward.

Milton and I were given a passkey for the hotel rooms. Armed hotel security guards, most of whom were former police officers, followed us. They needed to be kept in the loop so that they could keep their colleagues and supervisors apprised of the progress.

We kept our guns at low ready as we knocked on each door and yelled, "Police!"

When the guests opened their doors, we explained that we needed to search their rooms to make sure they were safe. Those who answered seemed confused, but none seemed offended.

If no one answered, we used the passkey to open the door.

During one particular room, we knocked on the door and were met by silence. We waited a few moments before walking in and interrupting a naked couple engaged in sex.

We obviously caught them in an extremely vulnerable state. Their moans of passion quickly evolved to gasps of embarrassment when they looked up and saw an audience of gun-toting people wearing tactical uniforms and standing inside their room.

This didn't stop Milton. He kept walking into the room as they pulled up their sheets to cover their nakedness. When I walked in behind him, I saw the female pulling the sheet up over her face.

We entered each room with a police technique called "slicing the pie," which consisted of performing an instantaneous quick look-peek procedure. This was a method we utilized for high-risk areas where the perpetrator might be a concealed threat. We then looked behind the bathroom curtains, behind the closet doors, and under all of the beds.

The hotel search lasted over eight hours, and we came up empty-handed. I began my ninety-minute drive home at two thirty in the morning.

The following day I went to the command post area at the MBPD police station. I wanted to check with the analyst maintaining the lead system. I started to ask her if the crime scene unit had followed up with examining the boat when I heard a dispatcher talk over the radio. She announced that shots were fired on a houseboat at the same marina where Anne and I had searched the previous day.

A caretaker had opened the front door of his boss's houseboat and saw signs of an intruder. When he heard a gunshot, he ran, and 911 was called.

I immediately knew the location of this boat. I noticed it because it was the only houseboat on the same dock as the sailboat.

Milton and I rushed out of the conference room. We drove to the vicinity of the boat and saw a couple of patrol units already on the streets. With our guns drawn, we ran up the sidewalk and took cover behind some foliage off to the side.

We waited anxiously for SWAT to enter the boat and solve the mystery.

They did. Inside the large, beige two-story houseboat, they found Andrew Cunanan dead from a self-inflicted .40-caliber bullet to his head. A handgun laid next to his body, the same type of handgun used in the murders.

The search was now over. Cunanan was dead.

If during the previous day, Anne and I had continued our search of those docked boats, we may have had a deadly confrontation with Cunanan. We'll never know, but we both were happy we were spared an armed encounter with this pathological, sadistic serial killer. An angel must have been looking over us that day.

With the death of Cunanan, the renowned murder of Gianni Versace and four other victims were solved, and another serial killer was no longer a threat to the public.

To this day, tourists still flock to the site of Versace's death. The mansion has since been auctioned off, and the Versace family no longer owns it.

The steps to the mansion have even been referred to as Miami Beach's "Strawberry Fields." This term came from the memorial in New York City's Central Park where fans of John Lennon often visited and took pictures.

At the conclusion of this case, I walked from the MBPD station to the Versace store located in Miami Beach. I then spent some of my overtime money on a Versace scarf to commemorate this investigation.

CHAPTER 9

Serial Burglars' Serial MO

The FDLE welcomed me to its Fort Lauderdale field office by throwing me into the midst of the "Spiderman Case," a full-blown cat burglar investigation that had already been ongoing for a year.

The burglar had been dubbed "Spidey" because of his modus operandi of scaling and climbing up the exterior of expensive high-rise condos in Miami, Fort Lauderdale, Palm Beach, and as far north as Vero Beach. He then gained access into the residences, mostly through open or unlocked balcony doors. He exited through the front doors and used either the stairs or elevators to leave the building through the garages.

Apparently, most people who lived on the third floor and above had a false sense of security, believing that their units were burglar-proof because they sat too high above ground level for anyone to access them. Many never locked their patio doors, even when they went out shopping or out to dinner.

Other residences did lock their doors, but that didn't stop "Spidey." He was resourceful and simply pried it open or lifted them out of the tracks to gain easy and quiet entry.

Once inside these units, Spidey stole jewelry, money, credit cards, and laptop computers. He then fenced them through a pawn shop owned by one of his Miami accomplices.

Spidey's skills extended beyond committing successful burglaries. He knew how to smooth talk the ladies. Later on, we discovered that he had seduced his parole officer while she supervised him on a previous criminal case. They had a baby and lived together in a Fort Lauderdale condo.

The Spiderman Task Force was comprised of about fifteen lead investigators from the FDLE, the Miami-Dade Police Department, and the Miami Beach Police Department. My role was to provide statewide jurisdiction and additional investigative assistance to the local police.

By the time I came onboard with this case, the task force had gotten a much-needed break that led them to narrowing their suspect list to one: a former Army paratrooper named Derrick James. This streak of luck started when a Broward County deputy pulled him over for speeding. He learned that not only was James driving with a suspended license, but he was in violation of his probation for other burglaries.

Of course, James was arrested. When the officer searched his car, he found a lot of expensive jewelry stashed under the front seat. This, of course, raised a red flag.

Task force detectives worked the case backwards, which is an investigative tool in crimes where stolen property was recovered, but the victim was unknown. They were able to identify the jewelry through burglary reports. They noticed that this jewelry was stolen about an hour before the cop stopped James.

They then acquired pawn shop documents that described items that were pawned, the date of the pawn, and the identity of the person who pawned the items with their addresses. With this information, they started following the paper trail that documented James' break-ins.

Once the police looked through case files of the identified burglaries, they located video tapes of the burglarized premises.

Even though the shadows kept them from being one-hundred percent sure it was James in those tapes, they couldn't help but feel optimistic that they probably had their Spidey in custody.

Because of the lack of clarity in the videos, one of my first assignments with this case came while Spidey was in jail as a result of this car stop. I had to obtain a court order for his clothing and shoes. We suspected they matched a video surveillance tape obtained from the garage of one of the burglarized buildings. This video showed him entering the garage right before the burglary took place.

Then a few days after my "visit," James was out on bail. The task force wanted to monitor his activities and further build a solid case against him. We hoped we could catch him in the act if we followed him to other high-rise apartments.

We planned to install a court-ordered covert GPS tracking device on his SUV. Installing the GPS needed to be done in the middle of the night while our subject and his neighbors slept peacefully.

So at two o'clock on a Tuesday morning, I met some members of the task force at Dunkin' Donuts. Involved in this meeting were FDLE tech agents Sam and Allen, Mark from the Miami field office, two Miami Beach Police Department detectives, a couple of Broward County Sheriff's Office detectives, and a Miami-Dade Police Department detective.

I decided that wearing black attire would be fitting for this night's activities. I chose a black bandana to cover my head. Not only did it keep my blond hair from being noticed, but it also saved me time from styling my hair. Albeit not a little black dress, it *was* an accessory to make me feel a little more feminine in this testosterone-fueled assignment

I drove into the donut shop parking lot and spotted the other agents standing near the rear of the building with coffee cups in hand. I recognized the tech team from working with them in Miami.

First things first. I strolled inside to get my mandatory caffeine dose in order to make it through a night that would require intense focus and alertness. On a whim, I also decided a dose of sugar would enhance my night's mission. Since my olfactory nerves caught a huge whiff of the delicious aroma of frying donuts, I decided to order a maple-frosted one. I would now be set to go, thanks to the soon-to-be caffeine and sugar high.

I climbed into a faded gray van with Mark and the two tech agents. The MDPD detective acted as our chauffeur. He drove us a couple of miles down the road before letting us out at the entrance of the middle-class neighborhood.

The other task force members followed us but stayed far enough behind so that they could warn us if someone entered the neighborhood. They knew we would need time to move out of sight to a hidden place.

Our strategic drop-off spot was far enough away from the cul-de-sac where the suspect lived so that we could covertly approach his residence. Mark and I exited the van and then separated to begin a slow progression to the target's house. We couldn't use flashlights, so it took a few minutes for my eyes to adjust to the dark streets. We then performed a low crawl through the dark night, keeping our torsos as low to the ground as possible and hiding behind the cars parked on the street and behind the bushes.

We spotted the suspect's SUV parked close to the small parking pad in front of his single-story grey condo. A porch light emitted a dim glare, but no lights were on inside the home.

After we established that it was safe, we radioed Sam to let him know that he could approach the SUV with his equipment. Allen and the MDPD detective stayed with the van so that they could be near us in case anything went wrong.

We kept a vigilant lookout as Sam slithered and disappeared under the car. Our job was to provide the essential eyes and ears to keep him safe in his mission since he was the one in the most danger. While maintaining my position, my body began to shake from the Dunkin' Donuts caffeine and sugar rush.

The installation only took a few minutes. With each ticking second, though, our muscles remained in a tense state. We knew that one barking dog could alarm our bad guy or his neighbors to our presence. We didn't want some crazed neighbor coming outside and waving around a shotgun, mistaking us for car thieves. If that happened, we would need to protect the tech agent under the car. Of course, bringing attention to ourselves could also disclose to our target that we were zeroing in on his criminal activities.

Our tech guy notified us that he was done, and we saw him coming out from underneath the car. The three of us crabbed our way back to the van and jumped in. We high fived each other, releasing relief that all had gone well without a hitch.

By the time I got home from this assignment, it was eight o'clock in the morning. I fell into bed hoping to get some sleep but instead tossed and turned for about half an hour. The caffeine and sugar I had consumed several hours earlier still rushed through my veins. I gave up and got up, changed clothes, and then went for a run to work it off and out of my system.

Our GPS tracker revealed that James was in the vicinities of some of the current burglaries. Then we learned through our investigations and background checks that James had served in the army. While there, he learned how to climb high and balance himself on thin railings. We documented multiple incidents where he scaled buildings as high as twelve stories, climbing from balcony to balcony.

This information allowed us to figure out his modus operandi (MO), explaining how he entered and burglarized his victims' residences. He modeled his routine after the notorious group of thieves called the Dinner Set Gang, who had operated in South Florida in the 1960s and 1970s.

Marrying the Love of My Life

On December 31, 1997, the FDLE gave me some time off in the midst of this intriguing "Spidey" case and for a very good reason: I was getting married to the love of my life—Gary Carmichael.

That morning, Gary and I packed up our car and drove from Boynton Beach to Beaufort, South Carolina, to elope. We chose this location because it offered the romantic setting we both desired and was only a day's drive away from South Florida. We had reservations at the same bed and breakfast inn where the movie *Prince of Tides* was filmed.

When I first saw the inn, I gasped. The photos didn't do it justice, and I could understand why. The picturesque colonial mansion and its marble steps that led to its front door could not be fully appreciated unless one saw it in person. For us, it was the perfect place to bring in the new—a new year and a new life together.

To begin, we celebrated New Year's Eve that night. When working in an environment that sucks the life of out you, allowing ourselves the rare pleasure of enjoying ourselves was an anomaly; being in love was a gift. We planned to focus solely on each other and leave the job behind, if only for a couple of days.

That night Gary and I enjoyed a wonderful sit-down dinner celebration with other inn guests. We were all in a party mood. After some jokes, we found our new friends to be lots of fun. In fact, we all engaged in an impromptu conga-line dance throughout the B&B.

At midnight when we toasted, Gary slipped a beautiful opal pendant on a gold chain around my neck as he kissed me. He chose this particular gem to pay tribute to our meeting and assignment together during Hurricane Opal.

That night turned out to be special. That night, life was good; life was special.

The next morning, I woke up and remembered that not only was it New Year's Day, but within a couple of hours I would be marrying my best friend. Butterflies fluttered inside my belly, not from nerves but from excitement.

I climbed out of bed. Not even the cold could keep me under the covers. After putting on my running gear, I stepped outside into the frigid temperatures. Thinking about the day's activities gave me an unusual amount of energy. In fact, I could have run further, but I had to get back to attend a wedding—mine.

After showering and putting on my makeup, I donned an off-white suit that I purchased from Ann Marie's, my girlfriend's bridal shop in Homestead. I picked up the bouquet of daisies that Gary had ordered, and Gary and I walked downstairs to the main parlor.

We entered a room filled with antiques from the Civil War era. Tall ceilings trimmed with crown molding balanced the Persian carpets that lay across pine floors. Elegant gold-framed mirrors completed the opulent interior.

During the ceremony, we stood in front of a mahogany fireplace mantel framed by green holiday garland. A large decorated Christmas tree that sat in front of a window provided a festive backdrop.

A minister from the local community officiated the ceremony. The witnesses consisted of the owners of the inn.

Gary and I looked into each other's eyes and pledged our love for each other. Nothing else entered my mind or thoughts, just him and I doing what had been ordained even before we met.

Taking our vows came naturally. Neither of us hesitated proclaiming our answer to the "Will you take ..." questions. For me, no other option existed. We were merely going through the formalities of uniting our lives to become one. In my heart, though, I was already forever one with Gary Carmichael.

I don't quite recall the minister saying, "I now pronounce you husband and wife," although I know that at one point he did. I just remember Gary giving me a long kiss, which brought me out of my daydream state.

When he released my lips, I teetered in my stance, overwhelmed by the emotion. I then looked around and saw our two witnesses smiling and heard them say, "Congratulations."

I was now indeed married. I was now indeed Mrs. Gary Carmichael (although I kept my legal name Turner). What just happened hit me, and I smiled at the realization.

Afterward, we went outside and posed for pictures on the front porch. I was so ecstatic that I didn't even feel the cold temperatures.

Then we went back inside and posed for pictures in front of the Christmas tree.

I truly found my soul mate with Gary. Without a doubt, I knew he was worth waiting for!

The End of "Spidey"

The Spiderman investigation ended up lasting a total of two years, although I was only involved with it for the last year. During this time period, James burglarized sixty homes and was credited with stealing millions of dollars in property.

I had never worked with any of the task force members until then, and I'm glad I had the privilege of doing so. I found them to be some of the most tenacious and smartest cops I have ever encountered, even though some of them appeared to be a ragtag group. The three who conducted surveillance seemed to live in the van and gave little to no consideration to their personal hygiene. They looked disheveled and unkempt. Everyone pardoned their appearances, though, and focused more on the fantastic job they were doing.

Their slapstick bantering amongst themselves reminded me of the Moe, Larry, and Curly of Three Stooges with one exception—they exhibited brilliance. Their like-mindedness created a cohesiveness that led to their jelling together and complimenting each other. They were all workaholics, totally submerged in their jobs and working nonstop.

James finally went to trial for most of the burglaries he was alleged to have committed. The judge didn't want to sway the jury, so he ruled that the use of the name Spiderman during the proceedings was inflammatory.

Because of my involvement with obtaining his clothing and shoes, I was subpoenaed to testify in a Miami courtroom. James' well-known successful Miami lawyer used every tactic he could during my testimony to discredit me. At one time while questioning me, he moved to the side and back of the witness box and asked me questions. Defense lawyers often use this tactic to get a witness to look away from the jury when answering questions. However, I never turned to look at him but kept my eyes fixed on the jury.

The lawyer asked me the date of James' arrest. I recalled that I had served the search warrant at the jail on June 28, but I couldn't remember with certainty the actual date of his arrest. I knew "Moe" was sitting outside the courtroom, and I knew he had the case file with him. I needed to retrieve it so that I could look over some of its contents.

I looked at the judge and said, "Your Honor, I'd like to go out to the hallway to review my report and refresh my memory."

The judge granted my request and gave everyone a short recess.

I got up from the witness stand and walked to the doors. Outside in the hallway, I saw Moe sitting on a long oak bench that contained years of dents, scratches, and deep trenches carved from heavy items embedding themselves into the wood. I sat next to him.

Since Moe had the files all organized and could easily find the report, I asked, "Can you please look for James' arrest report?"

After I read through it, I returned the report to Moe and walked back inside the courtroom. The tension was so thick, it was almost stifling. I could feel every eye on me as I made my way to the witness stand.

James' high-profile lawyer continued with his cross-examination. He accused me of breaking "the Rule," a slang term used for the state of Florida's rule that prohibits witnesses from discussing their courtroom testimony with each other during the trial. This was an obvious ploy to cast doubt on my integrity, and thus my testimony.

Evidently, the defense attorney had sent his junior lawyer into the hallway to spy on me. He then tried to spin and twist my asking Moe for the report into something sinister.

I had learned a long time ago that many defense attorneys will throw out these spike strips to try and take the focus of guilt off of their clients. Basically, it boils down to their using typical defense drama and tactics to make law enforcement look suspicious and unprofessional to the jury.

I wasn't concerned because I hadn't done anything wrong. The judge had given me approval to go into the hallway to locate and read the arrest report, and I didn't discuss the case with the agent in the hall who held the case file. I only asked him to let me review the report.

Still, the judge felt he had no choice but to address this allegation and ordered an additional hearing to do so. He sent the jury out of the courtroom to hear the argument.

The defense gave his position and the allegations against me, and the prosecutor and I gave our position and addressed the allegations. The judge then ruled in our favor, and the jury returned to hear the rest of the trial.

From then on, James gave me "the finger" every time I entered the courtroom, and of course, he made sure he gave me this special kind of welcome before the judge walked into the court.

When James' attorney cross-examined "Curly," he accused him of planting evidence and fabricating reports. Curly became so incensed with these allegations that he lost his temper and referred to the defendant as Spiderman.

The judge held Curly in contempt of court.

Curly humbled himself and apologized. "Your Honor, please forgive my slip of the tongue. I felt like the defense was beating me up and calling me a dirty cop. I'm extremely sorry, and it won't happen again."

The judge showed mercy on Curly and withdrew the contempt of court charge. Curly was very thankful, realizing that he had barely missed spending the night with the roaches and rats in the Dade County Jail at the taxpayer's expense.

The jury found Spiderman guilty of the burglary charges and convicted him. Both a Broward County judge and a Miami-Dade County judge sentenced him to a combination of lengthy state prison sentences.

In honor of Curly using the S-name during the trial, Moe had shirts created as souvenirs for the task force. He had the words

"Spiderman Task Force" and a darling little spider logo embroidered on the left chest on the front of the shirt.

The Back–Door-Entry Case

The Back-Door-Entry Case became my next burglary investigation.

I was the only FDLE agent assigned to this statewide investigative initiative that covered many counties. As a result, I worked with investigators all over Florida.

This case involved a man and a woman who were suspected of burglarizing high-end houses. They entered the gated neighborhoods of homes worth millions of dollars. The woman dressed as a maid, and the man drove a nondescript rental car, usually a black sedan. Just like in the Spiderman Case where residents felt safe living on upper floors, these residents felt a false sense of security from living in their gated communities.

I started off this investigation by viewing numerous videotapes of the black sedan piggybacking behind other vehicles sailing through the neighborhoods' gates. When the gate opened for a resident to enter, the burglars' car slipped through it as well before it had a chance to close.

We were able to get a plate number, but when I ran the number, we learned that it belonged to a rental car. Then when I called the rental company, I learned that a fake ID had been used to rent the vehicle.

The burglars' proficiency of getting past the gates and into the communities and the propensity of most people to just ignore the car rather than confront the driver helped these burglars achieve success.

After the couple entered a community, they continued forth with their MO. The man dropped the woman off near a target home. If neighbors saw her, they presumed her to be the maid.

She then walked to the rear of the mansions looking for an entry, such as a sliding back door. In some cases, she used a screwdriver to gain entry.

Once inside the homes, the woman went straight into the master bedroom, master closet, and master bathroom. She usually located high-dollar jewelry items quickly.

She scooped up the items, placing them in a booster garment worn under her skirt. Many shoplifters used this type of sling because its pockets could hold items as large and as bulky as a ham.

While the woman gathered her booty, the man cruised the neighborhood, waiting for her to return to the street. When he spotted her, he picked her up, and they left the neighborhood. Afterward they mailed the goods to their fence in Chicago.

One time the woman punctured the glass on the back door with a screwdriver and cut herself on the broken glass. This provided us with her DNA. I compared it to another case from Palm Beach County where she had already been identified. We got a match, providing us with a major piece of evidence that helped me piece together our case.

Then what added fuel to our evidence fire were the descriptions given by a few victims who had seen this woman leaving their homes or running out of their yards. Additionally, we had obtained pictures of the man from the videos of the unmanned gates. We were then able to identify our prime suspects as Boiko Dolinsky and Donka Lapinsky. Both turned out to be Romanian gypsies from Chicago.

I called the detective on the Chicago case involving Boiko and Donka. Our conversation proved very productive as he shared his extensive intelligence on organized crime with roots related to gypsies. I had no idea that Chicago had such a large gypsy population.

It turned out that our suspects were associated with a well-organized network of crooks who were now conducting criminal activities in high-end communities throughout Florida. Consequently, as the lead investigator, I eventually incorporated the Florida RICO Act and charged the couple with racketeering.

The Office of the Statewide Prosecutor (OSP) under the Florida Attorney General's Office assigned a petite black-haired beauty named Cathy Mueller as the prosecutor. During this case, Cathy and I became great friends and worked together for many years afterwards. She always dressed to the nines, wearing very high heels, almost as if compensating for her shorter stature. Long lashes framed her large dark eyes, and her skin glowed with a pale creamy texture. Her shiny dark hair swept down her back in a beautiful cascade of curls.

This case involved a lot of time, including hours on the phone calling alarm companies all over Florida and requesting video footage of the homes that had been burglarized. Then I tediously reviewed them. I looked for the suspects so that I could place them in the area of the crimes. This kept me in the office for days at a time, which I didn't like. Most cops prefer to be out on the street. I have always preferred that to sitting at a desk.

Cathy and I ended up putting together hundreds of cases involving these two burglars with the value of stolen property estimated to be at two hundred fifty million dollars. Since we were able to show that their network of organized crooks turned out to involve complex organized crime, we built a case to prove that it was an ongoing criminal enterprise.

The closed society that encompassed gypsy criminals made it difficult, if not impossible, to infiltrate. They only trusted their own blood. They lived together, worked together, and played together. If they got arrested and sentenced, they submitted to prison time rather than ratting each other out for a deal.

Eventually, an alert police officer and his K-9 finally arrested Boiko and Donka. First, he had to chase Donka when she tried to evade him. When he finally captured her, he frisked her and found jewelry worth a few thousand dollars hidden under her maid's skirt.

Both Boiko and Donka got convicted and sentenced to state prison on criminal RICO charges. Unfortunately, we never recovered most of the jewelry.

A few years after they went to prison, I learned that Boiko died while incarcerated. Someone told me that upon hearing this news, Donka screamed and collapsed.

She had just lost the love of her life.

The Hole-in-One Case

While working in my office on a beautiful spring morning, an FBI agent called me. She wanted me to look into another series of burglaries. Her request was both professional and personal because she herself had been a victim. Additionally, since this was a local case with no proof of it extending over state lines, it didn't meet the FBI criteria to get involved.

Apparently, her FBI credentials and wallet were stolen while playing golf in the Fort Lauderdale area. She received a two-week unpaid vacation from the Bureau for improperly storing her credentials, so she had some time on her hands to conduct some research of her own and pull related police reports.

I considered this to be a case that needed attention, especially since someone was out there running around with FBI credentials. I told her I'd get back to her after I ran this by my supervisor.

After disconnecting our call, I walked to my immediate supervisor's office. He was on the phone, but when he saw me, he mouthed, "Have a seat."

He hung up a couple of minutes later. "Hey, Floy, what can I do for you?"

"Agent Janey Rhodes from the FBI just called me. She told me about some thieves who are stealing jewelry, credit cards, and money from golfers while they're playing golf. In fact, they stole her ID card and badge. Do you mind if I work this case?"

"Sure," he said. "You can be the case agent too. Make sure you keep me apprised of your progress."

I called Janey back and let her know. I then began to collect the police reports for golf course burglaries.

My investigation, which soon became known as the Hole-in-One Case, caused me to pull together pieces of the puzzle that led to a lot more realizations and conclusions. I discovered that other golfers at some of the most posh, upscale golf-course communities had been burglarized in a similar manner all the way from Orlando to South Florida and on both the east and west coasts of the state.

As I kept reading police reports, I noticed that in addition to the gold Rolex Presidential watches and large diamond rings that the thief nabbed from the golf carts, wallets with credit cards went missing as well. He didn't waste any time using those credit cards either. Soon after leaving the golf courses, he went to local gas stations and purchased gas with them. Fortunately, we were able to gather video footage from the gas pumps attached to those cards.

Then on those days when there didn't seem to be any available golfing victims, pro golf shops had made reports that golf clubs had been stolen from their stores. I guess this burglar needed to make up for lost "income" by stealing *something*.

I wasn't surprised that the pro shops had been burglarized, though. They were actually easy targets since no one expected any crimes to occur within them. One person could easily distract the shopkeeper while another walked out with the clubs.

I called the golf courses that had been affected. One of the managers said that some of his customers reported seeing one of his former golfers by the name of Sergio acting suspiciously around their carts.

We then visited some local pawn shops. When we saw them selling some of the stolen items, we showed photos from the gas station videos, and the clerks identified the person in the videos as the seller.

Because of the Florida reporting requirements for pawn shops, those who fenced items must present an ID and fingerprints. As a result, I hit pay dirt. I was able to match some of the prints with Sergio's criminal record from past burglaries. Additionally, I was able to match Sergio's mug shot with the identified video photos and a copy of the ID he presented.

I talked to a golf pro at one of the Fort Lauderdale shops. He told me that Sergio had become addicted to crack and heroine.

In learning more about Sergio, it all made sense. Before he became addicted to drugs, he frequented golf courses as a golfer, not a thief. Therefore, the reason why he had been so successful in his MO was because he fit in perfectly with the golfing community. He knew how to dress like a golfer, walk like a golfer, and talk like a golfer, so no red flags were raised.

Interviews of more witnesses revealed that Sergio didn't act alone. He had accumulated a few other addicts to his "gang," and his wife Sugar filled in as his driver during these crimes on a part-time basis.

He and his band of losers honed in on expensive golf courses in affluent areas. Sergio knew how to select the target-rich holes where his victims couldn't easily spot him.

He then took full advantage of those golfers. He knew that while they were out on the course concentrating on their games, golfers placed their heavy jewelry, like rings and watches, along with their credit cards and money, in the golf carts so they wouldn't be weighed down while they played. For Sergio, the setup was like taking candy from a baby.

Before the golfers had a chance to report their cards stolen, Sergio went to Home Depot or Lowe's and purchased high-end items with them. He especially liked lawnmowers, blowers, and expensive weed trimmers. They were easy to sell and provided quick cash to support his and his friends' drug habits.

The thieves then took the stolen items and those they purchased with the stolen credit cards to some pawn shops. However, I assumed they probably preferred selling them to accomplices who were known to circumvent the Florida reporting requirements.

When all was said and done, Sergio and his crew fenced hundreds of thousands of dollars' worth of booty stolen during their burglary expeditions.

Once I obtained my evidence, I then filed my statement of probable cause with the Clerk of the Court. This turned out to be my second RICO investigation with the OSP. I also obtained my arrest warrants, which enabled me to find and arrest Sergio.

Using the information in the reports, the field interrogation reports from local police, and the analytical information about possible associates, I figured out where they were staying. The group frequented cheap motels in Fort Lauderdale after scoring their drugs.

Next I needed to locate Sergio's Cadillac. I thought he probably hid the stolen merchandise in his car, not in the motel room. I also needed to get some of my team together for the takedown. Of course, I always enjoyed that part of my job.

I called my buddies from the FDLE fugitive squad in Miami. When we barged into the room, we grabbed Sergio, his gang, and a woman, who I presumed to be Sergio's wife Sugar. Like a lot of drug addicts, she looked older than her actual late-twenties.

The chemicals she took into her body created bad teeth, a pimpled complexion, and a skinny frame.

Her tight strapless top revealed protruding ribs, and tight short shorts displayed a skeletal figure. Three or more inches of dark roots covered her frizzy hair.

My encounter with her reminded me of the woman who had hid dope in her privates when I was a trooper. Sugar's first statement brought back those memories of that case.

She said, "I need to use the bathroom."

I asked, "So you can take out your dope?"

She flinched. Her eyes darted around the room as she started fidgeting with her hands before bringing her fingers to her mouth and biting her nails.

In a stern voice, I said, "I'll request a cavity search at the jail."

She had to know that she would face additional charges for bringing contraband into the jail.

"I'm holding," she said in almost a whisper.

"Yeah, I know," I responded. "I'll go in the bathroom with you, and you can take out the dope there."

We did just that. I think she also realized the danger of keeping her stash inside her privates for too long. If anything leaked, she would die a painful and ugly death.

We drove the hole-in-one gang to the FDLE offices for interrogation. I took on the role of good cop, friendly and nice, knowing that I got better results that way.

When interviewing Sergio, I said, "If you cooperate, I'll try to keep Sugar out of jail."

He seemed to let out a much-needed breath of air. He nodded, and his facial muscles relaxed a little.

Sergio, Sugar, and I ended up getting along very well. Sergio cooperated by providing leads for the narcotics squad. I asked Cathy the prosecutor to go easy on Sugar, and she let her off the hook for her part in the crimes. On the other hand, Sergio received twenty years. Many criminal informants still go to jail.

About a year or more after Sergio's arrest, I went to the Everglades Correctional Institution to interview another prisoner on an unrelated case. I decided to have a quick visit with Sergio. He said he had found God while in prison. I've heard that from a lot of prisoners. I hope it's true.

He sent me a Christmas card during that first year of his incarceration and addressed it to the Broward Field Office. He wanted to take Gary and me out to dinner upon his release.

I heard from Sugar. She called me at the office from time to time. She reported she was doing well and looking forward to the day when Sergio walked away from prison, and they could be together again.

The Radio Shack Burglaries

Just about the time I wrapped up the Hole-in-One Case, Cathy Mueller called me regarding another series of burglaries.

She told me about an interesting racketeering case being evaluated by OSP attorneys. They had called it the Tandy-Bandits Case. The thief burglarized Radio Shacks all over South and Central Florida after disabling their alarm systems.

Police departments in a few of the jurisdictions had gathered intelligence information. Their reports contained a common thread: their officers had stopped a red four-speed Mustang for traffic violations throughout Florida in the vicinities of some of the burglaries and around the time they took place.

They had identified the driver as Rudy Smart. He lived in Pembroke Pines, not far from the location of Sergio and Sugar's arrest. I began to look at him and his wife Jennifer.

Then we got a break. One of the burglar's cohorts got caught red-handed while breaking into a Radio Shack because he didn't properly disconnect the alarm system. Lucky for us, he decided to come forward and become a "cooperating" witness. He alleged that he had some very interesting information to give us regarding the Radio Shack burglaries in return for a lesser charge in an unrelated crime.

According to our new snitch, "Mustang Rudy" had broken the 911-system transmission code and interrupted a series of broadcasts over the Pembroke Pines Police Department radio frequency. This information ended up landing on Cathy's desk.

Coincidentally, another broadcast interruption had occurred early one morning over the Broward Sheriff's Office (BSO) police radio system. A male claimed a hostage situation was occurring at the BSO headquarters.

As a result, the police evacuated the entire building while SWAT searched it. Not only did this claim jeopardize the safety of law enforcement officers, but it threatened the community's safety as well. If a serious threat had taken place elsewhere, SWAT would not have been able to respond since it was searching a major police headquarters building.

The Broward Sheriff got very upset that his "secure" radio system had been broken into and disrupted, especially since he had just mentioned in a public announcement that the BSO radio system was secure and couldn't be infiltrated.

The snitch said, "I was with Rudy in his Miami apartment when he broke into the system using a radio he built. After the sheriff's building got evacuated, we got in Rudy's car and drove to watch the evacuation. Rudy had a smile on his face the whole time he watched. Yeah, he really took pride in his handiwork. He thinks he's smarter than the cops."

I doubted that someone could actually break into a secure system. I just didn't buy it, not until I performed background checks.

First, I discovered that Rudy was a ham radio operator. I took this information and interviewed his colleagues from a ham radio organization with which he had been involved. I found out that Rudy was known to be a radio and computer genius. He had been thrown out of the local club, though. It seemed that whenever Rudy showed up, stuff went missing. They suspected him of stealing equipment from other operators during their meetings.

From what I learned, if Rudy had put his talents into legal enterprises, he could have supported his family without engaging in criminal behavior. However, he couldn't conform to society or be consistent with a normal living schedule. That led to his downfall.

Then I got another lucky break. Rudy's wife Jennifer was arrested for shoplifting at a grocery store. She got caught with stolen steaks in her toddler's stroller.

I learned that Jennifer also had other shoplifting convictions, and the Florida Department of Children and Families was investigating her for child neglect. On top of it all, she was pregnant again.

So while I was experiencing good luck with my breaks, Rudy was experiencing some bad luck. Surveillance cameras taped him breaking into an Office Depot in Miami during a burglary attempt. The film footage provided a clearly visible image of Rudy entering the back of the store as it closed. The video also showed him breaking out of the store, his arms loaded up with stolen merchandise. I now had enough probable cause for a search warrant on the Smarts' apartment.

I drove to his apartment building located in a low-economic area and made notes on its appearance. After returning to my office, I wrote the warrant and included the street number and described the outside of his building as having drab, beige concrete walls, a rear window, and a satellite dish attached to the part of the roof that covered his unit. I knew the dish's serial number would be a match to a serial number belonging to one of the many dishes stolen in the Radio Shack burglaries.

I gathered together five FDLE agents, and we drove to Rudy's apartment. After leading the caravan of agents, I parked in front of his building and stepped outside of my car, appreciating the cool breeze that could sometimes accommodate an overcast summer day in South Florida. All six of us agents converged in front of the Smarts' unit, and I took the initiative and knocked on the door.

Jennifer opened it, holding the toddler on the side of her hip. Her eyes went to our waists where we hung our badges. She then looked at us, her eyes a bit wider than when she first saw us.

She realized that six cops stood in front of her. Trying to put on a façade of confidence and anger, she rolled her eyes and shuffled the toddler to the other hip. Her eyes narrowed and her chin tilted up in defiance.

"What do you want?" she snarled.

I was more than happy to explain. "We have a warrant to search your house, Mrs. Smart."

"Well, you can't come in," she spat out, her eyes narrowing more.

I didn't know if she really thought we'd turn around and go away, but I guess as far as she was concerned, it didn't hurt to try to sound tough and confrontational. I ignored her bravado and patiently read her the search warrant and handed her a copy. I also suggested she call an attorney if she wanted.

"I don't care," she stated adamantly. "You can't come in."

"Ma'am, we can and we will. If you don't let us in, then I'll have no choice but to arrest you and call DCF to come and take your child into custody."

Her eyes widened a little, and she stepped aside. We walked past her and into a dirty kitchen with a breakfast bar that opened to the living room. Dirty clothes mingled with broken computers and computer parts were strewn everywhere.

To the right was a stairway that led to the second floor of her apartment. I stepped onto stained, threadbare carpet that covered each step. At the top, we found ourselves walking through a narrow hallway with dirty stained walls that I assumed used to be white.

In the rear bedroom, I saw several sealed boxes. The logos and information printed on them indicated that they contained satellite dishes.

We didn't see Rudy anywhere, so when we went back downstairs, I asked Jennifer where he was.

She said, "We had a fight, and he left. I don't know if he's coming back."

After I advised her of her rights, she agreed to cooperate. She and I sat on a dirty stained sofa in the middle of her living room.

I said, "I promise I'll try to help you with your legal problems, but you've gotta tell me the truth about the burglaries."

"Yeah?" she asked skeptically, her eyes searching my face. "How you going to help me?

"I'll go to bat for you with the prosecutor who's trying your case. I'll ask the prosecutor to give you probation so that you can stay out of jail and take care of your kids."

She looked away and stared out the window as she seemed to contemplate this offer. She then looked at her baby and down at her growing belly.

"I was the lookout. I took my son with me, and we'd sit in the car in the parking lot while Rudy broke into the Radio Shacks and stole stuff. There were a few times when the police saw me there.

They'd come over and ask me what I was doing. I'd tell them that I had to pull off the road to breastfeed my baby."

I tried to refrain from smiling as I pictured this conversation. I'm sure most of the police officers wanted no part of that situation and gladly left without asking anymore questions.

She admitted she had a nasty habit of shoplifting. She told me that she not only shoplifted for food, but any other items she decided she wanted to have.

She said, "I always take the stroller and place things under the baby."

Compulsions and Convictions

I arranged a road trip with OSP Prosecutor Cathy Mueller and Jennifer so that she could show us the stores that Rudy broke into and burglarized. Her mother and sister watched the toddler as we drove across the state to Naples and then drove north to Fort Myers.

When we passed by the Naples Outlet Mall and saw the Coach store, Cathy and I couldn't resist stopping and doing a little shopping ourselves. For about half an hour, Cathy and I took turns going into the store while the other stayed with Jennifer in my unmarked car. I ended up purchasing a black leather bucket bag that I thought would stand up to the weight of my gun.

A few weeks later, the police stopped Rudy in Orlando for speeding in the Mustang. They ran a computerized check on him and saw the charges and the arrest warrant I had entered into the FCIC (Florida Crime Information Center) system. They arrested him.

I talked Cathy into asking the judge to give Jennifer five years of probation for her cooperation. He agreed. By the time she was sentenced, baby number two—a strapping healthy infant—had been born.

Rudy was given a lengthy prison term. After his sentencing, Cathy and I left the courtroom and walked across the street to a popular Cuban restaurant. We decided to celebrate our victory by indulging in some mojitos.

Jennifer later experienced troubles with her probation because she just couldn't stop shoplifting. Even though a judge had given her a couple of chances to shape up or she would go to prison and lose her children, she couldn't help herself. He finally sent her to prison, and she left behind two children.

Cathy and I had already suspected that Jennifer probably wouldn't be able to make her probation. For a habitual shoplifter, five years may have been too long of a time to go without indulging in her compulsion. However, the only alternative was to sentence her to a lengthy sentence term alongside her hubby. We tried to keep her with her kids, though, and give her the chance to change. We should have followed our gut feelings because she went to prison anyway.

The last I heard, both Rudy and Jennifer were still in prison.

They deserved what they received. The sad part about this case was seeing two little children with parents who didn't look out for their best interest. I hoped they were too young to remember how their parents put themselves before them. I prayed they found a safe family who would protect and love them.

CHAPTER 10

Serial Kidnapper

I n July 1998, the coordinator for the FLDE Regional South Florida Crimes Against Children (CAC) announced that she would be retiring. Therefore, FDLE made the announcement that applications were being accepted for that position.

I knew that agent had worked some of the most abominable child crimes imaginable. Investigating some of the worst evils known to mankind takes its toll on a person. Next to the victim and the victim's family, law enforcement is as close to these atrocities as someone can get. Therefore, those who enter this arena are known to suffer from maladies created by a constant level of stress.

Although a bleak position, I knew it was a great opportunity for me to fulfill my calling of seeking justice for child victims. I wanted to continue with my former colleague's efforts; she had worked tirelessly for twenty years to right these evils. Consequently, I hoped I could sway my supervisor in the FDLE Broward Office to let me take it on.

I wasn't naïve in the least bit. I realized that in taking this agent's place, I too would be confronted with these appalling acts that affected our most innocent. These types of crimes never failed to have some effect on decent law-abiding citizens and police officers alike. Still, I knew in my heart that I could handle whatever came my way and that I possessed an inner fortitude to do this job.

This strength, which had enabled me to survive for the past sixteen years in law enforcement, would give me the resolve and ability to push aside my personal feelings and investigate the cases. I recognized how this same strength came from my faith in God, and it would continue to sustain me if given the chance to enter into this new endeavor.

Undoubtedly, the CAC coordinator was a very important position and one that the FDLE didn't fill without fully vetting the candidates. Although I possessed an excellent record as an investigator, I knew I'd have to prove myself just like everyone else. The chance to do just that came through an assignment I received on a Tuesday morning in early September.

I woke up and looked outside the window to check the weather and saw that a lovely clear morning awaited me. I donned my running attire and began my morning jog, enjoying the slight breeze. As I ran, I mentally focused on the path I wanted to follow in my career, which involved landing the position of Crimes Against Children Coordinator for South Florida. I considered how I could reach my goals.

After my run, I jumped into the shower, dressed in a pantsuit, and grabbed a cup of coffee and power bar. I then left for my forty-five-minute drive to work.

I walked into my office, which sure beat the desk I had in the midst of an open-squad bay when I worked in Miami. My private office was one of the perks of my transfer, and I loved it.

While getting situated for the day, I overheard my boss talking in the office next to mine. He was telling another agent about a kidnapping and brutal rape of an eleven-year-old girl that occurred the previous day. Fortunately, she wasn't killed during this heinous crime.

I walked into the next-door office to see if I could somehow join the investigation. I was so excited about the possibility of getting involved with this case that I didn't even knock; I just barged in like I belonged there.

Both my boss and the other agent merely glanced my way as if I belonged there too. So far, so good. We appeared to be on the same brain wave. Hopefully my luck would continue.

My supervisor asked the agent, "So, you interested in taking this case on?"

The other agent said, "I really can't right now. Just got a hot lead on my current homicide, and I really should follow through on that."

I thought, *This is great!* It was just want I wanted—the chance to succeed in a case that looked challenging.

I was so excited to have stumbled across this opportunity. I knew that if I did a good job on this case, I had a better shot of getting the CAC coordinator position and achieving my objective of further protecting children. More importantly, it would give me a chance to take this monster off the streets and prevent the victimization of more children.

I immediately spoke up and said, "Excuse me, but I have time. I'm in the process of working on my statement of facts for my third RICO. I feel I can take it on. I'd like to investigate this case."

My supervisor stopped and stared at me. I could almost see the wheels turning in his head.

While he pondered my offer, the other agent said, "I'd really appreciate your stepping in, Floy."

My supervisor added, "The investigation could be a dead end because there's not much information on the suspect. Right now, it appears to be a random crime of opportunity with no connection between the victim and the perp."

This comment actually caused me to want the case even more. I wanted to seek justice for this child by going after whoever committed this brutal attack.

I said, "I understand."

My supervisor said, "Okay, then go ahead and open this case with the FDLE. Then go to the North Lauderdale Police Station and meet with Detective Robert Peterson for a briefing."

Within an hour, I stood in a small muted-green carpeted office with beige walls covered by several award plaques, assorted diplomas, and a few Marine Corps paraphernalia, all of which belonged to Detective Peterson. A middle-aged man with a high-and-tight haircut and wearing a plaid shirt with rolled-up sleeves sat behind a battered gray metal desk with his reading glasses propped on top of his head.

"Detective Peterson?" I asked.

He smiled. "So I'm told."

I offered my hand out for him to take. "Hi, I'm Special Agent Floy Turner with the FDLE."

His initial smile turned into a big grin that spread across his face. He stood and walked over to me. Then he grabbed my hand and enveloped it with his own. In fact, his hand squeezed mine so hard I thought he would crush it.

I tried to prevent my smile from turning into a grimace. I couldn't help but have a quick flashback to my trooper days when Bear, a huge Rottweiler, almost broke my hand with his jaw's vice grip during one of our K-9 exercises.

"Hello," he said, "Glad to meet you."

He stood tall and straight as an arrow, which gave me the ability to sum him up. Upon noticing his slim stature and weathered face, I felt a slight chill run down my spine as I had another flashback. He looked so much like my late FHP squad partner, mentor, and great friend Pete Gannon, who died of cancer. The uncanny resemblance tugged at my heartstrings, causing a lump to form in my throat as I momentarily remembered my time with Pete. I thought about how Pete had influenced my early career, and I involuntarily closed my eyes when I remembered how I held his hand when he took his last breath. Although no one would ever take Pete's place in my heart, I did hope that Robert and I would become friends.

He said, "FBI Special Agent Karen Kool is a few minutes out. Once she arrives, I'll provide you both with our current details and status."

I nodded. I didn't want to get into the details of the case until the FBI agent arrived too, so I thought I'd get to know Robert a little bit in the meantime.

"Okay," I said. "Hey, I can't help but notice your wall hangings. I see you served in the Marine Corps."

"Yeah," he shrugged nonchalantly. "Nam."

I didn't ask any more about his military experience, although it did explain his haircut and rigid stance. I continued to read the plaques and awards.

"So, you were a homicide detective with Miami-Dade PD?"

"Yep, five years."

"What brought you here?" I asked.

"Well, I retired early. I got shot in my chest, just above my heart."

I flinched, and Robert didn't miss my reaction.

"Yeah, well, it happened in the late '70s during the Liberty City shootout. Three of us got shot."

My eyebrows shot up in recognition. "That was you?"

He nodded, and his eyes fixed on the wall above me. "My partner was the one who died. The other cop ended up with brain damage."

The room got eerily silent.

Robert took his eyes off the make-believe spot on the wall and placed them on me. He took in a deep breath. "So," he said in a lighter tone, "after the shooting, I went back to work for the MDPD, became a homicide detective, and a few years later decided it was time for me to go. And I did, and I planned on staying retired until one of my good friends, who just so happened to be the North Lauderdale Police Chief, kept harassing me to come back. I finally gave in just to keep him quiet." He rolled his eyes and smiled again.

I felt comfort in knowing that Robert possessed a wealth of experience because the MDPD Homicide Bureau was the finest homicide unit in the southeast. Its detectives may carry more than a dozen active cases at any given time. He would be a wonderful asset to this case.

Need I say that by now, Robert had my unwavering respect? He had accomplished a lot.

Although he emanated a gruff and crusty exterior, I was able to see beneath that facade as he spoke to me with respect, and that went a long way for me. Although women in law enforcement were progressing in that area, it was still a man's world.

About that time, a slightly overweight woman wearing the mandatory FBI navy-blue business pantsuit and white blouse walked into Robert's office. Her straight, dark-brown hair was cut short, and her ruddy complexion held beautiful light-blue eyes that twinkled when she smiled.

Robert greeted her just as warmly as he did me. He shook her hand. "Hi, Agent Kool. I'm Robert." He removed his hand from her and used it to point toward me. "And this is Special Agent Floy Turner with the FDLE."

Karen looked at me and turned her head to speak over her shoulder to Robert. "Please. Call me Karen."

She then took my hand and shook it. For some reason, I suspected she and I would make a good team.

Robert filled us in on what had transpired. "Here's what our investigative efforts have revealed so far. Eleven-year-old Ritha St. Claire had been walking home from school on Monday afternoon. About two thirty, she noticed a man in a small, white car driving slowly on the street as she continued toward her home.

"She became nervous and ran to the front-porch area of a nearby house to wait for the car to pass. After seeing it drive by, she resumed her walk home. The driver of the car must have gone around the block. When she was still a couple of blocks away from home, he sped up from behind Ritha, stopped the car, and jumped out with a gun."

He paused as he glanced back and forth between Karen and me. "The driver pointed the gun at Ritha and told her to get into the backseat of his car. She complied. He told her to keep her face down in her lap and place her hands over her eyes.

"She did peek up as he pulled into the parking lot of a nearby large discount store. He stopped behind its building.

"While he raped her, he instructed her not to look at his face. The initial officer's report says she concentrated on the tattoos on her attacker's arms and the car's interior layout and color.

"After an hour of brutally raping her, he drove Ritha back to the area where he had kidnapped her. He let her out of his car.

"At that time, Ritha ran to her home in a middle-class Haitian neighborhood, which is just a few miles from here. When she told her mother what had just happened, her mother called the police."

Robert shook his head. "I'm worried about the way Ritha's mother is handling this situation, though. I mean she did the right thing by calling the police, but she seems overly concerned that the neighbors are going to find out what happened and that it'll bring shame upon her daughter. I recommended that she get counseling for Ritha, but I think she just wants to sweep the whole thing under the carpet, kinda like out of sight, out of mind."

I felt sorry for Ritha for so many reasons. I knew that when something as traumatic as rape occurs, counseling is necessary. This child had been victimized, and she wasn't given a way to deal with it.

We strategized about our next steps. We agreed that we needed to bring Ritha in for an in-depth interview before too much time had lapsed, and family conversations swayed and modified her story.

Robert called Ritha's mother and told her to bring her daughter to the police department so that we could talk with her.

Both Karen and I had been trained in child-interview techniques. We used a room with a child-friendly décor that included teddy bears, walls painted with primary colors and a yellow brick road, plush blue carpet, and overstuffed red-and-green plaid comfy chairs. We told Ritha's mother that she could stay in the room with us while we talked with her daughter.

After Karen introduced us, she said, "Hi Ritha, would you tell us what you saw?"

She reiterated the story in the report. Then she added, "I know he told me to put my hands over my eyes when he made me put my head in my lap, but I peeked."

"Good job, Ritha," I said. "So what did you see when you peeked?"

She began providing details of her attacker. She described him as a short, hefty, balding man with lots of tattoos. She specifically recalled a spiderweb tattoo inked on his left upper arm along with tattoos of a dragon with wings and a flaming skull. She remembered another tattoo of a skull and chains on his right arm.

Ritha also described the car's interior in great detail. She said the gray-velour cloth had a swirl design. "The car looked new," she added.

We talked with Ritha for two hours, taking a couple of breaks along the way. We then dismissed Ritha and turned her over to her mother so that they could leave.

After Karen and I went back to Robert's office, the three of us began to formulate a case-management action plan. I called my squad's analyst and asked her to conduct computer checks on Broward County reports of peeping toms, loitering and prowling, attempted kidnapping, kidnapping, and rape. We hoped they would produce a database of possible suspects.

We got a hit. About an hour before Ritha's kidnapping, a fifteen-year-old girl reported an attempted kidnapping in nearby Fort Lauderdale.

Armed with the report's information, Karen and I headed to a state-operated group home where the other victim, Hattie Brown, lived.

We walked into the group home that smelled of food cooked in grease. A large, frumpy-looking white woman wearing a tropical-print moo-moo and silver scuff slippers opened the door. Between her gray hair, the wrinkles on her flushed face, and baggy eyes, I estimated her to be in her sixties. She expressed a pleasant, grandmother-type demeanor and didn't seem surprised that we were there. I supposed that running a state-run facility made her used to caseworkers and the police dropping by unannounced.

Karen and I showed her our credentials and told her why we were there.

She smiled. "Of course. Follow me. I'm Miss Riley, but everyone here just calls me Grandma."

Grandma led the way through what looked like a living room. The dim light emitted from the room's only lamp stand provided a glimpse of its dismal and sparse furnishings.

She turned and studied my face in the faint light. "I have six girls living here. Hattie's had a tough life, and she's a handful, but praise the Lord, she was spared from being abducted."

I liked Grandma.

She took us into a small bedroom with three sets of bunk beds. A small metal desk in the right corner was occupied by a slightly overweight African-American teenage girl.

Grandma said, "Hattie?"

The girl turned around. Her eyes opened slightly wider when they fell on Karen and me.

Grandma continued, her tone soft. "These two ladies are police officers and here to talk to you about what happened yesterday."

Hattie's dark eyes narrowed slightly as she looked at us, displaying a knee-jerk reaction of distrust. She involuntarily wrapped her brown arms around her waist as she glanced down briefly.

Grandma turned to leave. "I'll be right down the hall if you need me." Then she left the room.

I wasn't quite sure if she was talking to us or Hattie.

"Hi, Hattie," I said. "Want to go somewhere more private?"

Although we were alone with her in the room, I had the feeling that the walls and plywood door were thin enough for conversations to creep through.

"Yeah," she said sighing heavily. "We can go outside on the patio."

"Okay," Karen said. "We'll just follow behind you."

Both Karen and I wanted to display a very friendly and unassuming demeanor. We wanted to make Hattie feel at ease.

We all walked onto the patio and sat at a table with an umbrella to block the sun.

I started the interview. "Hattie, we want to get the person who did this to you, but we need your help. Can you tell us what happened?"

Her eyes went back and forth between Karen and me until they settled on me. "I was walking home from my morning class. It was around noon. A small white car stopped in front of me. A man got out of it and pointed a gun at me. He told me to get in his car."

She looked down for a moment. When she looked back up, both her eyebrows and her voice were raised. "I took off running as quick as I could and never looked back."

Karen looked in Hattie's eyes and softly asked, "Do you happen to know the type of car?"

Hattie nodded and surprisingly gave us a specific make and model.

Karen's gaze didn't alter or change as she pressed Hattie further. "Why are you so sure that was the type of car?"

"Because that's one of the kinds of cars I always stole."

I got the impression that Hattie was honest. Her street smarts must have been what kept her from becoming a rape victim.

As Karen and I left the group home, I called Robert to check in with him and convey what we had just learned. At the end of our conversation, I said, "Robert, we'll request a list from the Department of Motor Vehicles for all of these types of vehicle models registered in Broward County."

Karen said, "On my way home, I'll stop in at the local dealership closest to the crime scene to get one of their brochures. It should show the interiors for that current model. I'll see if I can get some older brochures for earlier models too."

Karen and I said good-bye. We agreed to meet the following morning at the North Lauderdale Police Department (NLPD).

When I got back to the office, I updated my boss and our analyst before calling it a day. Night was falling as I drove home. I thought about two very different girls with two very different outcomes and how both faced many adversities during their young lives.

The following morning, I parked in front of the sand-colored, one-story Public Safety Department building that held several government offices, including City Hall, Zoning, the fire department headquarters, and the NLPD. Each had their own separate section of the building.

When I reached the main door of the police station, someone buzzed me into its reception area. I immediately made my way to Robert's office. His door was open, and I knocked on the door jamb. He looked up from the papers he was reading on his desk and smiled when he saw me.

"Hey, Floy." He gestured toward a chair in front of his desk. "Can I get you a cup of coffee?"

"Sure."

"Be right back," he said.

Karen entered the office right after Robert returned with my coffee. I held the much-needed cup of high-test java and took in a deep breath, relishing in its aroma.

She glanced at my obvious pleasure and looked at Robert. "I need a coffee fix too, but I'm too excited to let you leave until I show you both the brochure for the new car models our perp is driving. It has the exact gray velour seats that little Ritha described."

According to what Karen learned at the dealership, this new design was created specifically for this current year. This discovery narrowed down our search drastically, so we could eliminate all of the previous years from our request to the Department of Motor Vehicles. It would also lessen our efforts to match the car with a possible attacker. We decided to look into reports made for new models that had been stolen.

Robert, Karen, a part-time FDLE analyst, and I comprised our small task force. Our mutual passion about this case made each of us willing to delve as deep as needed to find this guy before he hurt another child.

Karen suggested we have the analyst use the FBI Rapid Start lead tracking system. It would allow us to track and document the leads.

Agreeing to use it proved to be a very good plan. It streamlined the leads in an organized system, allowing easier retrieval of information and making our jobs less confusing. Over the course of this investigation, we eventually followed over eight hundred leads.

Karen and I began systematically conducting interviews of the owners of this specific car by their addresses. We started with those closest to the kidnapping location and worked our way outward.

We also looked at registered sex offenders. For the next several months, we spent days on end conducting interviews of registered sex offenders and those who lived in the neighborhood where Ritha was abducted. We came up empty-handed. We used other sources to generate leads, such as news reporters who appealed to the public for assistance, Crime Stoppers, and networking with other detectives in South Florida.

We then found ourselves faced with another problem. We learned that our possible star witness, Hattie, had fled from the group home.

We checked areas in the Pompano Beach area where she frequented in the past. By talking to some of her friends, we discovered that she prostituted herself at night near the projects.

Karen and I began to work the same hours that Hattie did and in what amounted to a mini "hood." We finally located Hattie on a back street wearing clothes and high-heeled boots similar to a prostitute's attire. Her tight blue-jean shorts rose way too high, and her tight V-neck shirt showed way too much cleavage.

We drove up to her, and she waltzed over to us, probably thinking we were a john.

Karen rolled down my window. When she saw us, she stopped in her tracks. She reared back, her eyes opened wide in surprise.

I yelled, "Hattie, come here."

She walked over to our car and bent down to get a better view of us.

Karen said, "You don't want to do this, Hattie. You don't *have* to do this. You have a choice. Prostituting yourself like this isn't the answer."

Karen and I then talked to her about the dangers in her choice of street survival. We explained the diseases and crimes involved in child exploitation.

I said, "Prostitution is not a victimless crime, and if we catch you doing this again, we won't be able to overlook it."

She said, "I just can't believe you actually looked for me."

Karen said, "Of course we did. We were concerned about you."

"Really?" Hattie asked, her eyebrows furrowed and her tone carried a mix of appreciation, confusion, and disbelief.

"Really," I stated firmly.

"You were worried about me?" She asked, her eyes softening as she gave a slight smile. Our actions had obviously cut right through her street-wise demeanor.

I thought, *Poor girl, she's had such a hard life that she can't believe someone actually cares about her.*

She climbed into our car without further prompting. She was still a kid and needed love and caring.

We then took Hattie to the receiving facility of the Department of Children and Families (DCF) that was located in a low-rent shopping center. They housed children in various emergencies until they could be placed in a group home or foster care.

"Hey," I said. "Don't be thinking about running away again. We'll be checking in on you for the next few days at your school."

Hattie gave another slight smile and nodded in understanding. I also think she nodded in confirmation and appreciation.

Once we got her checked into the DCF facility, we talked at length with the counselor on duty. We expressed our concerns about Hattie requiring close supervision. She needed to be in a program where she could be monitored and watched to prevent anymore runaway episodes.

We finished with DCF about two o'clock in the morning. As we were leaving their office, a pizza delivery guy drove up with five pies looking for the person who placed the order.

The DCF intake officer laughed and shook his head. "You must be new," he said. "These crazy kids are always ordering pizza, but they never have any money."

Karen and I looked at each other. Simultaneously, we started emptying out our pockets in an effort to find enough cash to treat these kids to fresh pizza. We didn't want them to have to steal money in order to eat it.

Between Karen and me, we were able to come up with enough money for the pizzas and a little bit for the tip. After that, we were cleaned out, but the delivery guy learned a valuable lesson regarding these specific local customers and their potential to pay.

Two-Legged Monsters

My case file bulged from all of our interviews with car owners. So far, we achieved zero results for our efforts.

We reached an agreement to widen the interview circumference areas to include Florida's southwest coast. Just as we expanded our area, we noticed a driver's license belonging to a male from Naples who owned a car that fit the suspect's car exactly. Furthermore, he resembled the composite that the police artist had drawn from Ritha and Hattie's input.

Our computer checks disclosed very relevant details about this man. He worked for a medical lab, so he frequently drove to

Broward County to pick up urine samples from drop boxes outside of doctor offices. He then returned back to the Naples lab.

Our experience and training told us that we had come up with a good lead. However, we couldn't explain the only missing component—this guy didn't have a criminal history. Most of these perverts start off as peeping toms, burglars, etc.

Karen and I drove to Naples and followed this man for three days in a row. He did nothing other than pick-ups at numerous offices and then return to Naples.

On the fourth day, we developed a plan to gather more information on our suspect. I had asked Jacob, my former partner from my FHP days, if he and his K-9 Sniffer would assist us since he drove a marked police vehicle. We would drive out to Alligator Alley, the main highway that connected Naples and Fort Lauderdale. Then all three of our cars would park on the side of the road and wait for our guy.

When it was time to carry out our plan, I rode with Karen. Robert drove behind us in his unmarked car.

When the suspect passed us in his car, Jacob pulled out and conducted a traffic stop. Robert then drove up behind Jacob and parked. He got out and joined Jacob, and they began to question our suspect.

Karen and I watched from her car. Robert and Jacob spoke to this guy for about a half hour, determining why he drove to Fort Lauderdale, his time schedule, and if he had been in any trouble with the law.

We observed his demeanor during their questioning. Although he seemed calm, his wrinkled nose and pulled-together eyebrows told us that he was obviously confused with this line of questioning.

Jacob and Robert let him go. Afterward, we all met at the Broward County Highway Patrol Office to discuss the questioning and decide our guy's status. Before entering the building, Jacob took Sniffer out of his cage and walked him over to us.

Sniffer made a beeline to me. I bent down to greet him, and he fervently licked my face as if to say, "Hi! Where you been? I sure have missed you."

Then he walked over to Robert's car, hiked up his right leg, and peed.

Robert watched in shock but let Sniffer finish taking care of business. No one really wanted to interrupt Sniffer from taking care of business or from anything else for that matter. His massive size was just too formidable.

All of us, including Sniffer, walked to an empty office that Joseph had reserved for our meeting.

Robert got straight to the point. "The guy seemed credible enough and forthcoming in answering questions about his daily trips to Fort Lauderdale. He said his tight schedule only allowed for pick-ups. He told us that his tight schedule didn't even allow him enough time to stop for lunch."

Jacob said, "Yeah. He even showed us his packed lunch that he would eat along the way since he couldn't stop to eat."

Robert continued. "I looked at his arms, and they didn't have any tattoos, and according to Ritha, our perp had numerous tattoos. Plus, this guy didn't look heavy enough."

Karen said, "Well, we need to check with his boss to collaborate his alibi. Until then, we can't eliminate him as a suspect, but we can't keep him in the number-one spot either."

We were all disappointed, hoping that our search had finally come to an end. Unfortunately, we would have to keep pounding the pavement.

The next morning, I called our courier's employer, and he confirmed his alibi. He also confirmed his tight schedule.

I asked, "Has he ever arrived late?"

The employer said, "No, never. He's a good employee. I don't understand why you're asking about him."

"He drives a car that's similar to one used in a crime, but I thank you, sir, for your time," I said and hung up.

We were now frustrated. The only good part of this entire operation turned out to be working with Jacob and Sniffer for a day.

Fortunately, we did have other leads, so we closely looked at the development of two in particular. The first one involved an emergency room doctor. Several preteen girls filed complaints against him for molesting them during medical exams. None of these complaints ever resulted in charges.

Karen and I interviewed the doc, and he supplied us with an alibi for the day of the rape. We verified it with documents that proved he had been out of town on the day in question.

Next we focused on another sleazy guy who lived near Hattie's group home. What caught our attention was how he used his job as a photographer to entice young girls with offers of modeling careers. What held our attention were the convictions of two counts of child abuse in the fourth degree that he had garnered a couple of years earlier in Michigan. His efforts had given him a stay in prison for a year.

Then Mr. Scumbag moved to Florida from Michigan a few months earlier. He didn't waste time. He went to the Plantation Mall, where he used his old tricks on a sixteen-year-old by telling her he was looking for young models. He promised that if he could take pictures of her in the mall, he could make her famous with the photos. She naively agreed.

After shooting the pictures, he told her that she needed a portfolio. He convinced her that in order to create one, she needed to go with him to his hotel room because that was where his photography studio and required equipment were located to perform her model photo shoot. She again naively agreed.

While in his hotel room, this scumbag persuaded his prey to take off her top and shorts. This left her wearing only her panties. He started taking pictures of her lying on the bed.

While adjusting her poses, he fondled her breasts. When this poor girl saw that he had become visibly aroused, she realized he was conducting much more than a model photo shoot.

She grabbed her clothes and ran out of the room screaming. The police arrived and arrested Mr. Scumbag for molesting this child, but she was too embarrassed to testify at a later trial. As a result, the case was dropped.

I really wanted to get up close and personal with this guy. We drove to Ritha's house and to the DCF facility to show both girls the photo array, which consisted of six pictures of six different men, including Mr. Scumbag.

Each girl studied the array, but neither of them was able to pick out the picture of their offender and identify him. We were then forced to eliminate Mr. Scumbag as our suspect.

We decided to look at other abduction attempts in Miami and Palm Beach. Karen and I drove to an elementary school in West Palm Beach to interview a nine-year-old girl, who while walking home from school, was chased by a creepy man on a bike.

A neighbor who witnessed the event chased the pervert away and reported it to the police. When we showed the composite of Ritha's rapist to this neighbor, she said it didn't resemble the suspect on the bike.

This incident also differed from the MO our pervert used and proved to be a dead end. Karen and I thanked this vigilant neighbor for intervening and drove back to my office.

As I dug through some files, Robert called. "You are *not* going to believe what I've just done. I got us booked on *America's Most Wanted* to air our case."

I froze. "What?" That was the only word that I could manage to spit out.

We had talked about trying to get on the show, but admittedly, I didn't believe our chances were good.

"Oh, *America's Most Wanted*?" he teased. "It's a television show that helps capture bad guys…and girls."

"I know what *America's Most Wanted* is."

"Good." I could hear the chuckle in Robert's voice.

It took only a few moments to process what he said. Then excitement overcame me. This show earned the well-deserved reputation of putting a lot of felons behind bars. I hoped it would now provide the lead to our suspect.

I smiled from the hope rising up inside of me because this was our chance of getting national attention for our case and getting a monster off the streets.

America's Most Wanted – A Dream Come True

A couple of weeks later on an already-hot Friday morning in May 1999, Robert and I boarded our flight at Miami International Airport. We were on our way to Washington D.C. where *America's Most Wanted* was filmed.

Although we wanted Karen with us, *AMW* had asked for only two detectives, and Robert asked me to go. Regardless, Karen was excited. For her, it didn't matter who went; her priority was just getting the word out there about this freak so that we could put him behind bars and keep him from hurting another child.

After settling in our seats, Robert asked, "Do you want to go with me to the National Law Enforcement Officers Memorial while we're in D.C.?"

"Of course I would," I responded, feeling touched by his question. I knew he wanted to view his late partner's name and pay tribute to his sacrifice.

Our trip turned out to be a whirlwind. After checking into the Marriott, we received a message that one of the show's representatives would pick us up for dinner in a few hours.

So that evening found Robert, the *AMW* rep, and me at Pier 7, a lovely restaurant located on the Potomac River. We enjoyed the ambiance of the river scenery while dining on a delicious dinner, sipping top-of-the-line drinks, and engaging in great company, thanks to *AMW*.

We discussed some of the show's protocols and where we would sit. The rep told us that Saturday would be a free day for us. Because the show aired live on Saturday nights, we wouldn't be needed until then. He also told us that the program manager expected us to stay on the set until after midnight to take leads from the West Coast since it aired later there.

As expected, they had put some post-show plans in place as well. He informed us that the filming crew, the staff, other law enforcement officers, and Robert and I would walk to a nearby Irish Pub for a late-night snack and some drinks.

On Saturday, we took full advantage of our free time. That morning we begin the day by taking in some tourist spots. First, we walked to the White House, then to the Capitol Building, and then to the Washington Monument.

Afterward we went to the Police Memorial in Judiciary Square. Four bronze statues of lions with inscriptions surrounded the walls. One of those inscriptions really captured my attention and held me spellbound. It said, "The wicked flee when no man pursueth: but the righteous are as bold as a lion (Proverbs 28:1)."

Robert and I walked along the reflecting pool on the sidewalk. He then searched the wall for the plaque that held the name of his fallen partner.

After locating it, he removed a pencil and oblong piece of the memorial's stationary from a container in front of the wall. He placed the paper over his partner's plaque and used the side of the pencil lead to color over the engraving.

He planned to take the small memento back to the officer's mother as a tribute to her son's memory. I can be a hardened cop, but as I watched him meticulously trace his fallen partner's name, a tear or two slipped down my cheeks.

We left after I located the names of some of the fallen officers I remembered from Miami. Then Robert and I walked in silence for a few blocks. We both thought about the men and women who gave their lives so that others could live in peace. I prayed for the families of those brave officers.

After arriving at the hotel, we got ready for an early evening ride to the studio. I knew we had a late night ahead of us, so Robert and I ate a light dinner before leaving for the show.

We entered the studio, and bright lights seemed to come from every direction to greet us. Tables and work stations lined each side of the room, and excitement filled the air.

We were swept into a frenzy of instructions and advice. Someone from the show told Robert and me to sit in front of the telephones and act as if we were writing incoming leads.

We met a Chicago Police Department homicide detective. He would be sitting next to me during the show to talk about the murder of a twelve-year-old girl.

When John Walsh walked in, I gasped. I couldn't believe I was in the same room with him. I considered him to be an American hero. As the father of an abducted and murdered son, he continued to fight tirelessly for justice through this show for the past eleven years, and he would continue to fight through this show for the next twelve.

John walked over to me and shook my hand. He thanked me for my work and for being on his show.

He immediately offered me a photo opportunity to stand with him in front of the large *AMW* stage plaque. He did this with all of the law enforcement guests. I didn't hesitate to accept. He also took time to speak with each one of us about our cases.

We ended up acquiring fifty leads during the program.

After the show, Robert and I walked to the pub. My steps seemed a little lighter.

I looked down at the folder I carried that held our leads, and I couldn't help but smile. Possibly, just possibly, in my hands was the break we needed.

It Ain't Over 'Til It's Over

The next morning, we grabbed a quick breakfast before heading to Reagan National Airport for our flight home. I knew we had a busy week ahead of us.

Karen joined us Monday morning at the NLPD, and we all began looking over the leads. For another month, we conducted numerous follow-up interviews. We still didn't have the one tip we needed, though.

We decided to keep track of all of the attempted abductions in South Florida. We all believed this bad boy would strike again.

A few weeks later, the tide turned. North Miami Beach Police Department (NMBPD) Detective Hal Cohen called me. I knew Hal from when we worked together on the murder of Department of Revenue tax collector Ronald Brooks. Sure, I had been upset with Hal at the time for what had transpired, but that was long over. Now wasn't the time to hold grudges but to come together to collaborate on getting a child predator off the street.

Hal learned about our search for a child abductor and rapist from the messages we had sent to other police agencies. We had asked them to contact us if they investigated a similar crime.

Hal said, "Floy, I've had two attempted abductions that I think you may want to know about. In one day, a man in a brown van approached two girls of color walking home together from school in North Miami Beach. Then about fifteen minutes later, he approached a third girl of color as she walked alone. During both incidences, he pointed a gun at the girls, and both times, the girls ran away.

"I need to meet with your team ASAP. I'm leaving the station now with my lieutenant to come your way."

"Okay," I said. "we'll see you in my office."

I called Karen and Robert, telling them what Detective Cohen had told me and that he was on his way to my office to meet with us. Within an hour, we had everyone together who needed to be there.

We all felt we were looking at the same person. The description from Hal's cases resembled that of our suspect's. Also, the MO seemed to be the same. This pervert approached only dark-skinned girls walking home from school, and he always pointed a gun at them.

We agreed to split up and start looking for a brown van, but we all wondered what had happened to the white car. Karen decided to stop in the same dealership where she had obtained the brochure a few months back. She wanted to ask if they had any missing vehicles. She just seemed to have a hunch about this car.

Within an hour, Karen called me on her cell phone. "Floy, I just left that Pompano Beach dealership. They told me they had recently performed an inventory check and discovered that a white car, same model used in the North Lauderdale and Fort Lauderdale crimes, was missing.

"They said that the last time anyone remembered seeing it was just before one of their salesmen, Adonis Kozma, was fired. I showed them the composite picture of our suspect. All of the salesmen said it looked like Adonis.

"The dealership gave me Adonis' address. Listen to this. He only lives a few miles from North Lauderdale and about a mile from the store where Ritha was raped."

Finally, we were getting somewhere. This was the best news we had gotten since the case began.

We all decided to meet up at the FDLE offices to move on this new information. My FDLE analyst, Terry, ran a computer check on Adonis. What we learned horrified us. Adonis had a total of thirty-two felony arrests. I found it interesting that none of the arrests were for sex crimes. Furthermore, I wondered how a person with that many felonies could still be loose and on the streets.

Robert said, "I'm going to leave now and drive by Adonis' house."

Karen said, "Right behind you."

We followed Robert in my car. When my cell phone rang, I heard Robert on the other end. He was very matter of fact when he announced, "There's the brown van sitting in Adonis' driveway."

I saw it too. I knew we were finally on target!

Now we needed a search warrant, so we left to go to the NLPD to write it. In the meantime, Karen pulled together an FBI surveillance team to locate and watch Adonis. Law enforcement uses this common procedure once it identifies a dangerous felon. They maintain a watch on the suspect to ensure public safety.

After putting the final markings on the warrant, I called the FDLE Regional Legal Advisor for the review process before taking it to the on-call judge. I wanted to make sure we had all of our ducks in a row and that there was nothing that could keep a judge from signing it.

My diligence paid off. The judge signed the warrant.

Robert then called. "Ladies, you are *not* going to believe this. Our friend Adonis is a drug informant for the Coral Gables Police

Department. I called their narcotics unit, and someone from there is driving up here to meet with us."

Within the hour, the detective who "handled" Adonis rushed into our meeting room. After talking with him, I could tell that he had no idea his source hurt and raped children. He felt terrible about it.

The detective shared with us all of the information he had on Adonis. Then he said, "Adonis has an uncle who works for a South Florida police department."

My stomach knotted up. I felt terrible that such a monster had a family member connected to law enforcement.

We knew the day was slipping away, so we got busy fast. We needed to get this guy off the streets before he could victimize another child.

The surveillance team followed Adonis to his stepfather's job site where he worked in construction. While watching him, the FBI agents witnessed him break into a car and steal it. They arrested him for auto theft.

At the same time the FBI arrested Adonis, Ritha was with Karen and me at the NLPD looking at a photo lineup. Her eyebrows furrowed as she stared at Adonis' picture. "That's the man who hurt me," she said in a matter-of-fact tone.

Ritha's ID was paramount for so many reasons. For one, she had seen the tattoos and could identify them. More importantly, though, her case would result in a life sentence due to her age.

Once Karen and I finished with Ritha, we drove to the area of the arrest. My supervisor had been monitoring the radio transmissions and was agitated that the FBI conducted this arrest.

He radioed me on a car-to-car channel, not realizing that I had Karen with me in the car. "I'm going to kill the FBI agent who made that arrest," he announced.

Karen never said a word or blinked an eye. Of course, my boss wasn't going to kill an FBI agent. He felt compelled to vent his frustration over the fact that he wanted to be the one to make the arrest. Many times, the bosses fight over the glory while those of us in the trenches work quite well together.

I said, "Sir, this arrest was for car theft, not the rape."

"Oh," he responded.

Actually, the FBI wasn't interested in charging and prosecuting Adonis for auto theft, either. They were merely there to help us and keep him under surveillance. It just so happened that they witnessed him committing a felony and couldn't turn a blind eye to it. After they arrested him, they drove him directly to the NLPD and turned him over to us at Karen's request.

Karen and I both knew that Hal and Robert were the ones who needed to interview Adonis. We suspected that he would be more likely to develop a rapport with the male detectives.

In the meantime, Karen, my supervisor, and I left to serve the search warrant on the small, concrete-block home where Adonis lived with his mother and stepfather. At thirty-nine years old, the man still lived with mom.

I knocked on the brown door. After a couple of moments, an ample-sized, curvy woman with big red hair answered the door. She wore a tropical top, several gold bangles on her wrist, and gold hoop earrings.

When she saw our badges, her colorfully made-up eyes widened.

Once she regained her composure, she asked with all of the innocence that a mother, blinded by love for her son, could muster, "May I help you?" She then tried to position her big red lips into a smile. However, the rest of her face didn't match her attempt.

I said, "Ma'am, we have a search warrant to search your home. Does Adonis Kozma live here?"

She nodded.

With a firm voice, I stated, "We have a warrant. Please step aside."

"What? Why do you want to search my home? What do you want with my son? Adonis is a good boy. He did nothing wrong."

"Ma'am, please step aside."

She finally moved out of the way, and I read her the warrant and then handed it to her as I walked past her.

Her eyebrows remained in a fixed raised position. "John," she yelled, "come here. The police want to search our home."

A thin and wiry man wearing painter pants and a dirty T-shirt walked into the room. His skin's dark tan and wrinkles were obviously the result of working out in the sun for hours at a time. His brown eyes looked sad, and he kept quiet.

Adonis' mother repeated several times, "But my Adonis is a good boy. He wouldn't do anything wrong. We're very close. He's a good boy."

Of course, we didn't tell her that her good boy was in our custody being interrogated for the rape of a child. We ignored her and continued on with our mission.

When I entered Adonis' bedroom, the first oddity I noticed was that it looked more like a teenager's room than a grown man's. For one thing, he had a collection of baseball hats decorating his walls.

We didn't discover any incrementing evidence, but we did gain a lot of insight into the family issues.

Adonis's mother said, "I watched *America's Most Wanted* and told my husband that the rapist looked like my son. But I knew the similarities were just coincidences. I knew that picture wasn't Adonis because he's a good boy."

I couldn't help but shake my head. Did she not realize that her utterance wasn't doing anything to help her son?

The stepfather repeated her affirmation in a monotone voice as if reading from a cue card. "Yes, it could not be Adonis because he is a good boy."

As we left the house, his mother still repeated, "He's a good boy."

Later that night in an interview at the NLPD, Adonis confessed to Robert and Hal. He told them that he ditched the car in a canal along with the gun.

When asked why he raped a little girl, he said, "I overpowered her."

His statement made me sick. Here was a grown man, and he got off by overpowering a little eleven-year-old girl. His confession was also a clue to his mindset, that rape was all about power and control.

Robert asked, "You seem to want to abduct only black girls. Why?"

He stared at him, his eyes fixed and his eyebrows raised. "Because I'm a white supremacist."

Karen and I went to Ritha's home. When she saw us, she welcomed us inside her home.

I said, "We just came by to tell you that we've got the guy who did this to Ritha. He's in jail now."

Her shoulders relaxed, and a grin spread wide across her face and revealed white teeth. "Follow me."

Karen and I looked at each other and complied.

Ritha's mom led us into her garage where we saw a small altar. A voodoo puppet of a man that was covered with pins laid on top of it.

She said, "Thank you. You were guided by my voodoo spirits."

Although I found her statement strange, I kept my mouth shut.

The following day, police divers located the white car in a canal within two miles of the scene of Ritha's rape. They didn't find the gun, though.

Consequently, I wrote a search warrant for Adonis's DNA and drove to the jail. I then entered the building with the warrant in hand and walked back to the gray and dreary health clinic where I presented the signed warrant to a large burley black prison guard.

I said, "Will you please bring Mr. Adonis Kozma down to the clinic so that I can swab his cheeks for a DNA comparison? Oh, and by the way, did you know he's the white supremacist who raped a little black girl?"

I guess that was the bad in me coming out. I wanted the prisoners and guards to know what Adonis did.

Family Betrayals

Once the arrest made the papers, Adonis' cousins contacted me. They were in their mid-twenties. Their father was the police officer.

They told me what they had never shared with their families. Adonis began raping them at three and four years of age until they were in their teens.

As a police officer, their father didn't trust anyone to babysit them but a member of their close-knit family. He had also used his position and community standing to get Adonis out of other possible arrests in the past.

These siblings had never dealt with the consequences of this childhood torture and kept it secret for over twenty years. One suffered from an eating disorder, and the other withdrew from social functions.

They agreed to wear a wire and visit Adonis in jail. They wanted to obtain evidence that he had sexually molested them as children.

Raping a child under the age of twelve doesn't have a statute of limitations and is considered a capital offense in Florida.

I had each of them sign a one-party consent form, which is required in order for the evidence to be admissible in a Florida court. Under the direction of law enforcement, a cooperating witness can wear a wire and tape a conversation.

As we wired them up, I instructed, "Tell Adonis you forgive him but that you just want to know why he raped you. I need you to mention how young you were when you were raped. Getting him to say the ages on tape will provide important evidence."

They both nodded.

"Any questions?"

They both shook their heads, so I sent them into the jail

My plan worked. Adonis apologized to his cousins for raping them when they were three and four years old and then continuing to do so for years. This indeed gave me what I needed to ensure that Adonis would never be free again. I've learned over the years that the best strategy for a conviction is to stack the cards in favor of justice.

Through my conversations with the cousins, I realized that Adonis and his mother shared an unusual relationship. They told me he slept with his mother in her bed well-past puberty. The family members speculated that incestuous relations occurred during this mother-son sleeping arrangement.

The evidence kept coming in. My analyst continued to perform searches on Adonis' background and discovered a woman in Mobile, Alabama, who used to go by the name of Randi Kozma. She now went by a different name that we assumed was her maiden name. Randi and Adonis got married when she was very young.

She was petrified of Adonis. She said he had locked her in their bedroom while he was away at work, padlocking the door from the outside. He also took the telephone away from her during the day.

I think she was so terrified of him that she was afraid to try to escape. Then one day she got the courage. She turned the doorknob and realized that Adonis must have forgotten to lock it. She flung the door open and then ran outside and to her mother's home.

During the night, Adonis broke into her mother's house and threatened to kill her and her mother if she didn't leave with him.

She said, "If you need me to testify, I will, even though Adonis still scares me."

I hadn't heard the worst at this time. I got notified that a Florida State prison inmate needed to speak with me. He and Adonis had shared a cell when he had temporarily resided at the Broward County Jail.

I arranged for the prisoner to be transferred back to the jail. When I interviewed him, he disclosed that Adonis tried to get a hit man to murder Ritha. He knew he could face a life sentence for raping a child under twelve, so he wanted to ensure she couldn't testify at his trial

Robert took our snitch into the Broward County Jail's health clinic and attached the recording device to the inside of the prisoner's thigh. We then sent him up to the recreation room where Adonis watched television.

When the snitch returned, Robert took him aside to remove the wire. Then Robert, Karen, and I went into the office at the jail and gathered around the digital recorder to listen to it from beginning to end. None of us wanted to miss one word of the conversation.

However, we ended up getting more than conversation. We discovered that our snitch had stopped by the jail cell toilet on the way to see Adonis. The device had been kept on, leaving any and everyone who heard this recording privy to his moaning and groaning as he took care of personal business.

I watched the color drain from Robert's face, and he squirmed in his seat.

He whispered, "I didn't wear gloves when I took the recording device off the snitch. Jeesh! I didn't expect him to go to the bathroom on the way."

He seemed to regain his color, though, as we listened to the conversation between the snitch and Adonis. Even with a lot of background noise, we still picked up some discussion about Adonis getting his mother to sell her jewelry and then making arrangements for her to pay the hit man to silence Ritha. However, from the snitch's tone, it wasn't clear if this was the snitch's idea or Adonis' idea.

We requested a hearing on the possibility that Adonis was tampering with the child witness. We didn't have clear evidence of who came up with the hit idea, so we didn't have enough to charge him with it. We needed the judge on the case to hear the recording. In making him aware of it, he could invoke some regulations as to Adonis' contacts.

When we presented this recording to judge, we achieved our goal. He ruled that due to that evidence, Adonis couldn't have any telephone calls, mail, or visits from or with anyone other than his lawyer. This included his mother and any hit man he may solicit to help him with his insidious scheme.

Although this may be construed as a small victory, we thought it would probably be enough to keep Ritha safe.

When at First You Don't Succeed...

Over a year and a half after initiating this investigation, Adonis' trial was about to commence.

Two weeks beforehand, however, Ritha ran away from home. I suspected she didn't want to face the court trial. Thankfully, she was quickly found. Her mother finally agreed to getting her counseling.

Due to the issues with Ritha running away and the fact that she hadn't received any counseling prior to the trial, the prosecutor offered, and the defense accepted, a plea deal for twenty-seven years on each count to be served consecutively. This translated into the assurance that Adonis would never walk the earth again as a free man.

On the morning of the sentencing, however, Adonis and his mother cooked up a last-minute deal. They now wanted him to withdraw the plea agreement and go to trial instead. We didn't feel it was in Ritha's best interest to face her rapist and testify since she already seemed so fragile.

I telephoned Adonis' cousins. I asked them if they would agree to press charges in their cases should the plea be withdrawn. They both said yes.

Armed with this information, I reminded the prosecutor about the cousins. He approached Adonis's attorney. He informed him about the covert operation where Adonis' cousins recorded their visit with him in the jail.

Adonis reconsidered his withdrawal plan and agreed to go forth with the plea after all.

During his sentencing, the judge said, "When you leave the Florida State Prison, it will be in a pine box."

Adonis turned around and looked at his mom, who was bawling like a baby. His eyebrows were raised in the middle, and his eyes pleaded with his mother to do something.

She did. She fainted.

The National Missing Children's Day Ceremony

In May 2000, a full year after my trip to D.C., I returned to attend the annual National Missing Children's Day ceremony and took

Gary's daughter Kellie with me. This event focused on the cases of missing, kidnapped, and murdered children and honored the law enforcement officers from across the U.S. who brought these cases to a conclusion.

We woke up to get ready for the event. I opened up our hotel room's curtains and noticed the lovely spring day. I smiled and hoped it would bring some encouragement to this somber event.

The ceremony started with the National Capitol Breakfast held at the Capitol building. Members of Congress congratulated us for being award recipients. At one point while Kellie and I were enjoying our delicious food, a Florida Congressman stopped at our table to greet us.

That afternoon, Robert, Karen, Hal, Kellie, and I were taken to the Department of Justice (DOJ) for a formal ceremony as part of the National Missing Children's Day. Its members and Attorney General Janet Reno presented us with an award for our investigative efforts with Ritha and Hattie's case.

Later on, our group sat at a round wooden table in the hotel lounge during happy hour. Hal's supervisor Lieutenant Lynn Russo joined us. She happened to be in the area attending the FBI National Law Enforcement Academy in Quantico, Virginia. I thought it appropriate that she celebrate with us since the North Miami Beach Police Department, where she worked, was involved in this case. Plus, Hal was one of her detectives.

We discussed the events that had brought us together. We joked and laughed. Then almost simultaneously, we all got quiet as we each stared pensively into our drinks.

I silently reflected back on this case, where we had started, what all we had done, the dead ends along the way, and finally our sweet victory.

This case had consumed my life for a year and a half, and I couldn't help but wonder, *What now?* Sure, I would always have cases, but those that involved injustices perpetrated upon children, well, those I could sink my teeth into because of my intense passion for the victims involved.

Robert cleared his throat, which jerked me out of my thoughts. I glanced over at him.

He looked around the table at each of his companions, ensuring he had our attention. He then stared off into the distance as he shifted in his seat as if trying to find a comfortable spot while searching for the right words. He took a sip of his drink.

We all looked at each other with raised eyebrows. I could tell everyone sitting at our table was intrigued and eagerly anticipated Robert's announcement. Whatever it was, it was serious.

"I need some help, folks." He then brought his glance back to his friends and colleagues, moving his eyes to each of us one at a time.

He raised his right eyebrow, cocked his head to the side, and then darted his eyes between Karen and me. "I've got a cold case homicide involving a five-year-old victim.

"Karen and Floy, would you look at the case file and help me with this investigation?"

CHAPTER 11

Who Murdered Little Nancy?

I arrived at my office at ten o'clock in the morning on the Monday after I returned from my Washington D.C. trip.

I had just started to get settled into my morning routine when I got a surprise visit from Robert. He arrived with a portable cart filled with four brown cardboard boxes with lids.

He smiled like the cat that just ate the canary. "I got off the phone a moment ago with Karen. She'll stop by before heading to her office."

Ever since Robert had mentioned this cold homicide case of five-year-old Nancy Goodyear while we were in D.C., I knew he'd be visiting me. He had definitely piqued my interest, so I told him I wanted to *learn* more. However, I didn't tell him I would help.

Admittedly, I wanted the case; I just didn't know if it met the current FDLE investigative focus. I even woke up in the middle of the night and made mental notes as to how the case would or could be accepted by FDLE.

So not even twenty-four hours after our plane touched ground in Miami, Robert barged into my office and stood, briskly rubbing his hands together while retaining that same smile. Since FBI Special Agent Karen Kool was on her way, I assumed he planned to brief both of us together.

It seemed to me that Robert had jumped the gun from casual talk to bringing the entire case file to me. I still needed to receive approval from my supervisor. I hadn't even had the chance to tell my boss, "Good morning; I'm back," let alone tell him about this cold case.

I said, "Sure, Robert, make yourself at home. Before we get started, I need to run this by my supervisor; otherwise, we're all going to be wasting our time if he doesn't agree to my working this case."

I left Robert sitting next to my desk, walked to my supervisor's office, and tapped on his doorjamb. He looked up from his desk and grinned from ear to ear.

"Congrats on your award, Floy. The SAC was so impressed that he decided to give you the position of Regional Crimes Against Children Coordinator."

Inwardly, I wanted to jump up and down and do a happy dance right there in my boss' doorway, but I refrained myself. This was a fantastic opportunity, not only for my career but because of my passion. I wish I could call Gary and tell him, but I needed to wait until after Robert and Karen left.

I did allow myself to smile, though, and say, "Thank you."

"Well, you deserve it. I've seen how much effort you put into your job. You go full force with every assignment we give you, regardless of what it is.

I replied, "This is great timing. I have Robert in my office with a child homicide cold case that happened almost six years ago."

He continued to smile. "Go for it then."

By the time I rounded the corner from my boss' office, I saw Karen talking with Robert in my office. Now *I* looked like the cat that swallowed the canary. I excitedly gave them the news about my new assignment of Regional CAC and that my boss authorized me to investigate this homicide.

Over the next three hours and with many cups of coffee under our belts, Robert told us the details of this homicide. He started off by giving the back story that led up to the murder.

According to Robert, the local police in the town of North Lauderdale knew the victim's family very well but not in a good way.

He said, "Nancy's parents, Dan and Sally Goodyear, married each other when both were only fifteen." He sighed and shook his head. "I don't get it. Evidently their parents gave the approval for this union because as we all know, they couldn't have legally gotten married in Florida without it. Go figure.

"Then in that same year when young Dan was still a newlywed, he accumulated a rap sheet full of violent encounters. For one, he fought with a friend and intentionally ran him over with a motorcycle and killed him. Dan got charged as a juvenile for vehicular manslaughter and then sentenced.

"After spending about a year in the Department of Juvenile Justice state system, Dan got paroled. He and Sally started a family, giving birth to their son Adam in 1986, and daughter Nancy in 1989.

"Later on when Dan was in his twenties, he and his family moved in with his grandmother. He didn't have much patience with her dementia, so he began hitting her. She died about a year after one of his battering episodes. There wasn't enough evidence to show that the blows actually caused her death, so they couldn't prove homicide. Instead they charged him with elderly abuse. This time around, though, he was over eighteen, and the state charged him as an adult.

"While Dan was in prison, Sally needed to support her children, so she found a quick and lucrative way to make money. She stripped at the Pussy Cat Club in Hollywood. She also took in a renter named Sam to help make ends meet.

"After Dan got released, he worked in yard maintenance. Sally continued to strip. Sam moved out.

"Fast forward to September 1994, when Nancy was only five years old, and she went missing."

I did some quick math in my head. Since that was almost six years ago, she would have now been an eleven-year-old little girl with her whole life ahead of her.

Robert said, "The evening before her disappearance, Dan and Sally had argued. What happened prior to the argument demonstrated the adage that life is stranger than fiction. You just can't make this stuff up.

"Around four o'clock that afternoon, Dan came home from work. He walked into his house and grabbed a beer.

"I'm sure their large above-ground pool in his backyard look inviting since the day was so hot. He walked outside and saw his wife Sally and her friend and coworker Laura Benton in the pool. They were engaging in girl sex with each other."

Robert paused and gave a half-smile. "Dan asked if he could join them, but they refused to let him. So Dan sulked, cursed, and went back into the house. Actually, this started a slow volcanic eruption within him.

"Later that evening, Sally walked to a neighbor's house and into the arms of another lover, this one of the male gender. In fact, she used the term *lover* rather loosely when referring to any male subject toward whom she showed affection.

"Something else Sally did loosely was openly tell her husband about her affairs. Knowing his wife was having sex with other men compounded Dan's emotional state and intensified his anger."

Robert stared at some of the file's photographs. "However, from what I've learned, Dan was always consumed with anger, and he and Sally had a volatile relationship with lots of violence. This night was no different and ended with another argument after Sally came back home, and Dan confronted her with her affairs.

"The following day, Sally and Dan went back to their routines. She went to work the afternoon shift at the Pussy Cat. Then that evening around seven thirty, Dan fed the children Chinese takeout food. Afterward about eight o'clock, he put the children to bed in Adam's room. Nancy slept on the bottom bunk, and Adam slept on the top bunk.

"He then left them alone to take the twenty-minute drive to pick Sally up at her job.

"Arriving back at the house, Dan and Sally argued again about her affairs. The argument soon escalated into a fight. Dan threatened suicide.

"Sally called her girlfriend Laura to come over to the house and help her smooth out the situation with Dan. According to investigators, Dan, Sally, and Laura never checked on or saw the children in their beds that evening.

"When Sally awoke in the morning, she walked into the kitchen. She noticed that the front door was wide open. Since they lived with all sorts of people coming and going, the house was never secured, so Sally wasn't all that alarmed initially.

"A few minutes later, Adam came out of his bedroom. Sally asked him where his sister was, and he said he didn't know. He told her that when he woke up, she wasn't in the bed where she had slept the previous night.

"Now Sally was getting concerned. She ran into Adam's room and saw the bottom bed empty. She yelled her daughter's name, but nothing.

"Sally panicked and ran to her bedroom and woke up Dan. They began to search their house and neighborhood for Nancy. About an hour later, Dan called the police to report his daughter missing.

"When the police interviewed Dan, they found him uncooperative. The officers called the detective unit. Of course, Dan berated them for wasting his time, saying that while they talked with him, they all could be out searching for his daughter.

"The detectives asked about his activities the previous night. He said that he fed the children dinner about seven thirty, put them to bed, and then drove over to pick up Sally."

I couldn't help but wonder why DCF didn't remove Adam from the home after learning that this eight-year-old was left alone at night with his younger sister. At this point, I guess the question was moot.

Robert glanced back and forth between Karen and me. "Dan continued telling the detectives that he and his wife returned home and enjoyed some great sex. He omitted telling them about the argument, what had caused the argument, and his threatened suicide.

"The detectives interviewed Sally, and she openly disclosed the issues that caused the argument. She told them about what had become known as 'the pool incident' and how Dan got mad because she and her girlfriend refused to let him join them, her visit to her lover-neighbor, and Dan's subsequent threat of suicide. She also told the detectives that after Laura left, she and Dan engaged in the best sex of their lives.

"The detectives thought Dan and Sally contrived the statement about their great sex. They believed it could have been rehearsed to cover up the facts of what had really caused their daughter to go missing.

"The house became chaotic as family and friends repeatedly disturbed it with their frequent incomings and outgoings. The responding officers lost the integrity of the original crime scene."

I asked, "Why didn't the police tape off the house as a crime scene. Why did they let anyone enter it?"

Robert shrugged. "Don't know. They should have, and that was a big mistake because it has caused some headaches as a result."

I shook my head.

Robert continued. "That same morning, a police search team discovered blood droplets on the walkway leading to the Goodyear house. They collected specimens to be analyzed and put a rush on it. A few days went by before they got the results back showing that the blood belonged to an animal.

"Later that morning, responding officers and detectives conducted a neighborhood canvass. They found the source of the blood. The Goodyears had kept their two pit bulls in the backyard. During the night, the dogs could go in and out of the house at will by jumping through a missing pane in the kitchen window.

"Because they didn't have a fence, the dogs could also roam the neighborhood at will. They got into a neighbor's backyard that had a rabbit cage. The dogs became excited and went into a barking frenzy as they ran around the cage trying to get to the rabbits. Fortunately for the rabbits, the dogs couldn't touch them, but the ruckus understandably woke up the rabbit owners.

"From then on, the detectives always referred to these rabbit-owners-turned-witnesses as Mr. and Mrs. Rabbit."

Robert gave another slight smile. I could tell he was trying to bring a little lightheartedness into this serious situation.

"Mr. Rabbit grabbed a BB gun while Mrs. Rabbit got the family truck in motion to drive it. Mr. Rabbit jumped on the tailgate and aimed and shot BBs at the dogs until the canines ran around the back of their home for safety.

"The Rabbits both said this occurred about four thirty in the morning. At the time, they recalled seeing the Goodyear's front door wide open and the interior lights on, but they couldn't remember if they saw Dan's red pickup truck and Sally's beat-up blue sedan in their front yard.

"At this point, the investigation had gotten nowhere, but the police weren't about to give up. Everyone was determined to find little Nancy, hoping she was still alive."

The Search Comes to an End

Admittedly, Robert had my complete attention.

Dysfunction with a capital D clearly defined the victim's family both paternally and maternally. Many of them, along with their friends, possessed histories of domestic violence, criminal activity, and illegal drug use. Nancy's two grandmothers were not excluded from this group. They were still young, both in their thirties, and one stripped for a living while the other was addicted to drugs.

Robert took a few sips of coffee and got pensive for a few moments before talking again. "The police thought that Dan and Sally were under the influence of drugs when they interviewed them. Neither was in the proper condition to take a polygraph that morning. As a result, the police couldn't eliminate them as suspects.

"Other family members started to discuss possible suspects with the police. A few of them mentioned Sam Andrews, the guy who rented a room from Sally while Dan was in jail for battering his grandma. Seems that Dan, Sally, and Sam had a bit of history together. They went to the same middle school, and they all three dropped out at the same time. None of them ever went back to school. They socialized together and remained close friends all of these years.

"Sally told the detectives that one time, Nancy left Sam's room with a large rubber dildo and showed it to her mother. When Sally confronted Sam about why her daughter came out of his room with a sex toy, he told her he didn't know that Nancy had found it. He said he had been keeping it in a suitcase under his bed."

Robert took a deep breath. "The police searched the vicinity, radiating outward from the Goodyear house. One woman told officers that while waiting at a bus stop early that morning, she saw Nancy walking nearby. Armed with her information, the search for Nancy focused on her neighborhood.

"After a couple of days, the woman recanted. She said she just made up that story. She ended up causing the police to go on a wild-goose chase. Aggravating I'm sure, but no one pressed charges against her because she was mentally disabled."

I knew I had my fair share of wild-goose chases. With high-profile cases, people come out of the woodwork and interject themselves into the investigation with fictitious stories. They wanted attention, just like this woman did, I'm sure.

Robert said, "The FBI joined in the initial investigation to provide assistance." He looked at Karen.

As if on cue, she answered his silent question as to where she was then. "Yeah, back in 1994, I was working in Detroit."

Satisfied with Karen's response, Robert said, "Massive efforts to coordinate a search for Nancy took place. The FBI brought their mobile command center to function as the command office in a shopping center close to Nancy's house."

Robert stared at a report as if reading its contents. "Three days later and about twenty-six miles away from Nancy's home, a jogger was running on a dirt road alongside an isolated wooded area near Boca Raton in southern Palm Beach County. He discovered Nancy's battered and crumpled body lying face down in a deep puddle of water created by the heavy two-day-long rainfall. He called 911."

He looked up at Karen and me. Neither of us said a word.

"A uniformed patrol sergeant from the Palm Beach County Sheriff's Office arrived at the scene first. She found a thin, green electrical-type wire wrapped around Nancy's neck and knotted.

"She managed to request homicide detectives to respond, but she became sickened over the horrific appearance of this young child. Her skin was decomposing due to the length of time her body was exposed to the elements.

"The sergeant had a daughter about the same age as Nancy. She ended up suffering from severe traumatic stress as a result of seeing this gruesome sight. A few years later, she turned in her badge saying she couldn't function as a frontline supervisor anymore.

"Homicide Detective Glenn Woodard from the PBSO responded to the site as the lead investigator for his department. Since he knew about the missing child in Broward County, he put two and two together and contacted me. He knew me and knew I was a homicide detective with Broward County. He said, 'I think this child might be Nancy Goodyear.'

"Glenn then requested that one of Nancy's parents respond to the Palm Beach County Medical Examiner's Office to identify the body.

"A family member drove Dan there, and he made the positive identification.

"With Dan's verification of his daughter, the case became a homicide, and I became the lead."

Sam and Eddie

Before continuing, Robert asked, "Any questions?"

Karen and I shook our heads.

Robert looked down at a few documents in front of him. "I've got a report from an interview with Eddie, one of Sam's friends. After Dan got out of jail and moved back home, Sam moved in with Eddie. They lived together in a seedy cheap motel room, and they worked together as house painters. They also indulged in uppers to keep up with their busy schedules."

I continued to take notes.

"Eddie said that Sam wasn't in their hotel room for most of the night when Nancy went missing. When one of our detectives asked him if he was sure, he told him yes because he never got to sleep that night. Seems his girlfriend was in the hospital having their baby, and she kept him on the phone in his motel room all night.

"In fact, Eddie said he didn't see Sam at all until about six thirty in the morning when Sam drove them to a paint job in his van.

"What's very interesting, though, is that later that evening after work, Eddie and Sam watched the evening news in their motel room. They heard the report about a missing child. Eddie said that even before the news gave any of the details, Sam told him the missing child was Nancy.

"Eddie didn't know how he could possibly know it was Nancy. He didn't know why he didn't mention anything about it during work that day. After all, they were friends, roommates, and coworkers, and Sam was close to the Goodyear family. With them being together all day, he would have thought that Sam would have at least mentioned that Nancy was missing if the Goodyear family had told Sam about it. So he didn't think Sam found out about Nancy through them.

"Eddie stated that after the news broadcast, Sam made a few calls to his mother and a preacher and sounded frantic when he talked to them. Next thing Eddie knew, Sam walked outside to the parking lot and cleaned out his van. Eddie thought his cleaning his van was really weird because it was always trashed.

"According to Eddie, and I quote, 'Sam never gave a shit about it being clean before.'"

Let's Do It!

I studied Robert as I processed all of this information.

I asked, "Where's Eddie now?"

"The last time I spoke to him, he had packed up his girlfriend, new baby girl, and moved as far away as he could get from Sam. Said he didn't want Sam anywhere near his baby."

Robert took in another deep breath before letting out a long exhale. I could tell that this was difficult for him. "The autopsy results determined Nancy's cause of death—strangulation by affixation from the wire ligature wrapped around her neck. The report from the medical examiner came back inconclusive about whether Nancy had been sexually assaulted, though.

"Glenn and I keep going back and forth as to who killed Nancy. We can't determine whether Dan did it or Sam."

I wanted to bring a prosecutor into my investigative efforts. A lot of unanswered questions remained. Since it was still a cold case, I felt having a prosecutor onboard for legal clarification was imperative.

The amount of time I anticipated spending on this complicated case would be in vain if some legal reason denied prosecution. This could become a grand jury case, and we would need a prosecutor anyway. In addition, this case covered two different counties, so I thought Cathy Mueller would be perfect.

Cathy and I had worked several burglary and racketeering cases together, and I liked working with her. More importantly, she had jurisdiction as the statewide prosecutor with the Attorney General's Office.

I said, "I'll go and see Cathy and try to get her onboard. Karen, you with us on this case?"

She nodded as she continued looking through the file.

I asked, "Robert, can you get us a meeting with Glenn?"

He looked between Karen and me with a smile spreading wide across his face. He got the answer he wanted—we were going to work this cold case with him.

"You got it," he said.

Robert, Karen, and I then put our investigative skills together. We knew we needed to reach out to the Medical Examiner who conducted the autopsy and speak with him.

We also decided to contact the Goodyear family and ask permission to visit their house where Nancy was abducted. Although the case file contained pictures of the house, physically walking through it would enhance our visual acuity. We needed to bring to it an investigative perspective of crime scene logistics. Hopefully Glenn and Cathy would join us.

Right now, though, my head spun with all of the information I had learned and the four bulging boxes of reports and videos that stood before me. I knew huge advances had been made with DNA evidence. Still, investigating a crime six years old always comes with its share of complexities. I hoped I could find that missing piece to finally solve this mystery and bring little Nancy the justice she deserved.

After Robert and Karen left, I allowed myself the luxury of letting out a big sigh. I accepted that I'd be spending the rest of my day organizing and reviewing six years of documented information.

Looking around my office, I made a mental note to request a tall four-drawer file cabinet just for this case. In the meantime, I got busy and opened a case file in my computer. I then took all of the names that Robert had included in his morning briefing and indexed them in the FDLE system.

Next I reviewed and digested one report at a time. I came across one that shocked me. Prior to the death of Dan's battered grandmother, she had made a report to the Department of Children and Families (DCF) about an incident that occurred in the backseat of her car. Nancy was only three years old, and her brother Adam was six. The grandmother was driving when she glanced in her rearview mirror and saw Adam's penis in Nancy's mouth.

Based on my experience in investigating crimes against children, this type of behavior is learned by young children. They either find out about it through direct exposure in their environment or through similar physical activity in which they have engaged.

Visiting the Scenes of the Crime

Within a couple of weeks, Detective Glenn Woodard joined our group of investigators, representing the Palm Beach County Sheriff's Office. Cathy also came onboard, representing the Office of Statewide Prosecution.

Our whole team gathered together for a trip to the Goodyear home. Cathy rode with me in my car. Karen rode with Glenn in his car, and Robert drove alone.

We parked in front of a one-story concrete-block house that sat among small, older homes. The front yard looked neglected. A few browning palm trees were scattered among grass entwined with weeds. The shrubbery was overgrown and in need of watering.

The exterior of the house cried for maintenance. In addition to the faded trim, the two front windows appeared to be a little cockeyed. They didn't look like they were securely attached to the ledge that held them.

I asked Robert, "Why do those windows look like that?"

He said, "They're the windows for the room where Nancy slept that night. They've never been installed properly. In fact, that's the same condition they were in on the night she went missing."

While we walked up the cracked concrete walkway, the stained and dirty white door opened. A short and somewhat plump woman wearing blue-jean shorts and a tank top stood in the gap.

Her brassy blond hair reached down her back. Her bangs hit the top of her large-framed red glasses. I assumed her to be Sally. However, if I saw her in the grocery store, I would never have imagined that she still stripped for a living.

Sally welcomed us. She seemed excited that we were taking a new interest in solving her daughter's murder.

We walked through her doorway and entered into a mess. I almost felt claustrophobic standing in the midst of the clutter, dirty dishes piled in the sink, and dog odor that came from two large dogs that still used the missing kitchen window as a doggie door.

While walking through the hallway, I noticed that the walls bore what appeared to be indentations from someone's fists. These holes continued into the master bedroom.

I asked Sally about these wall scars. She said, "Dan has anger issues. Every so often, he hits the walls."

I knew from reading some police reports in Robert's case file that Sally had also been on the receiving end of Dan's "anger issues." The ongoing family violence worried me.

I asked Sally, "How is Adam doing?"

She said, "He's in middle school now. He hates school and skips classes."

I wasn't surprised to hear this report.

She took us to Adam's room.

Karen asked, "Are these the same bunk beds where Nancy slept that night?"

Sally's eyes were fixed on the bottom bed. "Yes," she whispered.

We walked across the hall to Nancy's room. The bed still contained the same dingy pink and purple plaid bedspread that was in the case file photos. I glanced to the right wall and saw a white accordion door opened to a small closet that held her stuffed animals. Pictures of Nancy from when she was around three to five years old hung on the walls.

I didn't gather a lot of new information from our tour, but nevertheless we needed to do it. You never know if you may find something that had been overlooked.

After leaving the home, our group stopped by the Palm Beach County location where Nancy's body was recovered. In the past six years, a lot of things had changed, including this crime scene. Robert and Glenn confirmed that this once-wooded area had now been developed into a residential community.

Glenn said, "After Nancy's body was discovered, we canvassed the area. I saw a shack at the end of this paved road. At the time, though, this road was just a dirt road." He stared down the road and paused for a moment before continuing. "A one-armed painter lived in that shack. Coincidentally he had worked with Sam, and coincidentally both Sam and Dan visited him there to take hits of cocaine."

Once we finished inspecting the crime scene—or what was left of it—we left to go to the Palm Beach Medical Examiner's Office. The M.E. who had conducted the autopsy had died from a stroke a few years back, so we had arranged to meet with the head pathologist.

Unfortunately, the first M.E. didn't provide a time of death, but he did give a description of the digestion of the food in her stomach. The current M.E. took that information and gave an estimated time of death consistent with the undigested food.

We asked to review the report that listed the stomach contents found during her autopsy. We wanted to double-check to see if it matched what the detectives had compiled in 1994, regarding what she had eaten, when she had eaten, and its digestion level.

As we all eagerly read through the report, we saw that the current M.E. estimated the time of death to be between midnight and three o'clock in the morning on the day she was reported missing.

<u>One Angry Man</u>

I had asked Dan to come to my office one evening for an interview with Karen and me.

When he slowly shuffled in, his body was slouched, his lips were pushed to one side in a smirk, and his eyes drooped in boredom.

I asked, "Mr. Goodyear, can I get you some water?"

He shook his head, rolled his eyes, and sighed. His body language spoke loudly and screamed that he had better things to do than be here with us. He kept looking around the room, under his fingernails, at a piece of phantom lint on his shirt, all before looking at his watch.

I surely didn't expect this attitude from the father of a murdered child, so I asked, "Mr. Goodyear, are we boring you? Do you have some place you need to go?"

He put his hands in his lap and moved his unexpressive eyes to meet mine without giving me an answer. His short dark hair blended in with his ordinary face, and the tan he acquired from performing outdoor labor enhanced his average looks.

He obviously came here straight from work. His grass- and dirt-stained T-shirt detracted from its once-white color. The well-worn blue jeans and well-broken-in beige work boots had all seen better days.

Dan's demeanor didn't improve a bit throughout the entire interview. In fact, it sucked. His obnoxious attitude left no room for doubt that he didn't plan to cooperate one bit. He continued to slouch in his chair and stare into space, and he refused to engage in conversation, providing terse answers to our questions.

Karen asked, "Dan, will you take a polygraph? This will allow us to eliminate you as a suspect."

Dan's face reddened, and he jutted his chin forward. He narrowed his eyes and furrowed his brow.

Rising out his chair, he said in a menacing tone, "You bitches can go to hell." He then huffed and puffed out of my office.

Karen and I looked at each other and smiled. We knew we had hit a nerve with an obvious macho male who thought himself superior to females.

"Well, that went well," I said sarcastically.

"Yeah," Karen said, "I'm going to take a wild guess that he hates cops, I mean *really* hates cops, especially girl cops."

"You think?" I responded and shook my head.

Coincidences and the "Church Lady"

For two weeks, I continued to leave messages for Sam and drive by his house with no luck. But then fate provided an unexpected opportunity.

On a beautiful, windy September morning, I walked out of the Fort Lauderdale Courthouse to meet Cathy for lunch at one of our favorite riverfront pubs. As I passed by the jail, I spotted Sam about six feet away sitting on a bench. I've never seen him in person, yet I recognized him from looking at the multiple pictures of him in Robert's case file.

I found his visual appearance disgusting. His belly hung over his pants and hid any semblance of a lap. I guessed he weighed about three hundred pounds, which seemed to overload his five-foot-nine-inch frame.

The grease from his straight brown hair caused it to act like glue and stick to the sides of his moon-shaped face. His complexion seemed to contain just as much grease as his hair. A double chin replaced his neck.

I made a beeline for Sam, walked up to him, and introduced myself.

I asked, "Okay if I share this bench with you?"

He nodded without looking at me. He emitted a sickening body odor, so I kept a bit of a distance between us and tried to breathe through my mouth to avoid gagging.

"Whatcha doing here, Sam?"

I got the feeling introductions were not necessary. I obviously knew who he was, and his past experiences with law enforcement probably led him to know I was a cop. Regardless, he didn't question my identity, just answered my questions.

"My wife just bailed me out of jail."

I knew he wasn't married, so I assumed he was talking about his ex-wife.

"What were you in jail for, Sam?"

"Got arrested last night for gas skipping. They said I didn't pay for my gas."

At this point, I didn't want to debate whether or not Sam actually paid for his gas; I couldn't have cared less. I changed the topic to what I needed to know.

"Sam, I respect your love for Sally and Nancy. You must have loved little Nancy. She was such a cute child."

As I spoke I could see tears welling up in Sam's eyes. I turned my head away from him so that I could take in a deep breath and not breathe and smell him while facing him. Then I leaned into him and placed my hand on his hand that rested on the top of the bench backing. Holding my breath, I said, "Sam, will you take a polygraph to eliminate yourself as a suspect?"

He started crying. His chin dropped to his chest, causing his head to bend forward and look at his big abdomen. His shoulders jerked up and down, keeping rhythm with his sobs.

Finally, he heaved a big sigh and raised his head. His eyes were now red and flooded with tears. "Yes."

"Let's go to my office then, and I'll make arrangements."

Sam said, "I've been up all night. If you set it up, I'll come in."

Without saying another word, he got up and walked away, and I could do nothing to stop him.

That was the last time I saw Sam for a while. He never responded to my repeated phone calls offering him the polygraph. I expected he had too much time to think about it after leaving me on the bench that day.

Despite his rejection of me, I wasn't finished with him. I knew Sam and I would meet face-to-face again one day.

In the meantime, Karen and I wanted to interview Sam's ex-wife. We knew that when she was married to Sam, he and her adult son Matthias used drugs heavily. Also, they allegedly committed burglaries together. I learned from reading the detectives' interview reports from 1994 that Matthias and Sam worked together on painting jobs. Then afterward they returned to burglarize these homes. They were arrested on a few of them.

About a week after seeing Sam, I started reaching out and calling his ex-wife at work and at home. Admittedly, I made a pest of myself, and I intended to keep on until she agreed to an interview. Finally, my efforts paid off because she reluctantly came into my office.

We gave her the name "church lady" since she came to her interview carrying a Bible. Her neat attire was the complete opposite of Sam's. The length of her dark full-skirted outfit fell below her knees. She pulled her black hair tightly together to form a bun on top of her head. She wore no makeup or jewelry except for a small gold cross on a thin gold chain around her neck.

However, her demeanor resembled that of her ex-husband's. She too acted like she didn't want to deal with us.

After we began to interview her, she prayed. When we asked her about Sam's activities, she gave unenthusiastic answers that were anything but forthcoming and never spoke negatively about him. However, she treated Karen and me with disdain and like we were heathens.

I found her behavior insulting, not because of how she treated us. I didn't like the way she used the Bible and prayers as mere props to appear to be one persona when in actuality she came across as something else.

Most of all, I found her behavior appalling in that she seemed to care more about protecting a potential child murderer than she did about seeking justice for a little girl.

Did He Confess to the Preacher?

I reviewed the subpoenaed phone records from the motel room where Sam had lived at the time of Nancy's murder. I found out that he had called his ex-wife's pastor.

This preacher and Sam had a bit of a history because he had counseled Sam when he was a fifteen-year-old juvenile delinquent.

These phone calls were of great interest to me. I wondered why he would call a preacher. Did he feel guilty? Did he confess to the preacher?

While going over more old arrest reports, I saw that Sam was arrested for loitering and prowling. The narrative for this charge indicated that Sam was involved in a sexual encounter with another male. A police officer discovered them naked on the beach under the pier. They had been found breathing heavily and wrapped tightly in each other's arms.

Karen and I attempted to interview Sam's mother. She cracked open her front door and peeked through the four-inch gap, using the door as a protective barricade.

"Yes?" she asked with a smile. "Can I help you?"

I said, "Hi, I'm Special Agent Turner with the FDLE, and this is Special Agent Kool with the FBI."

Karen and I both showed her our identification.

"We would like to talk with you."

Her smile quickly turned into a frown. She refused to open the door further.

"Go away," she rudely ordered as she slammed her door shut.

Then we heard her yell, "Get off my property."

We did; we had no choice.

Those Pesky Affairs

A week after I spoke to Sam outside the jail, I heard that Sally and Dan were having issues once again.

Sally told Dan that she was about six weeks to two months pregnant, but it wasn't Dan's. Evidently, the daddy was another lawn-maintenance man obviously doing much more than maintaining lawns.

After a fight, Dan called the North Lauderdale Police Department and threatened to kill himself.

The police responded to his house, and he met them at his door with a CO_2-powered pellet gun in the shape of a semi-automatic pistol. When he started to raise it up to point it at the officers, they immediately drew their guns.

They yelled at Dan to drop his gun.

He complied. These responding officers came very close to shooting him. I wondered if Dan was actually contemplating suicide by cop.

About a week later, Sally miscarried and was taken to the hospital emergency room. While there with her new man, Dan burst in and attacked him. Dan broke the new boyfriend's arm and elbow before the responding officers arrested him.

Sally's new boyfriend didn't have medical insurance, so he never could get the much-needed surgery to fix his broken arm. As a result, his arm atrophied and never looked normal again.

Trick and Treat

In a brainstorming meeting with Robert and Karen, I came up with the idea of staging a false task-force conference room. We filled it with empty file boxes labeled as leads. We also put a dry-erase board in the room and wrote information about suspects, leads, and assignments on it.

I thought this might get a reaction out of Dan. Either it would scare him if he believed we might be getting close to arresting him, or it would make him feel guilty if he did murder his daughter. If he was innocent, then it might compel him to cooperate with us.

So, we put this room together in less than three hours. We asked Sally if we could borrow some of Nancy's photographs and favorite toys without telling her our plan. We placed them in the room. We hid a video camera that would record everything being said.

Since Dan was still in jail for the assault on Sally's man, Karen and I stopped by the court to get a judge to sign an order to release him into our custody for an interview. While we picked up Dan at the jail, Robert volunteered to pick up Miami's tried-and-true method for obtaining a confession: the Burger King hamburger. We threw in fries and a drink for good measure.

After placing a handcuffed and shackled Dan into the backseat of my car, we transported him back to the FDLE building. Along the way, we read Miranda rights to him in case he decided to give us his full and complete confession.

He shrugged, rolled his eyes, and then stared out the window. He ignored us during the whole drive.

Since the male detectives Robert and Glenn met us at my office, Karen and I thought it best they conduct the interview. We figured they may get more information from him since he apparently hated female cops immensely.

Karen and I watched the interview on the monitor. Robert and Glenn started off slowly, giving him time to eat his food, and eat he did. In fact, he ate with such gusto, making it obvious that he enjoyed every bite. I guess the fast food must have been an improvement over jail food.

Once he consumed the last fry, and nothing was left in the sandwich wrapper, his attention could now be placed on the conference room and its display. His smirk turned into a frown as he looked around, pausing on each one of his daughter's toys and pictures. I thought that perhaps our plan was working.

However, Dan kept insisting that he wasn't responsible for Nancy's murder. He then broke down and started sobbing. I guess the memories were too much for him emotionally.

I surprised myself for feeling sorry for him during the interview, but I would never forget the fact that he was a scumbag of the first order.

<u>Where's the Cooperation?</u>

The following Saturday afternoon, Glenn and I waited at the FDLE office for Sally to arrive. We chose a quiet day for this interview so that we wouldn't be interrupted. We wanted to have a chance to question her alone and in more depth.

I unlocked the front entryway so that she could enter. I had instructed her to use the buzzer to let me know when she arrived so that I could buzz her in.

I looked at the clock and saw that Sally was late. With each passing minute, I started to get concerned that she wasn't going to show up.

Finally, about an hour after our scheduled interview, I heard the outside door open. I looked on the monitor and saw Sally waltz inside our building wearing a tight low-cut T-shirt, cut-off jeans, and flip flops. She was holding hands with the boyfriend that had the atrophied arm.

I shook my head and thought, *This is* not *going to work*.

I buzzed her in and rose from my chair to greet her. I knew she wouldn't concentrate on speaking with us with her boyfriend there and that she would use him for a distraction.

I'm very sensitive to families of missing, abducted, and murdered children, but Sally had already pushed me away too many times by not scheduling an appointment for an interview sooner. I needed to connect with her and establish solid ground so that she could help us obtain justice. This required her complete focus on the circumstances of her murdered daughter.

When I saw her, she was smiling like a high school girl who had just landed the popular quarterback.

I raised my right eyebrow and cocked my head. I pointed at him and then used my thumb to point toward the door. "You, get lost. We only needed to talk to Sally."

She opened her mouth to protest, and my eyes landed on her. I tilted my chin up, silently daring her to say anything. She stopped and looked down.

The boyfriend looked at her. Seeing that she had succumbed to our rules, he stomped out of the room, slamming the door behind him.

"Follow me," I told Sally.

I led her down the hall to the interview room.

Along the way, she said, "Agent Turner, I've been given a court date to appear in family court because of Adam's ongoing school truancy."

She then dropped a bombshell. "I'm going to homeschool Adam."

I made a mental note to make sure Cathy and I attended this court date.

She sat in one of the seats, and I noticed her pout and hooded eyes. I knew she wasn't happy that her boyfriend couldn't be with her. I didn't care. I was more concerned about obtaining justice for Nancy than I was with pleasing Sally.

Once the interview began, Sally didn't get any happier. In fact, her pout evolved into just plain obnoxious behavior. She jumped up and cussed at Glenn. She then grabbed a wire basket off a desk and ran over to Glenn and tried to hit him over his head with it.

Why she attacked Glenn, I didn't know. He came across as the good cop, and I was the one who came across strong, starting with getting rid of the boyfriend. The only reason I could think of was that she was transferring her anger from me to him.

I ran to intervene and control Sally. I kept saying, "Don't attack a law enforcement officer. If you do, I will arrest you!"

She finally stopped her rage.

I thought, *That was a close call. I really don't want to arrest her.*

Our interview ended.

Not on My Watch!

The following week found Cathy and me in the Broward County Courthouse. The lovely fall day provided a cool breeze that blew across my neck and face. I hoped this weather was a preview of what could be a continued relief from a very hot summer.

Aesthetic differences existed between the Broward Courthouse located in downtown Fort Lauderdale and Miami's courthouse. Broward happened to be void of the litter, hot dog venders, and the general chaos that had become part of Miami's personality.

We entered the family courtroom. Looking around, I saw all of the Goodyear clan. Even the grandmothers attended in support of Sally's unacceptable agenda.

I had my own agenda too and that was to take a bold step that morning. After the family presented their argument for maintaining custody of Adam and Sally's plan for homeschooling, I addressed the judge.

I stood and said, "Your Honor, I know there's not a GED in the entire family. In my opinion, the family doesn't have the educational background to homeschool."

The judge paused as if considering my assertion and then agreed.

The court placed Adam in a charter school located close to where the family lived. The judge warned the Goodyears that she would be monitoring Adam's school attendance.

At the end of the proceeding, Cathy leaned over and whispered in my ear. "I know this judge. She and I were prosecutors together in our early years. She just got married to a DEA agent named Rios."

What a small world. The judge's husband was the same Agent Rios I knew from my Florida Highway Patrol Academy days. He had been a guest speaker at the FHP Academy when I was a cadet, and he told us some inappropriate things about our new job. The FHP subsequently banned him. Then years later, he ignored my attempts to get into the DEA narcotics school, making me his target of vengeance. Thank God my then-husband stepped in and went over his head, and I attended the school anyway, much to Rios' chagrin.

Of course, I wasn't about to share this back story with Cathy, and most definitely the judge wouldn't hear about it from me either.

Later that evening, Sally called me on my cell. "You're a fucking bitch. Keep out of my business."

I rolled my eyes and shook my head. "Call me back when you're sober. I want to solve your daughter's murder, but I will not tolerate your verbal bullshit."

I don't like using that kind of language, but I knew it was the only language she comprehended and respected.

That phone call established an understanding between us. From then on, most of our subsequent conversations were tolerable.

Ask the Polygraph

Late one morning, Cathy stopped in my office after finishing up with her morning court cases. She wanted to get wild and crazy and go on some interviews with me.

"Well," I said. "I think we need to find Laura from 'the pool incident' and interview her. I've been needing to go over all of the details of that incident and the night Sally called her to come over when Dan talked about suicide. Wanna take a trip with me to the Pussy Cat Club?"

She stared at me with a big grin. Even the dreary overcast fall day didn't seem to deter her enthusiasm.

I leaned forward and whispered, "I promise I won't tell any of the other prosecutors in your office about your adventure."

Leaning back, I saw that she still wore that same smile.

My analyst had run several computer checks to locate Laura. She came up empty-handed as if Laura had dropped off the face of the earth, so I knew I needed to do some old-fashioned detective work and pound the pavement. At this point, it seemed to be the best and only way to look for and develop clues as to how to find Laura.

I figured the best place to start would be Laura's last-known place of employment, which was the Pussy Cat Club. These girls moved from club to club, and hopefully I could gain some kind of intel. I wanted to ask the dancers if they knew her, if they knew where she might be now, and even if they knew whether she was still dancing.

When we arrived at the Pussy Cat, Cathy's demeanor changed to very reserved and cautious. She said, "I've never been to a strip club before."

I smiled inwardly, remembering back to my days as a field training officer with the Florida Highway Patrol. I recalled how Denny Romano, my obnoxious trainee, acted a whole lot differently than Cathy when entering a strip club. He didn't hesitate to run in the direction of the yelling and screaming going on at the back of the building. He ended up in the dressing room among a bunch of almost-naked women.

As soon as he saw the source of the ruckus, he ran over and squeezed between two tall strippers in an attempt to break up the soon-to-be cat fight. In fact, I had to admire his courage. He held them apart from each other, using his hands and arms as barriers.

I was sure Denny felt quite rewarded for his bravery as he stood up close and personal with their large breasts, which happened to fall within his line of vision. I watched how he was immediately transformed into a utopian trance. I think a bomb could have gone off just about then, and Denny wouldn't have noticed...or cared.

But now was different. Not only did my current partner not want to see naked women, but even the thought of seeing one embarrassed her.

Still, Cathy pushed aside her discomfort and followed behind me to the door. I showed the bouncers my credentials, and then using my experiences at having to visit these types of establishments, I pushed Cathy past the door bouncer and into the smoky, smelly, dimly lit room. This club contained the same components of all of the other clubs I've seen: a small bar, stools, some tables, and a raised dance floor where the girls performed.

We could see a very chubby woman swinging upside down on a pole. The red, green, and blue lighting didn't provide enough illumination to see much more than ten feet in front of us. This effect always made the dancers look better while providing some cover for the low-class clients.

Cathy moved her head every which way like a nervous cat on a hot tin roof. I smiled as I watched her expressions of shock, although I admit she hid most of them quite well.

One of the topless girls walked past us. I stepped in front of her and said, "Hey, can you tell me where we can find the manager?"

She said, "He's in the back" and continued on to her destination.

I gently pointed Cathy in the direction of the dressing room. Upon entering it, we saw a line of girls. They only wore a G-string and a pair of high heels. A well-dressed slender man sporting a small mustache stood in front of them. He gave each of them cash, which made me think he was the manager paying "his girls."

Cathy glanced back at me for reassurance. I nodded and said, "He's probably the manager."

The dressing room's bright lights didn't benefit these girls who worked the dayshift. It revealed their flaws. Not only did they look aged and used, but I thought they could use some exercise to tone up. I saw a lot of dimpled fat around their abs and bottoms.

Most had fallen breasts. All of us women experience these types of normal issues, but we wear clothes to cover them. I decided they would also look better in clothes.

Cathy's eyes bulged out, and her face turned bright red. She was definitely out of place with her gray Elie Tahari business suit, pink Brooks Brothers ruffled shirt, and brown soft-leather Cole Haan shoulder purse. She made an abrupt turn and tried to run out the door in her beige Prada high heels.

I smiled and shook my head, thinking, *Yeah, Denny Romano she's not.*

At times like this, I appreciated my nondesigner attire, but I was also more familiar with this environment than my colleague. Nothing surprised me, so I stayed in the room to talk to the dancers.

Upon asking the first girl if she knew where Laura Benton worked, several others clamored around me to join the conversation.

"Laura?" one of them asked.

"Girl, I haven't seen her in years," said another dancer.

They all looked back and forth between each other, chatting among themselves about Laura. Collectively, they all said they hadn't heard from her since she had left.

I then waited for the manager to give the last girl in line her money. At this point, he was my last hope in this club.

"Excuse me. Are you the manager?"

"Yeah," he said, looking me up and down.

I flashed him my credentials. "I guess you overheard that I'm looking for Laura Benton. Do you know where she works?"

He raised an eyebrow. "The only thing I know about Laura is that she left town a couple of years ago for a better dancing gig."

By the time I got back to the club's front door, I saw Cathy standing near the bouncer. Whereas her face had turned red inside, outside it was white. She nervously shook while inhaling a cigarette.

I said, "I thought you gave up smoking."

Her color now changed from white to a vile shade of green. "Bummed it from the bouncer."

When we got into my car, Cathy said, "I think I may be sick at my stomach."

"Not in my car," I said.

We pulled out of the parking lot, and I glanced over at my car's clock. It was a few minutes before four o'clock.

I said, "Let's drive by Sam's house to see if he's home."

I hoped I could catch him returning home from work.

As luck would have it, I saw Sam's car in his driveway. From our computer checks, we discovered that he and his divorced wife, a.k.a. the church lady, currently lived together because they used the same address.

I walked over to the passenger side and helped Cathy out of my car. Her green color had subsided, and her normal color seemed to be slowly but surely returning. Still, she seemed unsteady in her high heels.

Sam's pink house needed painting, and the yard was overgrown and neglected. After I knocked on the battered wooden front door, Sam answered. He wore a nasty-looking pair of navy sweatpants that fell below his Buddha belly and nothing else.

I said, "Hi Sam. Cathy and I want to talk to you."

Referring to the prosecutor by her first name was always a good technique to use in an effort to make a suspect feel comfortable. Using Cathy's title may have frightened someone like Sam, who had obviously been avoiding us.

He shrugged before grumbling, "Okay."

His "whatever" demeanor gave me the impression that having cops show up unexpectedly on his doorstep was more the rule than the exception.

I asked, "Is your wife home?"

"No. She's working out of town."

Sam turned, and we followed him to the kitchen. Since I walked behind him, I got a chance to see his plumber's crack. I found it to be exceptionally gross.

I turned my head to look back at Cathy. Her green color returned with a vengeance. Cathy's wild and crazy adventure was becoming more than she had bargained for.

Sam's concrete floors were covered with a peeling dark-red paint. I wondered if the color was left over from one of his painting jobs or if he stole it from his employer.

He sat at a small kitchen table, and we joined him.

Cathy gained her composure. She pulled out a legal pad and began asking a series of detailed questions.

As time went by, I saw more and more small roaches making their ascent up the legs of the table to its top. I had already pushed as far away as I could from the table because my olfactory nerves couldn't tolerate anymore of Sam's body odor. He smelled just as bad as he did during our post-jail encounter. Fortunately, Cathy remained focused on maintaining her meticulous note-taking process.

Cathy finally asked, "Sam, will you agree to clear yourself with a polygraph?"

"Yes."

I got excited, momentarily forgetting his body odor and the roaches. I forced myself to remain calm and nonchalant. "We'll have a detective come to your house with a portable polygraph machine."

Before he could object, we excused ourselves for a few moments and walked to the front-door stoop. Since Cathy didn't wear a gun, I wouldn't leave her alone with Sam. She did carry a gun in her purse, which many prosecutors do. However, I didn't know how proficient Cathy was with her weapon.

As soon as we stepped outside, Cathy and I quickly checked our clothes for roaches. Thank God, none of them had made their way onto our persons.

I called Karen. "Hey, can you get one of your FBI polygraphists to come to Sam's house ASAP?"

"Let me check. I'll get back to you as soon as I can."

Within five minutes, Karen called back. "Agent Thomas is on his way. He's coming from his home, which is just west of Fort Lauderdale. He should be there within thirty minutes. I'll brief him about the case details during his drive to your location."

"That would be great because we need to get right back in with Sam before he changes his mind again."

We then walked back into the kitchen to keep Sam busy by talking. We didn't want to give him enough time to think and change his mind.

FBI Special Agent Thomas arrived within the promised thirty minutes. In his hand, he carried a black Pelican hard case that housed and protected his polygraph machine.

Agent Thomas stood about five-feet-eleven inches. I thought him to be an attractive man in his late forties with thinning blond hair. A pair of tortoise glasses framed his light blue eyes, and his smile revealed very white teeth.

His dark pants fit well on his slender frame. He rolled up the sleeves of his white shirt that was complimented by a red-and-blue striped tie hanging loosely around his neck. He reminded me of an Ivy Leaguer and exhibited professionalism.

His easy way of engaging Sam was nothing short of amazing. He began by offering Sam a cigarette. I was afraid Cathy would grab one too.

As Agent Thomas placed his polygraph machine on top of the roach-laden table, he said, "If you ladies would like to take a break and leave, that's fine. I'm good here with Sam."

I knew this was a hint for us to get out so that he could continue to build a rapport with Sam. I was glad to leave. I watched Cathy's eyes fix on the cigarettes as if contemplating whether she should ask Agent Thomas for one too. I wanted to get her away from him before she decided to take up smoking again.

We waited in our car outside the house for about an hour. Agent Thomas finally strolled out of Sam's house around eight that evening. He was shaking his head and smiling.

We heard Sam screaming at the top of his lungs from his doorway, "Get the fuck out of here, and none of you ever come back! Fuckin' cops." Then the door slammed so hard, his whole house appeared to wobble.

We followed Agent Thomas to a donut shop a few blocks away. Before sitting down at a booth, we all brushed our hands over our clothes again, searching for bugs but hoping to find none.

Agent Thomas cut to the chase. "Sam failed the polygraph. He became upset when I told him that not only did he fail it, but he failed it miserably."

We all knew polygraphs weren't admissible in court because they weren't flawless. Agent Thomas had earned the reputation of being excellent at his craft, though. The most important part is the interview itself. Within that, the examiner must select important questions and phrase them in just the right way.

I drove Cathy back to her car parked at my office. After she left, I called Robert, Karen, Glenn, and my supervisor. I needed to keep them all in the loop about what had transpired and that we should promote Sam to the number-one suspect position on all of our flow charts.

The following morning, Robert, Karen, and I met at my office. Cathy couldn't make it. She wanted to recover from her nicotine fix that still made her feel ill and dizzy.

Now that we could shift the spotlight off of Dan in our investigation, we could focus on Sam as our person of interest.

We decided to locate Eddie, Sam's former roommate when Nancy was kidnapped and murdered. We wanted to wire him with a recording device and have him talk to Sam. We wanted to capture an admission of guilt from Sam that he was responsible for Nancy's death.

Fortunately, we found him quite easily. He was sitting in a state prison in the Florida panhandle. Apparently, Eddie had committed one too many burglaries and got caught along the way.

I called my friend the prison inspector. When I was a trooper, Jacob, Sniffer, and I had helped him by searching for contraband in his women's prison.

Inspector Tom Watts jumped on my request to interview Eddie. He started the paperwork to move Eddie to a closer prison where we could have easy access to him.

In the meantime, Sam was dealing with the stress of his failed polygraph by indulging in an excessive drug binge. But drug binges cost money, and Sam chose to pay for his implosion by embarking on a series of six bank robberies.

Big Boy Bandit

Work issues had been pushed to the back of my mind as I enjoyed my morning jog in Boynton Beach.

The cool morning in November 2000, almost took my breath away. The scenery only added to the ambiance with the vibrant pink and blue sky acting as a colorful background for the rising sun.

I looked forward to Christmas shopping. I kept myself preoccupied with constructing a gift list in my mind.

After getting back home, I took a shower before putting on a black pantsuit for the day. One hand grabbed my gun, and the other grabbed my coffee. I could now begin my drive into the FDLE Fort Lauderdale field office.

Just as I took my last sip of coffee while crossing from Palm Beach County into Broward County, my cell phone rang. Karen called to give me some earth-shattering news.

Sam had been arrested about an hour earlier in Pompano Beach. He had abducted and raped an eleven-year-old child walking to school with her sister. Reports stated that Sam had been driving a red van and pulled this little girl into it.

Two hours after the reported kidnapping, someone spotted him near the abduction area where he had already dropped off the victim. Fortunately, she was alive. A brief car pursuit ensued with the police and ended with Sam's capture.

The Broward Sheriff's Office (BSO) took Sam to their detective bureau located in its headquarters building for an interview. Karen and Agent Thomas were driving up from the Miami FBI Office to the BSO. I told her I would meet them there.

This terrible turn of events devastated me. Another precious child had become a victim, suffering from a horrific crime. The thought that I may have had a hand in pushing Sam over the edge with the polygraph crushed me.

What could I have done to stop this attack short of not giving Sam a polygraph? I had been working on Nancy's case for eighteen months. Although Sam was a strong and viable suspect, we couldn't arrest him because we didn't have enough evidence, and now he hurt another child.

Of course, I knew what I would have done had I suspected that Sam posed any immediate danger toward children. I would have put him under constant surveillance twenty-four-seven, but that would have been manpower intensive.

Without a crystal ball, I would never have been able to convince my supervisor to support these efforts. Suffice it to say, though, that I would have moved heaven and earth to avoid a helpless child from being hurt. I reminded myself that I had no control over the evilness of a child predator.

Karen, Agent Thomas, and I arrived at the BSO headquarters simultaneously and just in time for a command briefing about Sam's activities. The press had given the robber the name "Big Boy Bandit" when no one knew his identity. We now realized that Sam and this "Big Boy Bandit" were one in the same.

Our team waited in the conference room for the BSO to finish up with Sam. Robert joined us, and we filled him in on the details.

We discussed who would interview Sam when our time came. We knew that Sam hated Robert from when he questioned him with vigor in 1994. He didn't know Karen. On the other hand, Agent Thomas had developed a relationship of sorts with him, even though Sam had kicked him out of his house after the polygraph. Lastly, Sam was familiar with me, and he tolerated me, so we decided that Agent Thomas and I would handle the interview.

Unfortunately, that interview wouldn't happen for quite some time. We ended up sitting in that room for so long that lunchtime had come and gone and so had dinnertime.

A burley BSO captain who looked more like a football player than a cop came into the conference room. He said, "Sam confessed to kidnapping the girl and taking her to an isolated area in Boca Raton where he sexually assaulted her. Afterward, he returned to the same location where he had abducted her and dropped her off."

I felt horrible and very sorry for this young girl. I just wished that we could have made a case against him before he kidnapped this other child. Maybe if Sam was in such a confessional mode, maybe just maybe we could get him to confess to Nancy's murder.

As if reading my thoughts, the captain said, "You can now have your turn to interview Sam."

Agent Thomas and I walked into the small confined space of the claustrophobic interview room. Immediately, Sam's intense body odor hit me like a ton of bricks. His smell penetrated my nose and gave me an instant headache. Some of my reactions might have been psychological as I pictured Sam's scent entering my pores and penetrating my hair.

Agent Thomas shocked me when he pulled out a pack of cigarettes and a lighter and offered Sam a smoke. I thought, *Agent Thomas has got to know this is a smoke-free workplace.*

However, I did understand his methodology. I hated one thing more than Sam's odor. I detested the smell of a burning cigarette and exposure to its second-hand smoke.

I took one for the team, though, but I mostly wanted to wrap up my case with a confession. I wanted justice for the children who this poor excuse for a human had hurt.

After enjoying his smoke, he rose from his seat and got down on the floor. He then faced the wall, curled up in a fetal position, and ignored us.

I was really getting tired of looking at his plumber's crack. If I didn't know any better, I would have thought he tried to gross me out. We ended up leaving that interrogation room without the confession we so desperately coveted.

We decided to try to obtain the confession from another angle. We arranged for a BSO officer to go undercover as another prisoner. Maybe Sam would make some admission that could lead to a confession. We had nothing to lose.

We wired the UC with a recording device and put him and Sam alone in the back of the jail transport van. A sheet of plexiglass separated them from the driver, although back then, no expectation of privacy existed inside a police car. We hoped Sam didn't know that because anything he said in the car could be used against him.

On the way to jail, the undercover started a conversation with Sam, trying to acquire some incriminating evidence. Hopefully Sam would feel free to chat with our UC about his charges, and maybe he would mention Nancy.

Unfortunately, this effort didn't reveal any further information. However, Sam's body odor and foul smells in the back of the van did manage to thoroughly gross out the undercover police officer.

Our next tactic involved me writing a court order about a week later. I found an on-call judge to sign the order, giving us permission to take Sam on a field trip.

How did I get so lucky as to be the one to have Sam and his B.O. ride in the backseat of my car? Of course, poor Robert had to sit back there with him. Karen and Glenn followed in her FBI car and were able to breathe.

We drove by the Goodyear home. We then took him to the site where Nancy's body was dumped. Lastly, we drove him to her gravesite.

He seemed sad at the grave but still didn't offer up a confession. As a last-ditch effort, we fed him a Burger King meal before returning him to jail.

This time around, the BK meal held no magic. Sam refused to confess.

A Well-Rehearsed Story

By January 2001, Nancy's murder was well over six years old.

We still couldn't make a case against Sam. During the past several weeks since taking him on that trip down Memory Lane, we managed to conduct a series of interviews with his past associates. We learned that when committing any illegal activities such as burglaries, he used the names of his friends as aliases. This information became very important, especially after Sam called and summoned us to the jail.

For some strange reason, he wanted to speak with Agent Thomas and me. I called Agent Thomas. He came by my office to pick me up and drive us to the Broward County Jail, arriving within an hour of Sam's call.

My curiosity motivated me. Did Sam want to confess, or did boredom overcome him, and he beckoned us because he merely wanted company?

We were led to an empty interview room. A few moments later, Sam walked in looking slimmer and cleaner than normal. He also appeared calm, cool, and collected.

"I've got something to tell you," he started, his eyes going back and forth between Agent Thomas and me, seemingly searching our faces for a reaction. I refused to give him one, so I stared back at him with a blank expression.

Sam then provided us with quite an interesting story. "That night when Nancy got taken, I was driving around Pompano Beach. I happened to see Dan Goodyear driving his truck and turning into a gas station. I pulled into the same gas station and parked my van next to Dan's truck."

I asked, "Sam, was your van white?"

He nodded.

I asked, "Did it have some dents and scrapes on it?"

He nodded again.

He then said, "Dan was upset and began to cry. He told me that Nancy's body was in his truck wrapped in a blanket. He said she had been sleeping on the bottom bunk bed when her brother Adam rolled off the top and fell on her and killed her.

"I told Dan, 'Let's drive to the Sleep Inn Motel by the Florida Turnpike. We'll smoke some weed while we decide what to do with Nancy's body.'

"I went in and registered at the motel around two in the morning. They gave me a room on the first floor and down at one end of the building. Dan followed me to the room."

Sam remained calm and composed. He fixed his eyes on Agent Thomas' eyes as he continued.

"Dan carried Nancy's body into the room and put her on the bed. We watched some porn movies on TV, got high, and decided to dump the body in Boca Raton.

"Dan put Nancy into the back of my van. I drove north on the turnpike and got off in Boca, headed east until I got to a dirt road and stopped. Dan carried Nancy's body down the road and came back about ten minutes later with her clothes and blanket. I thought that Dan might have taken some of the extra green wire out of my van, but I didn't see him with it.

"We drove to a gas station a couple of miles away. We dumped Nancy's clothes and blanket into a trash can there before we bought some smokes. Then around four, I dropped Dan off at the motel and went back to my place."

I didn't believe any of his story, and he sounded as if he had rehearsed this speech a few times prior to relaying it to us. I still believed Sam abducted Nancy, took her to the motel, murdered her, and dumped her body in Boca Raton. As much as I despised Dan, I couldn't imagine him dumping his own daughter naked.

The next morning, Karen and I braved the rain and thunderstorms and drove to the Sleep Inn Motel to look over their records. We discovered that they kept the older records in a truck trailer behind the motel.

We walked in the hard rain through the mud to this storage unit. The less-than-enthusiastic manager led the way. He fumbled with his keys before unlocking a rusted door that gave a high-pitched squeal as it opened. A small rat took advantage of this opportunity to escape and scampered out into freedom.

We peered into a mountain of boxes. Raindrops fell inside this cramped structure.

Karen and I realized that we needed a dry day and a bigger team to go through all of these records. The manager appeared reluctant to this idea, taking in a long, deep breath, so I called Cathy on my cell phone as soon as we left the motel. I explained the situation and our need for a subpoena.

When I arrived back at my office about fifteen minutes later, the subpoena was waiting for me in the fax machine. Karen and I then looked at the weather forecast and selected a day for the next week to go through the motel's records.

Fortunately, the day we chose turned out to supply the perfect weather—clear and crisp. I had hoped to get some of my FDLE squad members to help, but they were all busy on their own cases. Their absences didn't stop Karen, Robert, Glenn, and me. We arrived early in the morning to begin our search.

We all wore old jeans, long-sleeve shirts, and work boots. We spent hours removing boxes littered with rat droppings, mold, and waterlogged pages. We formed a line, and I was in the middle. I passed all of the moldy boxes to a table that we had set up outside. For sure, this task didn't possess any of the glamour you see depicted in television cop shows.

We examined each box to find the year, the month, and the day that coincided with the date Sam stated they checked in. We also double-checked by flipping through some of the contents in each box to ensure they weren't misfiled.

We were all very focused and took this job very seriously. Enough was enough, and it was now time to give little Nancy justice.

After about five hours of searching, I finally discovered a box with the correct date, time, room location, and porn-movie charge. The name on the room registration didn't read Sam Andrews but David Walters.

I knew from my interviews that Sam had worked for a painter named David Walters. I suspected Sam used David Walters' name as an alias. I was relieved to have made this connection.

Confession Is Good for the Soul

Karen and I attended Sam's trials from beginning to end. He was found guilty and sentenced to life without parole for the six bank robberies and the abduction and rape of the eleven-year-old child. I discovered that Sam was also suspected of molesting a three-year-old child.

Karen and I took our case summary of Nancy's murder to the prosecutors in both Broward and Palm Beach counties. Both jurisdictions declined to go further without a confession.

They didn't feel we had enough evidence, including DNA, for a conviction. Everything was circumstantial. Without a confession, they wouldn't proceed to a grand jury for an indictment. Plus, we couldn't completely rule out Dan as a suspect.

We later flew to the Florida Panhandle and visited Sam in Century Prison. We had hoped that after he had sat in jail and realized he was never getting out, he would give us a confession.

He met him in a small eight-by-eight-foot concrete-block room with a table and three chairs. He had lost a lot of weight and looked cleaner. Prison seemed to serve him well.

He held a Bible and said, "I found Jesus, and the Lord's now using me to save other prisoners."

Like all prisoners, he appreciated the distraction from his prison routine and enjoyed chatting about how he walked around talking to other prisoners. He told us about his activities like someone bragged at parties and night clubs about what he did for a living.

Karen said, "Sam, we know you love Sally, and for her sake, you need to confess for what you did to Nancy."

I piped in. "Sam, we also know you're a Christian man, and as a Christian man, in telling us what really happened, you would be making peace with God and helping the Goodyear family."

I glanced over at Karen and then back to Sam. I asked, "Sam, do you mind if we pray with you?"

The center of his eyebrows raised, and he nodded.

Karen and I looked at each other, and the three of us bent our heads in prayer.

I said, "Lord, we pray for Sam, and we pray he comes clean."

He opened his eyes, jerked his head up, and yelled, "I didn't kill Nancy!"

Karen and I opened our eyes at the loud and harsh sound of his voice.

His eyes were narrowed. "I'm done dealing with you. Don't ever come back here again."

He stood up and headed for the door. Before walking out of the room, he turned back to look at us. "By the way, ladies, Adonis Kozma is an inmate here."

Evidently, he didn't realize I already knew that the North Lauderdale child pervert resided here.

I guess he wasn't through trying to shock me because he then said, "Mrs. Turner, Adonis Kozma hates your guts."

Again, he evidently didn't realize I already knew this too.

Sam's final parting words were not uncommon of inmates. "Now that I've found Jesus, I carry my Bible with me at all times."

I responded in an emotionless tone. "Even with your Bible, Sam, you won't be saved. You need to confess in order to save your soul. Haven't you heard that confession is good for the soul?"

All I wanted was for Sam to confess, yet in reality, he really didn't have any reason to tell the truth. It wasn't that I needed to hear the truth. As far as I was concerned, once he was arrested for the kidnapping and rape of a child, I knew that he murdered Nancy. I wanted the confession so that this case could be solved and closed. Mostly, I wanted the confession so that Nancy and her family could get justice.

I gave the situation one last-ditch effort. About a month after our visit with Sam, I asked Sally to write him a letter to tell him to confess so that she could live in peace. She promised to let me know if he replied, and I also checked back with her periodically just in case. Sam never responded to her plea.

At the writing of this book, Sam had never confessed. Sally went on with her life and now has a precious new daughter. She is very protective over her. I pray this child will grow up to be healthy, happy, and safe.

Dan passed away in 2010, of a drug overdose. I hope he is now resting in peace. He didn't find peace here on this earth, especially since he never got to witness and experience justice for his little girl.

Sam can never hurt another child. With the sentence he received, we'll all rest easier because Sam will die in prison.

Evil Persists in Many Forms

Nancy's case was the one that would haunt me for the rest of my career and beyond because it was never closed.

I truly felt that if I had taken the evidence I had compiled to another jurisdiction, then they would have prosecuted it, and Sam would be sitting in prison today for her murder. Nancy was robbed of getting the justice *she* deserved. Still, I received some solace in knowing that her murderer would never see the outside of those prison walls.

In the meantime, I will always carry the hope that sometime in the future, Sam will leak information to another inmate or even resort to simply telling the truth.

For now, it was time for me to move forward. As the Regional Crimes Against Children Coordinator, I knew other children needed me. In doing my job, I would be passionate in my fight to protect them to ensure that what happened to Nancy wouldn't happen to them.

At least that was my plan. However, if I thought that I would be able to throw myself full force into my position, I would soon discover that I was wrong. If I thought I had seen evil at its worst, I would soon discover I was sorely mistaken.

Unbeknown to any of us, the world was about to see evil like never before. The world was about to have a horrific ordeal unleashed upon it that would shake it to its very core. The world was about to learn that nightmares were real indeed, and it would experience one that it would never, could never forget.

Because unbeknown to any of us as we all woke up on September 11, 2001, our country was about to experience its first terrorist attack on its soil, and I would be thrust headfirst into its aftermath.

About the Author
FLOY TURNER

FLOY TURNER began her twenty-five-year career in law enforcement in Miami during the volatile cocaine-wars era as a trooper with the Florida Highway Patrol. After eleven years in this position, she served as a special agent with the elite Florida Department of Law Enforcement (FDLE) for the next fourteen years. She has been assigned to joint task forces at the international, federal, state, and local police levels, such as the 9/11 Counter Terrorism Task Force and the Belle Glade Prison Escape Task Force. These assignments have included complex investigations of serial homicides, kidnappings, missing children, child homicides, human-trafficking cases, and illegal narcotics smuggling cases.

As a FDLE Special Agent, Floy served as the Regional Crimes Against Children Coordinator in the Miami Region of Southeast Florida and was also a member of an Internet Crimes Against

Children Task Force, the Law Enforcement Against Child Harm (LEACH) Task Force, the Miami-Dade County and Broward County Child Death Review Boards, U. S. Immigration and Customs Enforcement Human Trafficking Task Force, and Homeland Security Task Force. She assisted in the development of the human-trafficking curriculum for Basic Law Enforcement Training and Incentive Classes for Florida Police Officer's Standards and has been a guest speaker at many local, state, and federal training sessions, including the FBI's Women in Law Enforcement Conference in 2004. She was awarded the State Law Enforcement Officer of the Year at the Florida Missing Children's Day in 2004, for her criminal investigations that located and recovered multiple missing children who were reunited with their families.

She was responsible for coordinating local AMBER Alerts with the FDLE Missing Children Information Clearinghouse and established a Child Abduction Response Team (CART) for the South Florida Region.

After her retirement, Floy served as a consultant for Fox Valley Technical College on the development and implementation of various training initiatives for the National AMBER Alert Training and Technical Assistance Program, U. S. Department of Justice, Office of Justice Programs.

Floy became the AMBER Alert Liaison for the Southern United States and Caribbean and created and coordinated the Child Abduction Response Team (CART) Certification program. She also continued to provide instruction in many AMBER Alert training courses until 2012.

From 2010 through 2013, Floy trained law enforcement officials and nongovernmental organizations in conducting human trafficking investigations for the Organization of American States throughout the Caribbean and Central and South America.

Currently, Floy consulted for the International Center for Missing and Exploited Children in a global AMBER Alert Training Initiative.

In September 2016, Floy was awarded the John and Reve' Walsh Award at Florida Missing Children's Day for her continued efforts of protecting children.

Floy is the co-author of bestselling book **BEHIND HER MIAMI BADGE**.

About the Author
SHERRIE CLARK

SHERRIE CLARK is the co-author of the best-selling book **BEHIND HER MIAMI BADGE**. Through her unique descriptive writing style, she brings reality to stories by putting readers in the shoes of the characters so that they can experience what the characters see, hear, and feel.

Sherrie is a former police officer with the NYPD, a writer, a book editor, and the author of the award-winning book **SMALL VOICES SILENCED**. She is also a coach and consultant for authors all across the country. As cofounder of Storehouse Publishing, she educates authors and aspiring authors through conferences, workshops, and online classes, sharing her expertise and knowledge on how to write and publish their books.

Sherrie has written, bylined, and ghostwritten over 200 articles, stories, blog posts, press releases, website content, bios, and such, all of which have been published online or in print. Some of the publications for which she has written include the award-winning newspaper *Victims' Advocate*. She served as the Jacksonville Christianity & Social Issues Examiner for examiner.com, a niche she created but has since been used by other writers, and was a volunteer writer and editor for the international organization Stop Child Trafficking Now.

Sherrie created, produced, and hosted the weekly online radio show *God, Where Were You When?* This show aired throughout Europe and as far as Japan and into Africa. She has a Masters of Arts in Clinical Christian Counseling and is a Licensed Clinical Christian Counselor with the NCCA.

When not writing and working with other authors, Sherrie enjoys spending time with her family.

www.ingramcontent.com/pod-product-compliance
Lightning Source LLC
Chambersburg PA
CBHW031117020426
42333CB00012B/117